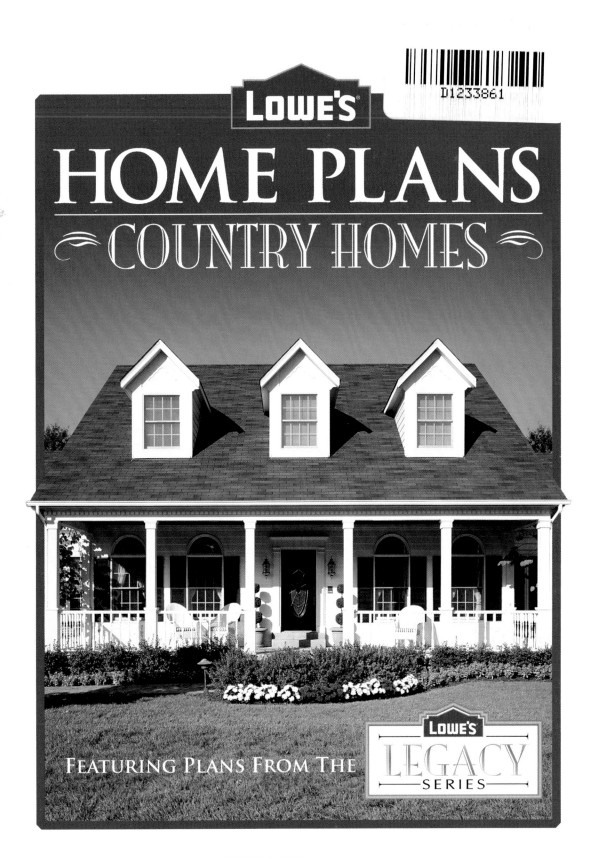

LOWE'S

HOME PLANS

❦ COUNTRY HOMES ❧

FEATURING PLANS FROM THE

D1233861

HDA
INC

HDA, Inc.
Saint Louis, MO

COVER HOME - The house shown on the front cover is Plan #533-021D-0003 and is featured on page 16. Photo courtesy of Edsel Breland.

LOWE'S LEGACY SERIES: COUNTRY HOME PLANS is published by HDA, Inc., 944 Anglum Road, St. Louis, MO, 63042. All rights reserved. Reproduction in whole or in part without written permission of the publisher is prohibited. Printed in U.S.A. © 2006. Artist drawings and photos shown in this publication may vary slightly from the actual working drawings. Some photos are shown in mirror reverse. Please refer to the floor plan for accurate layout.

ISBN-13: 978-1-58678-061-6
ISBN-10: 1-58678-061-1

Current Printing
10 9 8 7 6 5 4

HDA, Inc.
944 Anglum Rd.
St. Louis, Missouri 63042
corporate website - www.hdainc.com

CONTENTS

It's what separates you from the have knots.

We understand that it is difficult to find blueprints for a home that will meet all your needs. That is why HDA, Inc. is pleased to offer home plan modification services.

Typical home plan modifications include:

• Changing foundation type
• Adding square footage to a plan
• Changing the entry into a garage
• Changing a two-car garage to a three-car garage or making a garage larger
• Redesigning kitchen, baths, and bedrooms
• Changing exterior elevations
• Or most other home plan modifications

Home plan modifications we cannot make include:

• Reversing the plans
• Adapting/engineering plans to meet your local building codes
• Combining parts of two different plans (due to copyright laws)

Our plan modification service is easy to use. Simply:

1. Decide on the modifications you want. For the most accurate quote, be as detailed as possible and refer to rooms in the same manner as the floor plan (i.e. if the floor plan refers to a "den" then use "den" in your description). Including a sketch of the modified floor plan is always helpful.

2. Complete and e-mail the modification request form that can be found online at www.houseplansandmore.com.

3. Within two business days, you will receive your quote. Quotes do not include the cost of the reproducible masters required for our designer to legally make changes.

4. Call to accept the quote and purchase the reproducible masters. For example, if your quote is $850 and the reproducible masters for your plan are $800, your order total will be $1650 plus two shipping and handling charges (one to ship the reproducible masters to our designer and one to ship the modified plans to you).

5. Our designer will send you up to three drafts to verify your initial changes. Extra costs apply after the third draft. If additional changes are made that alter the original request, extra charges may be incurred.

6. Once you approve a draft with the final changes, we then make the changes to the reproducible masters by adding additional sheets. The original reproducible masters (with no changes) plus your new changed sheets will be shipped to you.

Other Important Information:

• Plans cannot be redrawn in reverse format. All modifications will be made to match the reproducible master's original layout. Once you receive the plans, you can make reverse copies at your local blueprint shop.
• Our staff designer will provide the first draft for your review within 4 weeks (plus shipping time) of receiving your order.
• You will receive up to three drafts to review before your original changes are modified. The first draft will totally encompass all modifications based on your original request. Additional changes not included in your original request will be charged separately at an hourly rate of $75 or a flat quoted rate.
• Modifications will be drawn on a separate sheet with the changes shown and a note to see the main sheet for details. For example, a floor plan sheet from the original set (i.e. Sheet 3) would be followed by a new floor plan sheet with changes (i.e. Sheet A-3).
• Plans are drawn to meet national building codes. Modifications will not be drawn to any particular state or county codes, thus we cannot guarantee that the revisions will meet your local building codes. You may be required to have a local architect or designer review the plans in order to have them comply with your state or county building codes.
• Time and cost estimates are good for 90 calendar days.
• All modification requests need to be submitted in writing. Verbal requests will not be accepted.

2 EASY STEPS FOR FAST SERVICE

1. Visit www.houseplansandmore.com to download the modification request form.

2. E-mail the completed form to customize@hdainc.com or fax to 913-856-7751

If you are not able to access the internet, please call 1-877-379-3420 (Monday-Friday, 8am-5pm CST)

Choosing a home plan is an exciting but difficult task. Many factors play a role in what home plan is best for you and your family. To help you get started, we have pinpointed some of the major factors to consider when searching for your dream home. Take the time to evaluate your family's needs and you will have an easier time sorting through all of the home plans offered in this book.

BUDGET: The first thing to consider is your budget. Many items take part in this budget, from ordering the blueprints to the last doorknob purchased. Once you have found your dream home plan, visit your local Lowe's store to get a cost-to-build estimate to ensure that the finished product is still within your cost range.

FAMILY LIFESTYLE: After your budget is deciphered, you need to assess you and your family's lifestyle needs. Think about the stage of life you are at now, and what stages you will be going through in the future. Ask yourself questions to figure out how much room you need now and if you will need room for expansion. Are you married? Do you have children? How many children do you plan on having? Are you an empty-nester?

Incorporate in your planning any frequent guests you may have, including elderly parents, grandchildren or adult children who may live with you.

Does your family entertain a lot? If so, think about the rooms you will need to do so. Will you need both formal and informal spaces? Do you need a gourmet kitchen? Do you need a game room and/or a wet bar?

FLOOR PLAN LAYOUTS: When looking through our home plans, imagine yourself walking through the house. Consider the flow from the entry to the living, sleeping and gathering areas. Does the layout ensure privacy for the master bedroom? Does the garage enter near the kitchen for easy unloading? Does the placement of the windows provide enough privacy from any neighboring properties? Do you plan on using furniture you already have? Will this furniture fit in the appropriate rooms? When you find a plan you want to purchase, be sure to picture yourself actually living in it.

Experts in the field suggest that the best way to determine your needs is to begin by listing everything you like or dislike about your current home.

EXTERIOR SPACES: There are many different home styles ranging from Traditional to Contemporary. Flip through and find which style most appeals to you and the neighborhood in which you plan to build. Also think of your site and how the entire house will fit on this site. Picture any landscaping you plan on incorporating into the design. Using your imagination is key when choosing a home plan.

Choosing a home plan can be an intimidating experience. Asking yourself these questions before you get started on the search will help you through the process. With our large selection of multiple styles we are certain you will find your dream home in the following pages.

THE LOWE'S LEGACY SERIES

LEG·A·CY: SOMETHING THAT IS HANDED DOWN OR REMAINS FOR GENERATIONS

HDA, Inc. is proud to introduce to you the Lowe's Legacy Series. The home plans in this collection carry on the Lowe's tradition of quality and expertise, and will continue to do so for many generations.

Choosing a home plan can be a daunting task. With the Legacy Series, we will set your mind at ease. Selecting a plan from this group will ensure a home designed with the Lowe's standard of excellence, creating a dream home for you and your family.

This collection of Legacy Series plans includes our most popular country-style home plans. Browse through the pages to discover a home with the options and special characteristics you need.

Along with one-of-a-kind craftsmanship, all Legacy Series home plans offer industry-leading material lists. These accurate material lists will save you a considerable amount of time and money, providing you with the quantity, dimensions and descriptions of the major building materials necessary to construct your home. You'll get faster and more accurate bids from your contractor while saving money by paying for only the materials you need.

The Lowe's Legacy Series is the perfect place to start your search for the home of your dreams. You will find the expected beauty you want and the functional efficiency you need, all designed with unmatched quality.

Turn the page and begin the wonderful journey of finding your new home.

Photos clockwise from top: 533-027D-0007, page 10; 533-017D-0006, page 9; 533-007D-0015, page 15; 533-023D-0001, page 24.

LOWE'S LEGACY SERIES

SPECIAL FEATURES

1,721 total square feet of living area

Roof dormers add great curb appeal

Vaulted dining and great rooms are immersed in light from the atrium window wall

2" x 6" exterior walls available, please order plan #533-007E-0010

1,604 square feet on the first floor and 117 square feet on the lower level atrium

3 bedrooms, 2 baths, 3-car garage

Walk-out basement foundation, drawings also include crawl space and slab foundations

Rear View

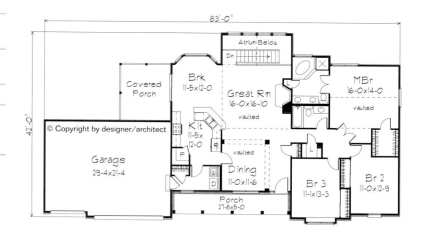

© Copyright by designer/architect

83'-0"

42'-0"

Atrium Below
Dn

Covered Porch

Brk
11-5x12-0

Great Rm
16-0x16-10
vaulted

MBr
16-0x14-0
vaulted

Kit
11-5x
12-0

Garage
29-4x21-4

Dining
11-0x11-6

vaulted

Br 3
11-1x13-3

Br 2
11-0x12-9

Porch
27-8x5-0

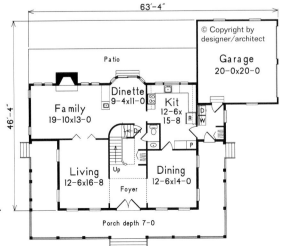

SPECIAL FEATURES

- 3,006 total square feet of living area

- Energy efficient home with 2" x 6" exterior walls

- Large all-purpose room and bath on third floor

- Efficient U-shaped kitchen includes a pantry and adjacent planning desk

- 4 bedrooms, 3 1/2 baths, 2-car side entry garage

- Basement foundation, drawings also include slab foundation

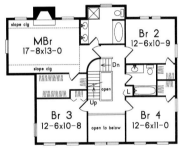

Second Floor
1,138 sq. ft.

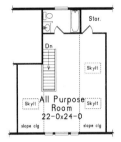

Third Floor
575 sq. ft.

First Floor
1,293 sq. ft.

SPECIAL FEATURES

2,444 total square feet of living area

Laundry room with workspace, pantry and coat closet is adjacent to the kitchen

Two bedrooms, a study, full bath and plenty of closets are located on the second floor

Large walk-in closet and private bath make this master bedroom one you're sure to enjoy

Kitchen enjoys a cooktop island and easy access to the living area

3 bedrooms, 2 1/2 baths, 2-car side entry garage

Basement foundation

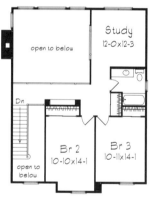

Study
12-0x12-3

open to below

Dn

Br 2
10-10x14-1

Br 3
10-11x14-1

open to below

Second Floor
772 sq. ft.

64'-0"

48'-0"

Great Rm
17-0x15-9

skylt

Brk
11-8x11-6

Patio

Kitchen
11-8x11-0

© Copyright by designer/architect

MBr
13-8x
20-0

Dn

Up

Dining
14-1x11-11

Garage
19-8x19-5

Porch

First Floor
1,672 sq. ft.

SPECIAL FEATURES

1,698 total square feet of living area

The massive great room runs the entire depth of the home offering a view of the front porch and easy access to the backyard

The adjacent breakfast area offers a relaxed atmosphere and enjoys the close proximity of the U-shaped kitchen

All bedrooms are located on the second floor, including the master suite that features a deluxe bath and walk-in closet

The optional bonus room over the garage has an additional 269 square feet of living area

3 bedrooms, 2 1/2 baths, 2-car side entry garage

Basement foundation, drawings also include crawl space foundation

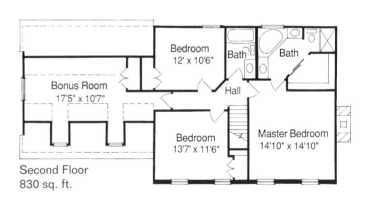

Second Floor
830 sq. ft.

© Copyright by designer/architect

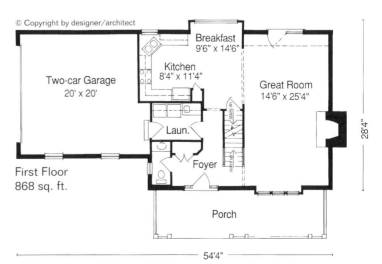

First Floor
868 sq. ft.

SPECIAL FEATURES

3,095 total square feet of living area

Arched entries add character to the private study and the formal dining room

The master bedroom is privately located and pampers the homeowners with lavish amenities

A built-in desk and island with cooktop and seating offers ultimate convenience to the combined kitchen and breakfast nook

The future recreation room on the second floor has an additional 403 square feet of living space

4 bedrooms, 3 1/2 baths, 2-car side entry garage

Slab foundation

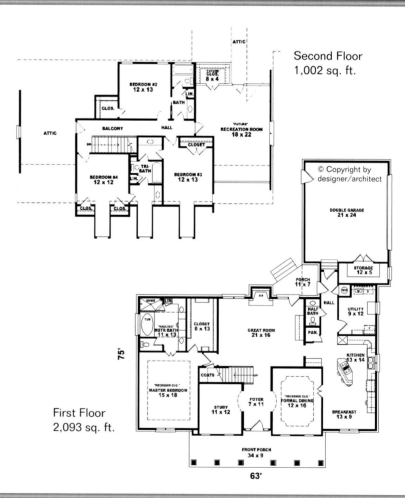

Second Floor
1,002 sq. ft.

© Copyright by designer/architect

First Floor
2,093 sq. ft.

LOWE'S
LEGACY
SERIES

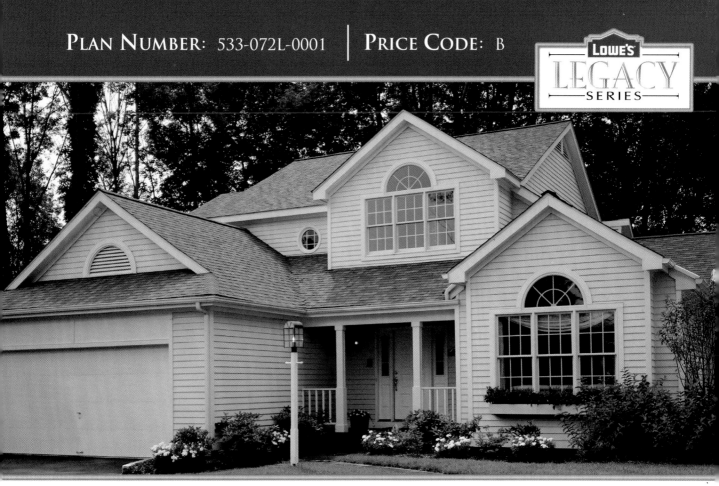

SPECIAL FEATURES

1,724 total square feet of living area

Beautiful palladian windows
enliven the two-story entry

Sliding glass doors in the formal dining
room connect to the large backyard deck

Second floor master bedroom
boasts corner windows, large
walk-in closet and a split bath

3 bedrooms, 2 1/2 baths, 2-car garage

Basement foundation

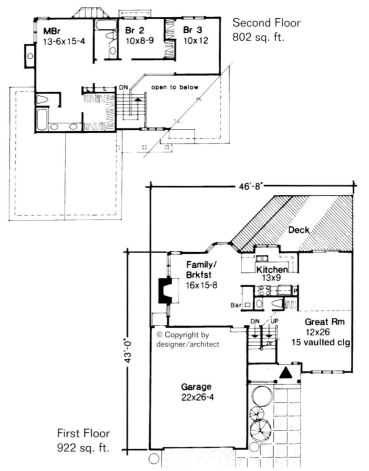

Second Floor
802 sq. ft.

MBr
13-6x15-4

Br 2
10x8-9

Br 3
10x12

DN   open to below

46'-8"

43'-0"

Deck

Family/
Brkfst
16x15-8

Kitchen
13x9

Bar

DN UP

Great Rm
12x26
15 vaulted clg

© Copyright by
designer/architect

Garage
22x26-4

First Floor
922 sq. ft.

SPECIAL FEATURES

2,874 total square feet of living area

Large family room with sloped ceiling and wood beams adjoins the kitchen and breakfast area with windows on two walls

Large foyer opens to the family room with a massive stone fireplace and open stairs to the basement

Private master bedroom includes a raised tub under the bay window, dramatic dressing area and a huge walk-in closet

4 bedrooms, 2 1/2 baths, 2-car side entry garage

Basement foundation

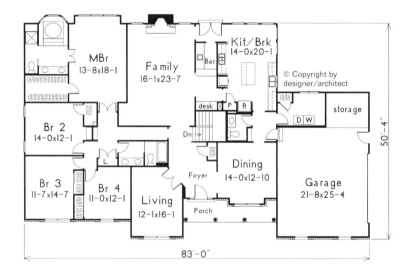

SPECIAL FEATURES

2,828 total square feet of living area

Popular wrap-around porch
gives home country charm

Secluded, oversized family room with vaulted
ceiling and wet bar features many windows

Any chef would be delighted to cook
in this smartly designed kitchen
with island and corner windows

Spectacular master bedroom and bath

2" x 6" exterior walls available, please
order plan #533-007E-0015

5 bedrooms, 3 1/2 baths,
2-car side entry garage

Basement foundation, drawings also
include crawl space and slab foundations

Second Floor
822 sq. ft.

First Floor
2,006 sq. ft.

© Copyright by designer/architect

SPECIAL FEATURES

3,035 total square feet of living area

Energy efficient home with
2" x 6" exterior walls

Front facade includes a large porch

Private master bedroom with
windowed sitting area, walk-in closet,
sloped ceiling and skylight

Formal living and dining rooms adjoin the
family room through attractive French doors

4 bedrooms, 3 1/2 baths,
2-car detached side entry garage

Crawl space foundation, drawings also
include slab and basement foundations

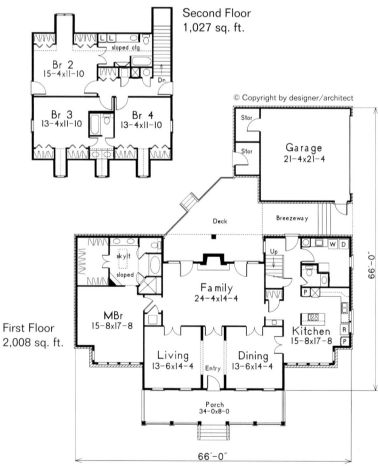

Second Floor
1,027 sq. ft.

© Copyright by designer/architect

First Floor
2,008 sq. ft.

SPECIAL FEATURES

2,301 total square feet of living area

Energy efficient home with
2" x 6" exterior walls

Formal dining room has lovely views into
the beautiful two-story great room

Second floor loft area makes a perfect
home office or children's computer area

Bonus room on the second floor has an
additional 300 square feet of living area

3 bedrooms, 2 1/2 baths, 2-car garage

Basement foundation

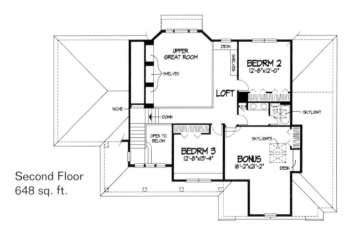

Second Floor
648 sq. ft.

Rear View

First Floor
1,653 sq. ft.

© Copyright by designer/architect

SPECIAL FEATURES

1,475 total square feet of living area

Family room features a high ceiling and prominent corner fireplace

Kitchen with island counter and garden window makes a convenient connection between the family and dining rooms

Hallway leads to three bedrooms all with large walk-in closets

Covered breezeway joins main house and garage

Full-width covered porch entry lends a country touch

3 bedrooms, 2 baths, 2-car detached side entry garage

Slab foundation, drawings also include crawl space foundation

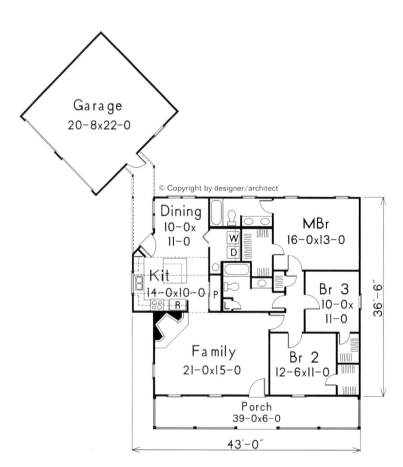

Garage
20-8x22-0

© Copyright by designer/architect

Dining
10-0x 11-0

MBr
16-0x13-0

Kit
14-0x10-0

Br 3
10-0x 11-0

Family
21-0x15-0

Br 2
12-6x11-0

Porch
39-0x6-0

36'-6"

43'-0"

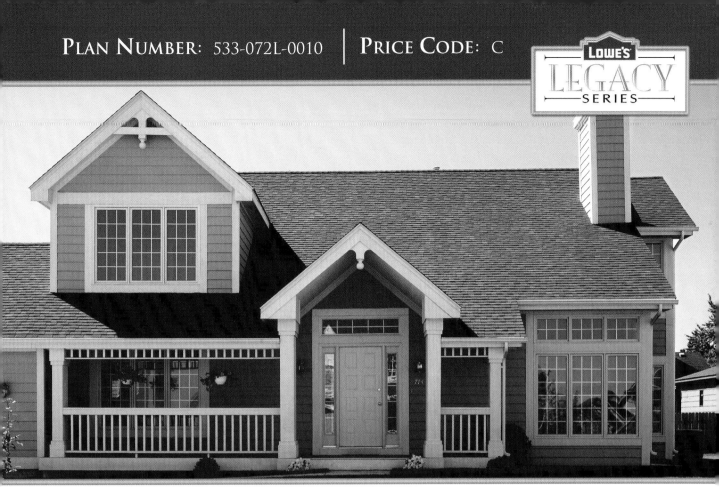

SPECIAL FEATURES

2,198 total square feet of living area

Sunken living room has a vaulted ceiling, a corner fireplace and eye-catching windows with transoms

A china hutch services the quiet dining room

Well-planned and stylish, the kitchen offers a snack bar and a built-in desk

3 bedrooms, 2 1/2 baths, 2-car garage

Basement foundation

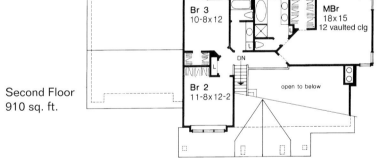

Second Floor
910 sq. ft.

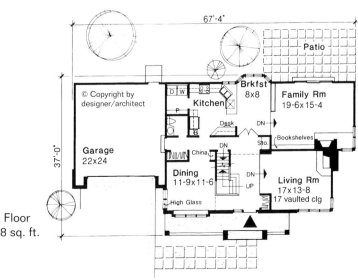

First Floor
1,288 sq. ft.

SPECIAL FEATURES

2,935 total square feet of living area

Gracious entry foyer with handsome stairway opens to separate living and dining rooms

Kitchen has a vaulted ceiling and skylight, island worktop, breakfast area with bay window and two separate pantries

Large second floor master bedroom features a fireplace, raised tub, dressing area with vaulted ceiling and skylight

4 bedrooms, 2 1/2 baths, 2-car side entry garage

Basement foundation

Second Floor
1,320 sq. ft.

MBr
20-1x15-0

Br 2
11-7x15-4

Br 3
10-10x
12-1

Br 4
13-7x12-1

Dn

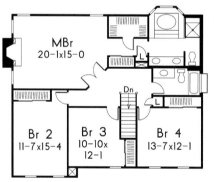

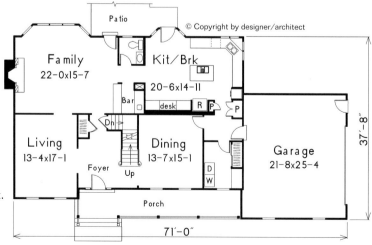

© Copyright by designer/architect

Patio

Family
22-0x15-7

Kit/Brk
20-6x14-11

Bar

desk

R P

P

Living
13-4x17-1

Dining
13-7x15-1

Garage
21-8x25-4

Dn

Foyer

Up

D W

37'-8"

First Floor
1,615 sq. ft.

Porch

71'-0"

LOWE'S LEGACY SERIES

SPECIAL FEATURES

2,730 total square feet of living area

Spacious kitchen features an island and generous walk-in pantry

Covered deck offers a private retreat to the outdoors

Large master bedroom has a bath with a corner whirlpool tub, separate shower and double walk-in closets

Oversized laundry room is conveniently located off the kitchen

4 bedrooms, 2 1/2 baths, 3-car side entry garage with storage area

Basement foundation

Rear View

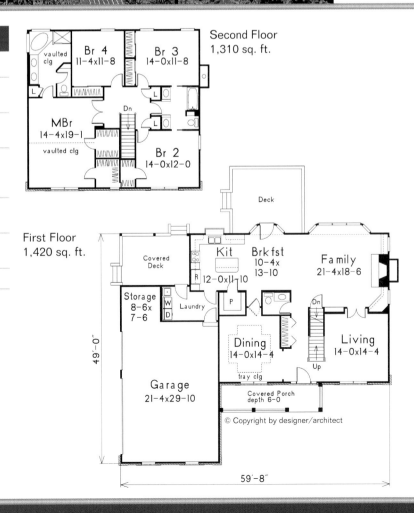

Second Floor
1,310 sq. ft.

Br 4
11-4x11-8
vaulted clg

Br 3
14-0x11-8

MBr
14-4x19-1
vaulted clg

Dn

Br 2
14-0x12-0

First Floor
1,420 sq. ft.

Deck

Covered Deck

Kit
12-0x11-10

Brk fst
10-4x
13-10

Family
21-4x18-6

Storage
8-6x
7-6

Laundry

Dining
14-0x14-4
tray clg

Living
14-0x14-4

Up

Dn

Garage
21-4x29-10

Covered Porch
depth 6-0

© Copyright by designer/architect

49'-0"

59'-8"

SPECIAL FEATURES

1,926 total square feet of living area

A breathtaking wall of windows brightens the great room

A double-door entry leads to the master suite which features a large bath and walk-in closet

An island cooktop in the kitchen makes mealtime a breeze

3 bedrooms, 2 1/2 baths, 2-car garage

Basement foundation

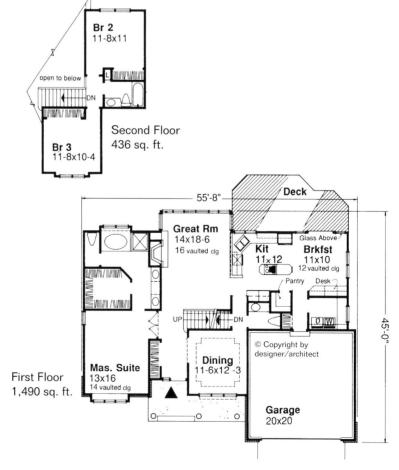

Br 2
11-8x11

open to below

DN

Second Floor
436 sq. ft.

Br 3
11-8x10-4

55'-8"

Deck

Great Rm
14x18-6
16 vaulted clg

Glass Above

Kit
11x12

Brkfst
11x10
12 vaulted clg

Pantry   Desk

UP   DN

D W

45'-0"

© Copyright by
designer/architect

Mas. Suite
13x16
14 vaulted clg

Dining
11-6x12 -3

First Floor
1,490 sq. ft.

Garage
20x20

SPECIAL FEATURES

- 2,255 total square feet of living area
- Energy efficient home with 2" x 6" exterior walls
- Master bedroom with adjoining bath has an enormous walk-in closet
- Deluxe kitchen features a planning desk and a convenient eating area
- Balcony library overlooks the family room
- Formal dining area has easy access to the kitchen
- 3 bedrooms, 2 baths, 2-car side entry garage
- Crawl space foundation, drawings also include slab and basement foundations

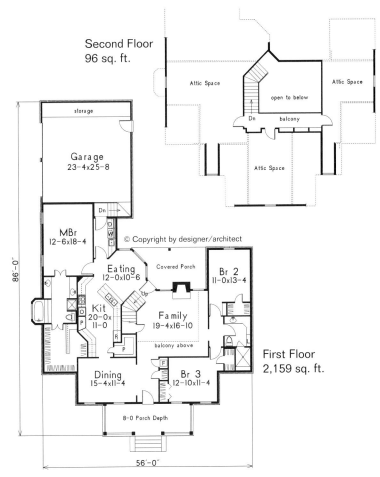

Second Floor
96 sq. ft.

Attic Space open to below Attic Space

Dn balcony

Attic Space

© Copyright by designer/architect

storage

Garage
23-4x25-8

MBr
12-6x18-4

Eating
12-0x10-6

Covered Porch

Br 2
11-0x13-4

Kit
20-0x11-0

Family
19-4x16-10

balcony above

Dining
15-4x11-4

Br 3
12-10x11-4

86'-0"

8-0 Porch Depth

56'-0"

First Floor
2,159 sq. ft.

Lowe's LEGACY SERIES

SPECIAL FEATURES

3,149 total square feet of living area

10' ceilings on the first floor and 9' ceilings on the second floor

All bedrooms include walk-in closets

Formal living and dining rooms flank the two-story foyer

4 bedrooms, 3 1/2 baths, 2-car side entry detached garage

Slab foundation, drawings also include crawl space foundation

Rear View

Second Floor
1,116 sq. ft.

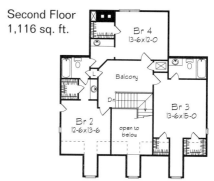

First Floor
2,033 sq. ft.

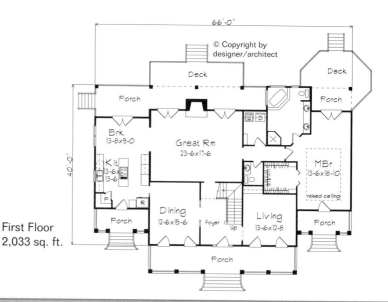

LOWE'S
LEGACY
SERIES

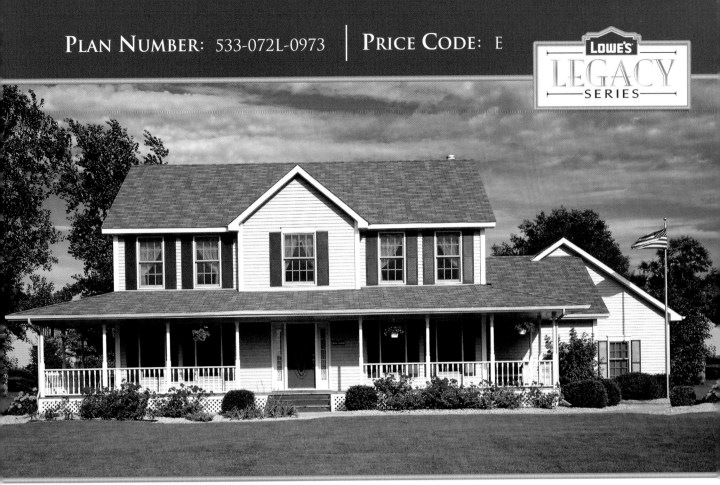

SPECIAL FEATURES

2,144 total square feet of living area

Formal living and dining rooms flank the foyer and offer stunning spaces for elegant entertaining

The more casual family room and dinette flow together with the kitchen for a spacious family gathering space

All the bedroooms are located on the second floor for extra peace and quiet

4 bedrooms, 2 1/2 baths, 3-car side entry garage

Basement foundation

Family Room - Interior View

Second Floor
988 sq. ft.

BEDRM 2
11⁴ x 11⁰

MSTR SUITE
12⁰ x 17⁴
10⁰ VLTD CLG

BEDRM 4
9⁸ x 11⁴

BEDRM 3
11⁴ x 11⁴

© Copyright by designer/architect

GARAGE
25⁸ x 35⁴

Width: 70'-3"
Depth: 60'-0"

KITCHEN

FAMILY RM
17⁶ x 13⁴

DINETTE
10⁰ x 11⁴

10⁰ x 13⁴

LAUN

LIVING RM
14⁴ x 11⁴

FOYER

DINING RM
11⁴ x 11⁴

COVERED PORCH

First Floor
1,156 sq. ft.

SPECIAL FEATURES

2,464 total square feet of living area

Energy efficient home with
2" x 6" exterior walls

The dining room is perfect for
hosting elegant meals

Master bedroom is oversized and offers a
large shower and a separate dressing area

The family room features a second fireplace
and is open to the spacious country kitchen

4 bedrooms, 2 1/2 baths, 2-car garage

Basement foundation

Second Floor
1,176 sq. ft.

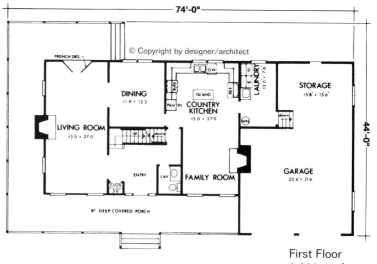

© Copyright by designer/architect

First Floor
1,288 sq. ft.

SPECIAL FEATURES

2,847 total square feet of living area

Secluded first floor master bedroom
includes an oversized window
and a large walk-in closet

Extensive attic storage and closet space

Spacious second floor bedrooms,
two of which share a private bath

Great starter home with option to
finish the second floor as needed

4 bedrooms, 3 1/2 baths, 2-car garage

Basement foundation, drawings also
include slab and crawl space foundations

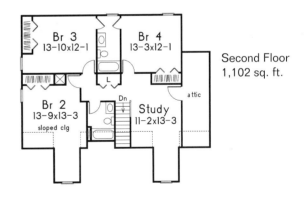

Second Floor
1,102 sq. ft.

Br 3
13-10x12-1

Br 4
13-3x12-1

Br 2
13-9x13-3
sloped clg

Study
11-2x13-3

Dn

attic

L

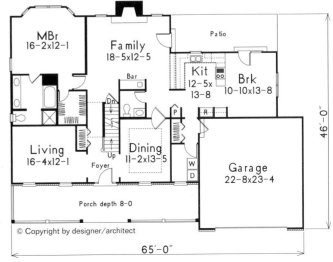

First Floor
1,745 sq. ft.

MBr
16-2x12-1

Family
18-5x12-5

Patio

Kit
12-5x
13-8

Brk
10-10x13-8

Bar

Dn

Living
16-4x12-1

Dining
11-2x13-5

Up

Foyer

W
D

Garage
22-8x23-4

Porch depth 8-0

46'-0"

65'-0"

© Copyright by designer/architect

LOWE'S LEGACY SERIES

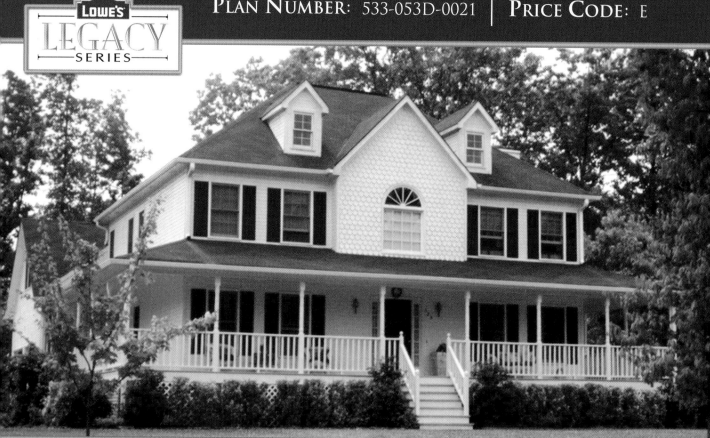

SPECIAL FEATURES

2,826 total square feet of living area

Wrap-around covered porch is accessible from the family and breakfast rooms in addition to the front entrance

Bonus room, which is included in the square footage, has a separate entrance and is suitable for an office or private accommodations

Large, full-windowed breakfast room

4 bedrooms, 2 1/2 baths, 2-car side entry garage

Basement foundation

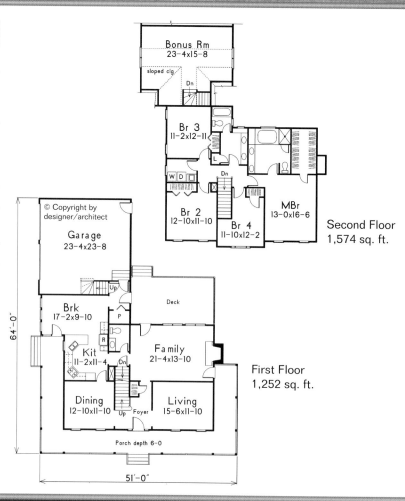

Second Floor
1,574 sq. ft.

First Floor
1,252 sq. ft.

SPECIAL FEATURES

2,445 total square feet of living area

A dramatic, skylighted foyer preludes the formal, sunken living room, which includes a stunning corner fireplace

A built-in desk and a pantry mark the smartly designed kitchen which opens to the breakfast room and beyond to the family room

Sunken and filled with intrigue, the family room features a fireplace plus French doors that open to the backyard deck

4 bedrooms, 2 1/2 baths, 3-car garage

Basement foundation

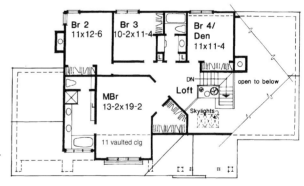

Second Floor
1,155 sq. ft.

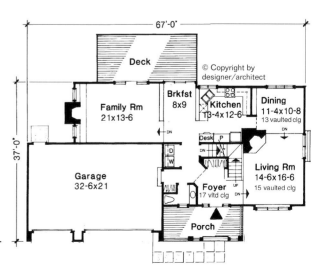

First Floor
1,290 sq. ft.

LOWE'S LEGACY SERIES

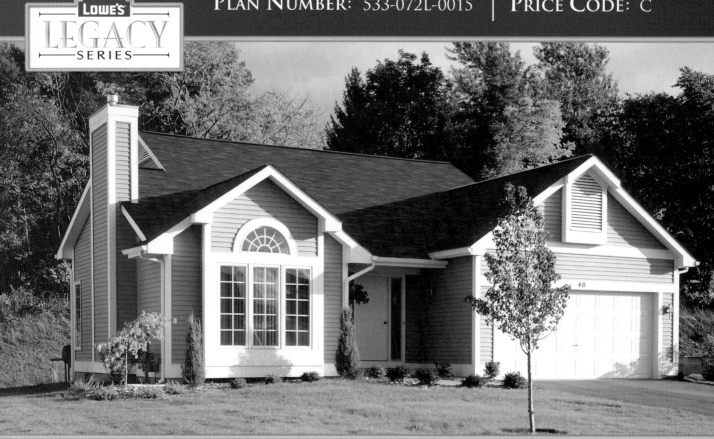

SPECIAL FEATURES

1,252 total square feet of living area

This delightful ranch features stylish amenities provided for easy family living

The living room shares a vaulted ceiling and high plant shelf with the dining room, along with a fireplace and sliding glass doors to the deck

The centrally located kitchen is open to the dining room for easy serving

3 bedrooms, 2 baths, 2-car garage

Basement foundation

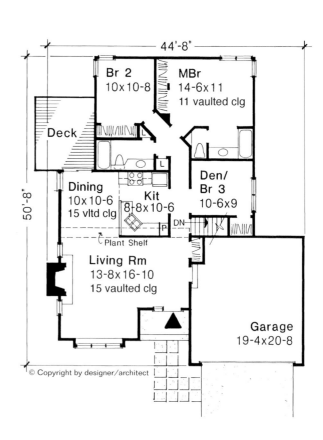

44'-8"

50'-8"

Br 2
10x10-8

MBr
14-6x11
11 vaulted clg

Deck

Dining
10x10-6
15 vltd clg

Kit
8-8x10-6

Den/
Br 3
10-6x9

L

P

DN

Plant Shelf

Living Rm
13-8x16-10
15 vaulted clg

Garage
19-4x20-8

© Copyright by designer/architect

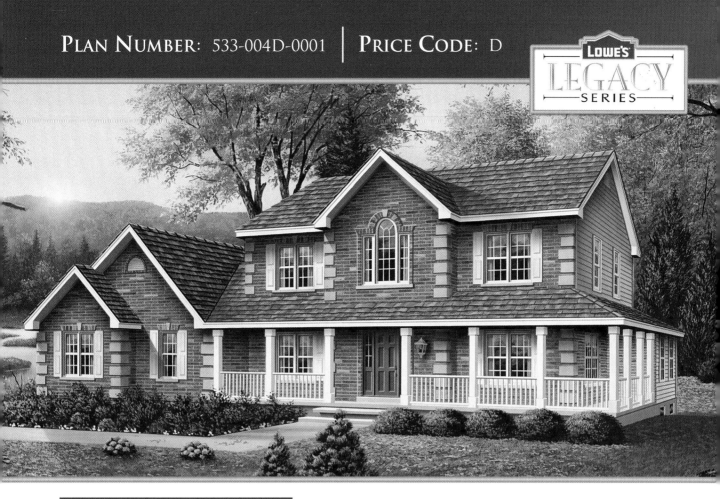

SPECIAL FEATURES

2,505 total square feet of living area

The garage features extra storage area and ample workspace

Laundry room is accessible from the garage and the outdoors

Deluxe raised tub and an immense walk-in closet grace the master bath

3 bedrooms, 2 1/2 baths, 2-car side entry garage

Basement foundation, drawings also include crawl space foundation

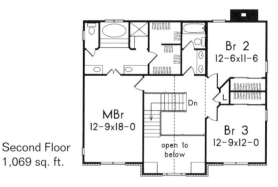

Second Floor
1,069 sq. ft.

MBr
12-9x18-0

Br 2
12-6x11-6

Br 3
12-9x12-0

open to below

Dn

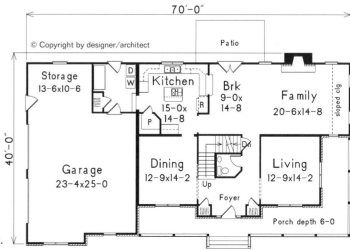

© Copyright by designer/architect

70'-0"

40'-0"

Patio

Storage
13-6x10-6

Kitchen
15-0x
14-8

Brk
9-0x
14-8

Family
20-6x14-8

sloped clg

Garage
23-4x25-0

Dining
12-9x14-2

Living
12-9x14-2

Up

Dn

Foyer

Porch depth 6-0

First Floor
1,436 sq. ft.

Lowe's LEGACY SERIES

SPECIAL FEATURES

1,400 total square feet of living area

Master bedroom is secluded for privacy

Large utility room has additional cabinet space

Covered porch provides an outdoor seating area

Roof dormers add great curb appeal

Living room and master bedroom feature vaulted ceilings

Oversized two-car garage has storage space

3 bedrooms, 2 baths, 2-car garage

Basement foundation, drawings also include crawl space foundation

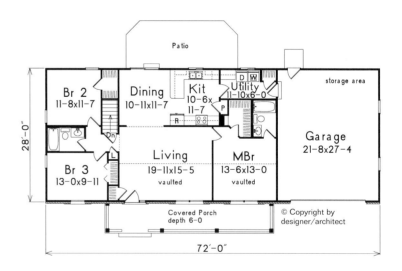

Patio

Br 2
11-8x11-7

Dining
10-11x11-7

Kit
10-6x
11-7

Utility
11-10x6-0

storage area

Br 3
13-0x9-11

Living
19-11x15-5
vaulted

MBr
13-6x13-0
vaulted

Garage
21-8x27-4

28'-0"

Covered Porch
depth 6-0

© Copyright by designer/architect

72'-0"

Lowe's LEGACY SERIES

SPECIAL FEATURES

1,814 total square feet of living area

Vaulted master bedroom features a walk-in closet and private bath

Exciting two-story entry with views into the dining room

Kitchen, family and dining rooms combine to make a great entertaining space with lots of windows

3 bedrooms, 2 1/2 baths, 2-car garage

Basement foundation

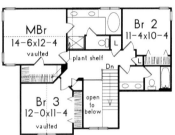

MBr
14-6x12-4
vaulted

Br 2
11-4x10-4

plant shelf

Dn

Br 3
12-0x11-4
vaulted

open to below

Second Floor
890 sq. ft.

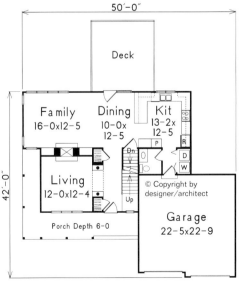

50'-0"

Deck

Family
16-0x12-5

Dining
10-0x
12-5

Kit
13-2x
12-5

42'-0"

Living
12-0x12-4

Dn

Up

© Copyright by
designer/architect

Garage
22-5x22-9

Porch Depth 6-0

First Floor
924 sq. ft.

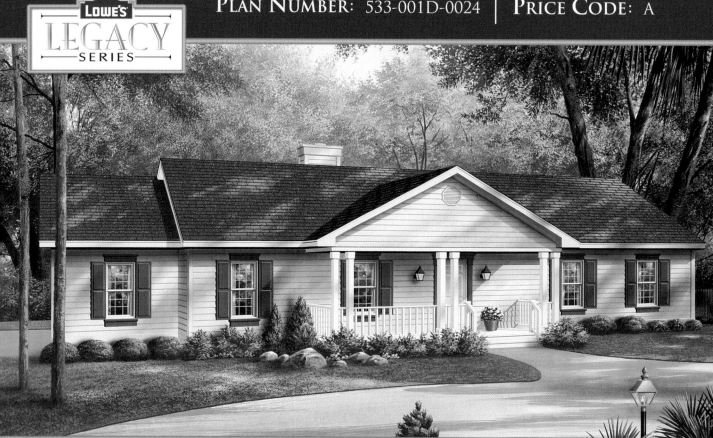

LOWE'S LEGACY SERIES

SPECIAL FEATURES

1,360 total square feet of living area

Kitchen/dining room features an island workspace and plenty of dining area

Master bedroom has a large walk-in closet and private bath

Laundry room is adjacent to the kitchen for easy access

Convenient workshop in garage

Large closets in secondary bedrooms maintain organization

3 bedrooms, 2 baths, 2-car side entry garage

Basement foundation, drawings also include crawl space and slab foundations

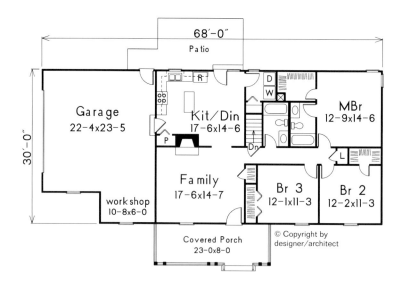

68'-0"

Patio

Garage
22-4x23-5

Kit/Din
17-6x14-6

MBr
12-9x14-6

30'-0"

Family
17-6x14-7

Br 3
12-1x11-3

Br 2
12-2x11-3

work shop
10-8x6-0

Covered Porch
23-0x8-0

© Copyright by designer/architect

SPECIAL FEATURES

1,672 total square feet of living area

The living room and breakfast nook are bridged by a handsome fireplace

The master bedroom enjoys a lovely bayed window and private bath with decorative glass block window

The formal dining room features a built-in china cabinet for beauty and function

3 bedrooms, 2 1/2 baths, 2-car garage

Basement foundation

© Copyright by designer/architect

Lndry

Kit
10-9x13-9

Brkfst
12-7x11-10

Br 2
11-8x9-2

Bath

Bath

Garage
21-2x23-2

Dining
9-7x10-7

Living
10-11x18-2

Foyer

Br 3
11-6x9-6

MBr
12-1x13-2

Porch
24-8x5-4

32'-0"

82'-8"

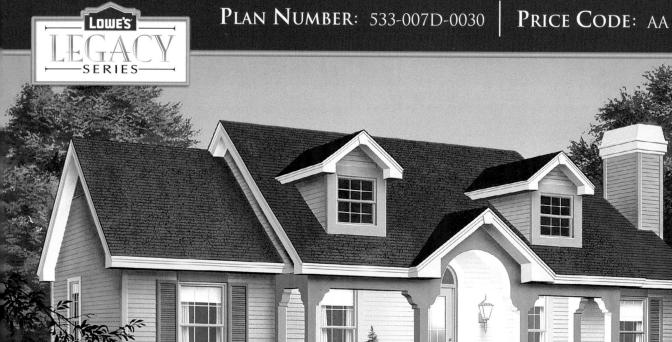

SPECIAL FEATURES

1,140 total square feet of living area

Open and spacious living and dining areas for family gatherings

Well-organized kitchen has an abundance of cabinetry and a built-in pantry

Roomy master bath features a double-bowl vanity

3 bedrooms, 2 baths, 2-car drive under garage

Basement foundation

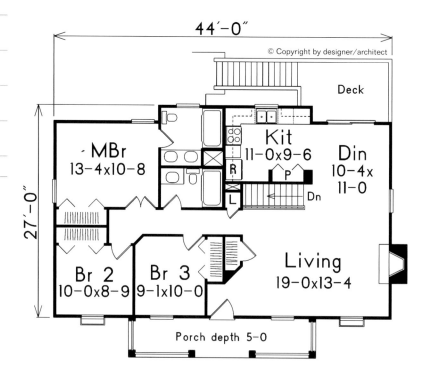

SPECIAL FEATURES

1,227 total square feet of living area

A coffered ceiling tops the master bedroom adding style and elegance to the interior

The dining area flows effortlessly into the coffered family room with fireplace

The U-shaped kitchen is compact, yet keeps everything within reach

3 bedrooms, 2 baths

Slab foundation

© Copyright by designer/architect

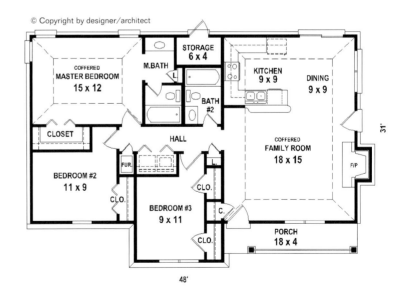

SPECIAL FEATURES

2,212 total square feet of living area

Louvered shutters, turned posts with railing and garage door detailing are a few inviting features

Dining room is spacious and borders a well-planned U-shaped kitchen and breakfast room

Colossal walk-in closet and an oversized private bath are part of a gracious master bedroom

3 bedrooms, 2 1/2 baths, 2-car garage

Partial basement/crawl space foundation, drawings also include crawl space foundation

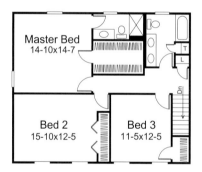

Second Floor
952 sq. ft.

Master Bed
14-10x14-7

Bed 2
15-10x12-5

Bed 3
11-5x12-5

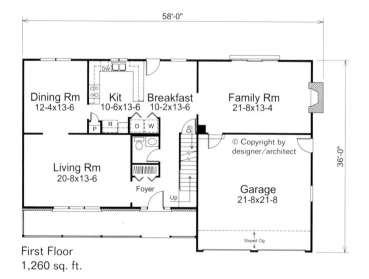

58'-0"

Dining Rm
12-4x13-6

Kit
10-6x13-6

Breakfast
10-2x13-6

Family Rm
21-8x13-4

Living Rm
20-8x13-6

Foyer

Up

Garage
21-8x21-8

© Copyright by designer/architect

36'-0"

Sloped Clg

First Floor
1,260 sq. ft.

Lowe's LEGACY SERIES

SPECIAL FEATURES

1,639 total square feet of living area

The great room has a trayed ceiling and a welcoming fireplace

The kitchen is well designed with plenty of counterspace and conveniently placed pantry and refrigerator

The eating area opens onto the back covered porch through beautiful French doors

3 bedrooms, 2 baths, 2-car side entry garage

Slab foundation, drawings also include crawl space foundation

© Copyright by designer/architect

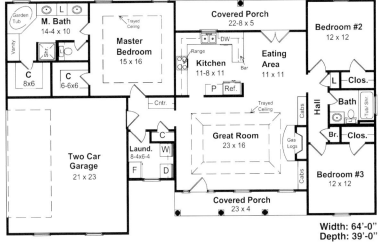

Width: 64'-0"
Depth: 39'-0"

SPECIAL FEATURES

1,655 total square feet of living area

Master bedroom features a 9' ceiling, walk-in closet and bath with dressing area

Oversized family room includes a 10' ceiling and masonry see-through fireplace

Island kitchen has convenient access to the laundry room

Handy covered walkway from the garage leads to the kitchen and dining area

3 bedrooms, 2 baths, 2-car garage

Crawl space foundation

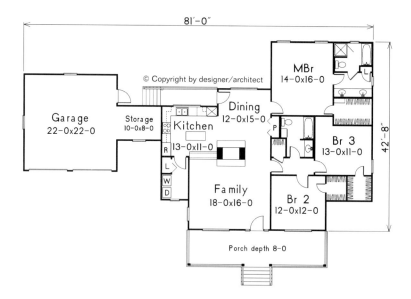

© Copyright by designer/architect

SPECIAL FEATURES

2,137 total square feet of living area

Elegant double-door entry with large foyer and double coat closets opens into the grand-size great room

Master bedroom features large double walk-in closets, dressing area and private bath

U-shaped kitchen has a breakfast bar and adjacent breakfast nook

Extra large laundry room

2" x 6" exterior walls available, please order plan #533-001D-0128

3 bedrooms, 2 baths, 2-car side entry garage

Crawl space foundation, drawings also include basement and slab foundations

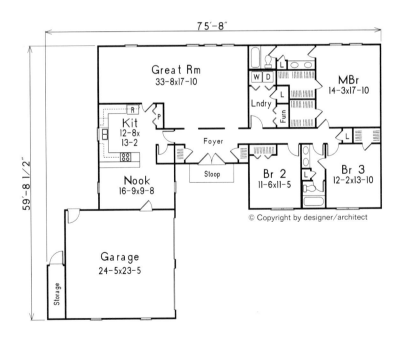

© Copyright by designer/architect

SPECIAL FEATURES

2,645 total square feet of living area

Second floor has a second washer and dryer area for convenience

Second floor casual family room is ideal for a children's play area with adjacent computer room

First floor master bedroom has a luxurious private bath with corner tub and walk-in closet

Bonus room on the second floor has an additional 438 square feet of living area

3 bedrooms, 2 1/2 baths, 2-car side entry garage

Basement foundation, drawings also include crawl space and slab foundations

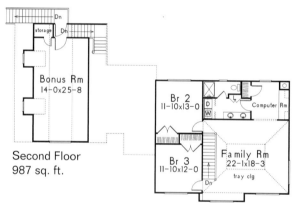

Second Floor
987 sq. ft.

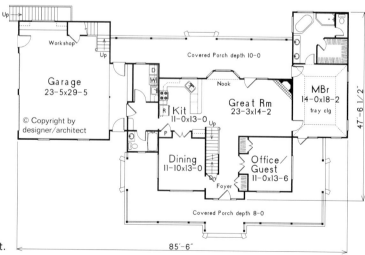

First Floor
1,658 sq. ft.

SPECIAL FEATURES

2,029 total square feet of living area

Stonework, gables, roof dormer and double porches create a country flavor

Kitchen enjoys extravagant cabinetry and counterspace in a bay, island snack bar, built-in pantry and cheery dining area with multiple tall windows

Angled stair descends from large entry with wood columns and is open to a vaulted great room with corner fireplace

Master bedroom boasts two walk-in closets, a private bath with double-door entry and a secluded porch

4 bedrooms, 2 baths, 2-car side entry garage

Basement foundation, drawings also include crawl space and slab foundations

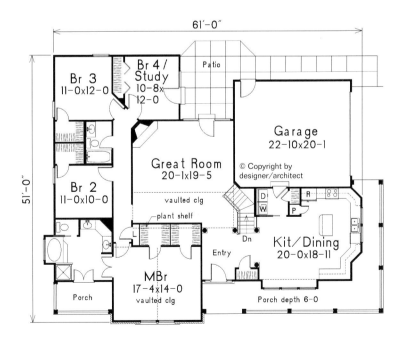

SPECIAL FEATURES

1,800 total square feet of living area

The wonderful family room boasts a 10' ceiling and opens nicely to the eating area and cozy kitchen

The chef of the family is sure to love this cheerful kitchen equipped with a uniquely-shaped island, plenty of counterspace and a functional pass-thru to the formal dining room

Luxurious master suite includes two closets, a separate shower, a double-bowl vanity and access to the screened porch

The optional bonus room has an additional 503 square feet of living area

3 bedrooms, 3 baths, 3-car side entry garage

Crawl space foundation

Rear View

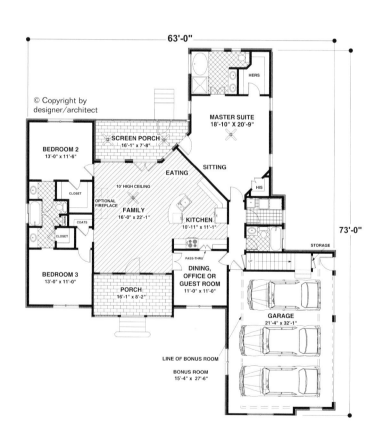

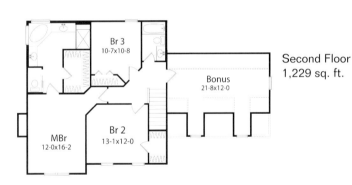

Second Floor
1,229 sq. ft.

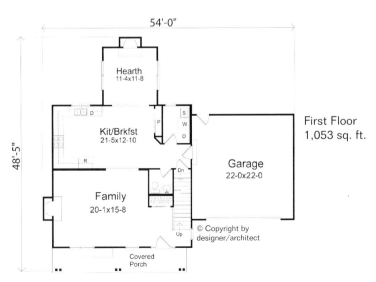

First Floor
1,053 sq. ft.

SPECIAL FEATURES

2,282 total square feet of living area

The kitchen/breakfast room is expansive in size and leads to an exquisite hearth room with plenty of sunlight and a large centered fireplace

The master bedroom contains a private bath with a large corner whirlpool tub, a separate shower, a double vanity and enclosed toilet room

The two secondary bedrooms share a full bath and can also be found on the second floor for privacy

The bonus room on the second floor has an additional 260 square feet of living area

3 bedrooms, 2 1/2 baths, 2-car garage

Basement foundation

SPECIAL FEATURES

1,751 total square feet of living area

A wide front porch and decorative window above the entry adds a country flavor to this home

The kitchen enjoys an abundance of counterspace and includes an island that opens to the spacious dining room

The master bedroom is privately located on the first floor while two additional bedrooms are located on the second floor

3 bedrooms, 2 baths

Basement foundation

Second Floor
561 sq. ft.

BED RM. 2
12'-0"x16'-0"
8' CEILING

SITTING

BED RM. 3
12'-0"x13'-4"
8' CEILING

OPEN TO BELOW

PLANT SHELF

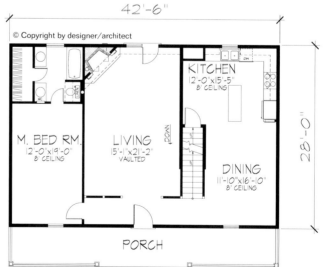

42'-6"

© Copyright by designer/architect

First Floor
1,190 sq. ft.

KITCHEN
12'-0"x15'-5"
8' CEILING

M. BED RM.
12'-0"x19'-0"
8' CEILING

LIVING
15'-1"x21'-2"
VAULTED

DOWN

DINING
11'-10"x16'-10"
8' CEILING

28'-0"

PORCH

SPECIAL FEATURES

2,363 total square feet of living area

Energy efficient home with
2" x 6" exterior walls

Covered porches provide
outdoor seating areas

Corner fireplace becomes focal
point of the family room

Kitchen features island cooktop
and adjoining nook

3 bedrooms, 2 1/2 baths, 2-car garage

Partial basement/crawl space foundation

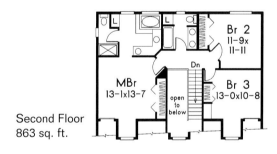

Second Floor
863 sq. ft.

Br 2
11-9x
11-11

MBr
13-1x13-7

Br 3
13-0x10-8

open to below

Dn

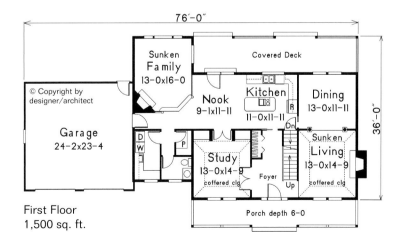

First Floor
1,500 sq. ft.

76'-0"

Sunken Family
13-0x16-0

Covered Deck

Nook
9-1x11-11

Kitchen
11-0x11-11

Dining
13-0x11-11

Garage
24-2x23-4

© Copyright by
designer/architect

Study
13-0x14-9
coffered clg

Sunken Living
13-0x14-9
coffered clg

Foyer

Up

Dn

36'-0"

Porch depth 6-0

Lowe's LEGACY SERIES

SPECIAL FEATURES

1,818 total square feet of living area

Useful and beautiful cabinetry flanks a center fireplace in the vaulted great room

A highly functional screen porch will be enjoyed year round

A corner whirlpool tub highlights the master bath, along with a walk-in closet and double-bowl vanity

3 bedrooms, 3 baths, 2-car side entry garage

Basement foundation

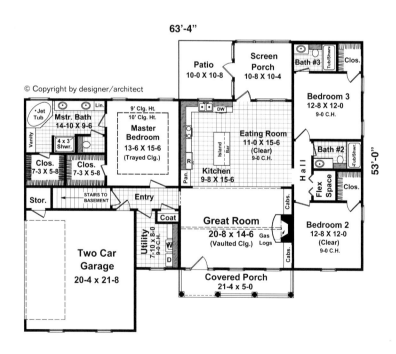

© Copyright by designer/architect

63'-4"

53'-0"

Patio 10-0 X 10-8

Screen Porch 10-8 X 10-4

Bath #3 · Tub/Shwr. · Clos.

Bedroom 3 12-8 X 12-0 9-0 C.H.

Bath #2 Tub/Shwr.

· Jet Tub · Vanity · Lin.

Mstr. Bath 14-10 X 9-6

4 x 3 Shwr.

9' Clg. Ht. 10' Clg. Ht.

Master Bedroom 13-6 X 15-6 (Trayed Clg.)

DW

Eating Room 11-0 X 15-6 (Clear) 9-0 C.H.

Island Bar

Hall

Flex Space

Clos.

Clos. 7-3 X 5-8

Clos. 7-3 X 5-8

Pan.

R

Kitchen 9-8 X 15-6

Cabs.

Bedroom 2 12-8 X 12-0 (Clear) 9-0 C.H.

Stor.

STAIRS TO BASEMENT

Entry

Coat

Great Room 20-8 x 14-6 (Vaulted Clg.)

Gas Logs

Cabs.

Two Car Garage 20-4 x 21-8

Utility 7-10 x 8-0 9-0 C.H.

W

D

Covered Porch 21-4 x 5-0

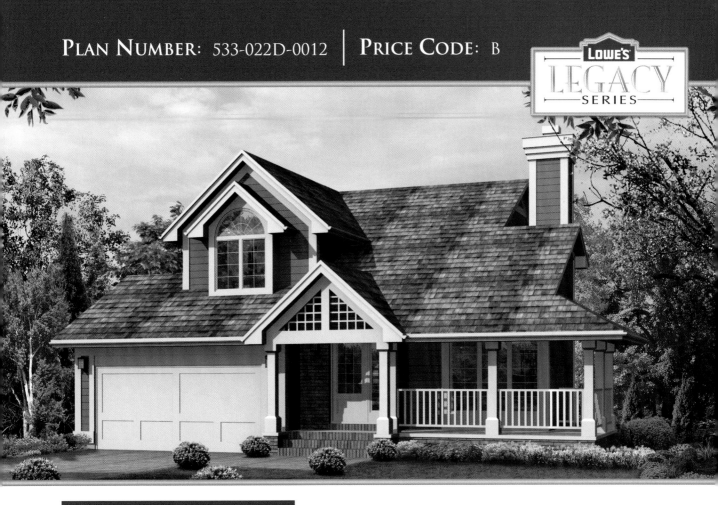

SPECIAL FEATURES

1,550 total square feet of living area

Impressive front entrance with a wrap-around covered porch and raised foyer

Corner fireplace provides a focal point in the vaulted great room

Loft is easily converted to a third bedroom or activity center

Large kitchen/family room includes greenhouse windows and access to the deck and utility area

The secondary bedroom has a large dormer and window seat

2 bedrooms, 2 1/2 baths, 2-car garage

Basement foundation

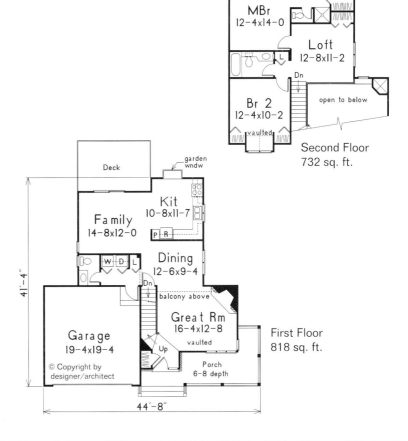

MBr
12-4x14-0

Loft
12-8x11-2

Br 2
12-4x10-2

open to below

vaulted

Second Floor
732 sq. ft.

Deck

garden wndw

Kit
10-8x11-7

Family
14-8x12-0

P R

Dining
12-6x9-4

W D L

Dn

balcony above

Great Rm
16-4x12-8
vaulted

Garage
19-4x19-4

Up

Porch
6-8 depth

© Copyright by designer/architect

41'-4"

44'-8"

First Floor
818 sq. ft.

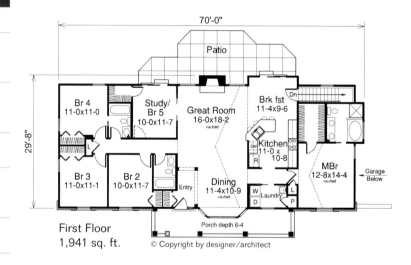

SPECIAL FEATURES

1,941 total square feet of living area

Interesting roof lines and a spacious front porch with flanking stonework help to fashion this beautiful country home

The vaulted great room has a separate entry and bayed dining area suitable for a large family and friends

The master bedroom enjoys a big walk-in closet and a gracious bath

Four additional bedrooms complete the home, one of which is ideal for a study off the great room

5 bedrooms, 3 baths, 2-car side entry drive under garage

Walk-out basement foundation

First Floor
1,941 sq. ft.

© Copyright by designer/architect

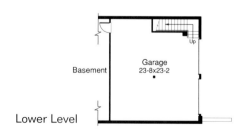

Lower Level

SPECIAL FEATURES

1,501 total square feet of living area

Spacious kitchen with dining area
is open to the outdoors

Convenient utility room is
adjacent to the garage

Master bedroom features a private
bath, dressing area and access
to the large covered porch

Large family room creates openness

3 bedrooms, 2 baths, 2-car side entry garage

Basement foundation, drawings also
include crawl space and slab foundations

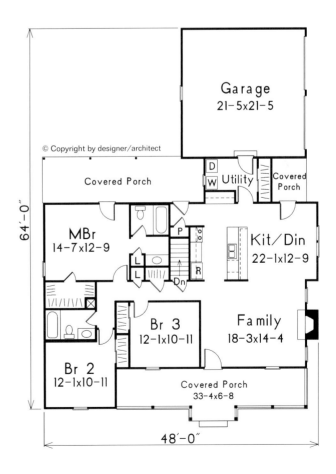

© Copyright by designer/architect

Garage
21-5x21-5

Covered Porch

D W Utility Covered Porch

MBr
14-7x12-9

Kit/Din
22-1x12-9

Br 3
12-1x10-11

Family
18-3x14-4

Br 2
12-1x10-11

Covered Porch
33-4x6-8

64'-0"

48'-0"

SPECIAL FEATURES

2,321 total square feet of living area

Energy efficient home with
2" x 6" exterior walls

Fully appointed kitchen is highlighted by a
convenient center island with snack counter

Spacious, yet cozy, family room

Second floor is open to living areas below

4 bedrooms, 2 1/2 baths, 2-car garage

Basement foundation

Second Floor
1,136 sq. ft.

© Copyright by designer/architect

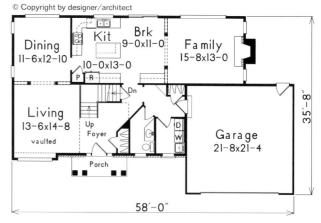

First Floor
1,185 sq. ft.

SPECIAL FEATURES

- 1,582 total square feet of living area
- Conservative layout gives privacy to living and dining areas
- Large fireplace and windows enhance the living area
- Rear door in garage is convenient to the garden and kitchen
- Full front porch adds charm
- Dormers add light to the foyer and bedrooms
- 3 bedrooms, 2 1/2 baths, 1-car garage
- Slab foundation, drawings also include crawl space foundation

Second Floor
745 sq. ft.

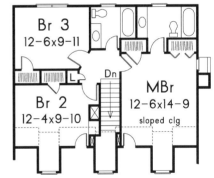

Br 3
12-6x9-11

Br 2
12-4x9-10

Dn

MBr
12-6x14-9
sloped clg

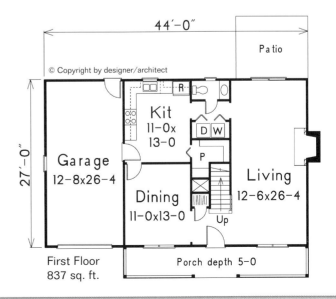

44'-0"

Patio

© Copyright by designer/architect

Kit
11-0x
13-0

D W

Garage
12-8x26-4

27'-0"

P

Living
12-6x26-4

Dining
11-0x13-0

Up

First Floor
837 sq. ft.

Porch depth 5-0

SPECIAL FEATURES

1,384 total square feet of living area

Wrap-around country porch
for peaceful evenings

Vaulted great room enjoys a
large bay window, stone fireplace,
pass-through kitchen and awesome rear
views through an atrium window wall

Master bedroom features a double-door
entry, walk-in closet and a fabulous bath

Atrium opens to 611 square feet
of optional living area below

2 bedrooms, 2 baths, 1-car side entry garage

Walk-out basement foundation

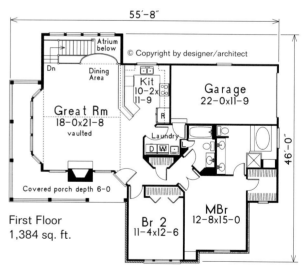

First Floor
1,384 sq. ft.

© Copyright by designer/architect

Atrium below

Dn

Dining Area

Kit
10-2x
11-9

Garage
22-0x11-9

Great Rm
18-0x21-8
vaulted

Laundry
D W

Covered porch depth 6-0

Br 2
11-4x12-6

MBr
12-8x15-0

55'-8"

46'-0"

Rear View

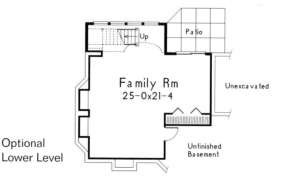

Optional
Lower Level

Up

Patio

Family Rm
25-0x21-4

Unexcavated

Unfinished Basement

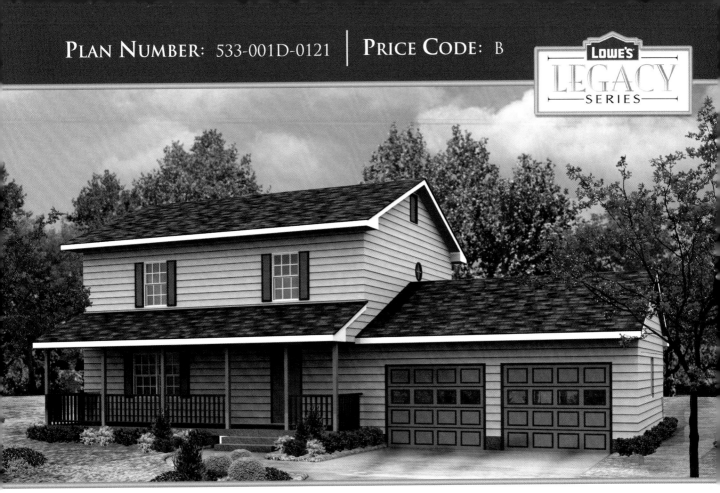

SPECIAL FEATURES

- 1,664 total square feet of living area

- Energy efficient home with 2" x 6" exterior walls

- L-shaped country kitchen includes pantry and cozy breakfast area

- Bedrooms located on second floor for privacy

- Master bedroom includes walk-in closet, dressing area and bath

- 3 bedrooms, 2 1/2 baths, 2-car garage

- Crawl space foundation, drawings also include basement and slab foundations

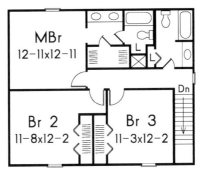

MBr 12-11x12-11

Br 2 11-8x12-2

Br 3 11-3x12-2

Dn

Second Floor
832 sq. ft.

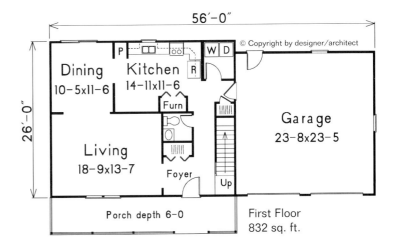

56'-0"

26'-0"

P

Dining 10-5x11-6

Kitchen 14-11x11-6

W D

R

© Copyright by designer/architect

Furn

Living 18-9x13-7

Garage 23-8x23-5

Foyer

Up

Porch depth 6-0

First Floor
832 sq. ft.

SPECIAL FEATURES

3,782 total square feet of living area

Stylish staircase in the foyer ascends to the second floor balcony overlooking the great room below

Lower level includes a media room with built-in cabinets, fireplace and ceiling mounted projector and screen

The formal dining room is decorated with an impressive tray ceiling drawing the eye upward

Massive 42" direct vent fireplace and expansive window wall helps bring the outdoors into the vaulted great room

4 bedrooms, 3 1/2 baths, 2-car garage

Basement foundation

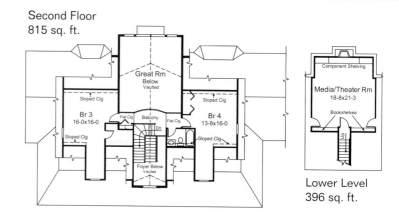

Second Floor
815 sq. ft.

Lower Level
396 sq. ft.

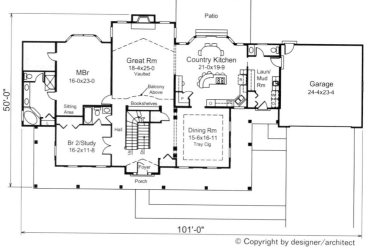

First Floor
2,571 sq. ft.

© Copyright by designer/architect

LOWE'S
LEGACY
SERIES

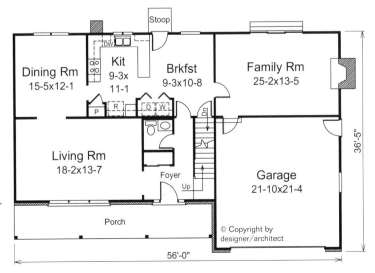

SPECIAL FEATURES

2,258 total square feet of living area

Kitchen is nestled between the dining room and breakfast area for convenience

Master bedroom has a large walk-in closet and private bath

Second floor bedrooms share full bath featuring double-bowl vanity

3 bedrooms, 2 1/2 baths, 2-car garage, plan also includes 4 bedroom option

Basement foundation, drawings also include crawl space and slab foundations

Second Floor
970 sq. ft.

MBr
14-1x13-5

Br 2
10-7x10-3

Br 3
10-7x10-3

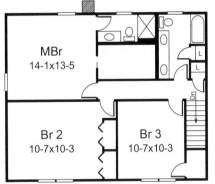

Stoop

Dining Rm
15-5x12-1

Kit
9-3x
11-1

Brkfst
9-3x10-8

Family Rm
25-2x13-5

Living Rm
18-2x13-7

Foyer

Garage
21-10x21-4

36'-5"

First Floor
1,288 sq. ft.

Porch

© Copyright by designer/architect

56'-0"

SPECIAL FEATURES

2,138 total square feet of living area

The vaulted sunroom is an enchanting space to dine and it accesses two covered porches

The master bedroom enjoys his and her baths and walk-in closets as well as access to one rear porch and an optional storage, lounge or office space

The bonus room on the second floor has an additional 302 square feet of living space

3 bedrooms, 3 baths, 2-car garage

Basement foundation, drawings also include crawl space and slab foundations

Optional Second Floor

© Copyright by designer/architect

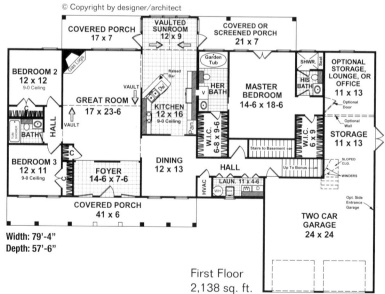

Width: 79'-4"
Depth: 57'-6"

First Floor
2,138 sq. ft.

SPECIAL FEATURES

2,449 total square feet of living area

Striking living area features a fireplace flanked with windows, a cathedral ceiling and balcony

First floor master bedroom has twin walk-in closets and large linen storage

Dormers add space for desks or seats

3 bedrooms, 2 1/2 baths, 2-car detached garage

Slab foundation, drawings also include crawl space foundation

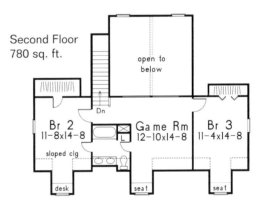

Second Floor 780 sq. ft.

open to below

Dn

Br 2
11-8x14-8

Game Rm
12-10x14-8

Br 3
11-4x14-8

sloped clg

desk

seat

seat

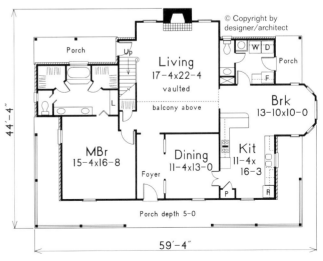

© Copyright by designer/architect

Porch

Up

Living
17-4x22-4
vaulted

W D

F

Porch

balcony above

Brk
13-10x10-0

44'-4"

MBr
15-4x16-8

Dining
11-4x13-0

Foyer

Kit
11-4x
16-3

P

R

First Floor
1,669 sq. ft.

Porch depth 5-0

59'-4"

SPECIAL FEATURES

2,806 total square feet of living area

Harmonious charm throughout

A sweeping balcony and vaulted ceiling soar above the spacious great room and walk-in bar

Atrium with lower level family room is a unique touch, creating an open and airy feeling

4 bedrooms, 2 1/2 baths, 2-car garage

Walk-out basement foundation

© Copyright by designer/architect

First Floor
1,473 sq. ft.

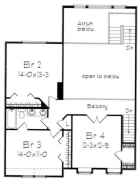

Second Floor
785 sq. ft.

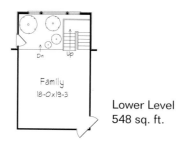

Lower Level
548 sq. ft.

SPECIAL FEATURES

1,802 total square feet of living area

Front and rear covered porches offer enchanting outdoor living spaces

The kitchen enjoys a snack bar counter open to the dining room as well as a window above the sink overlooking the backyard

The relaxing master bedroom features a vaulted ceiling, two walk-in closets and a majestic bath

3 bedrooms, 2 baths, 2-car side entry garage

Slab foundation, drawings also include crawl space and basement foundations

© Copyright by designer/architect

COVERED PORCH 12' x 10'

CLOS. 5' x 6'

M. BEDROOM (VAULTED) 14'6" x 16'

M. BATH 10'6" x 16'

CLOS. 5' x 6'

KIT. 12' x 11'

DINING ROOM 11' x 16'

BED #2 12' x 12'

STOR. 11' x 8'

UTIL. 6'6" x 8'

ENTRY

COAT

MEDIA 8' x 9'

GREAT ROOM 23' x 16'

BATH

HALL

2 CAR GARAGE 22' x 22'

ATTIC ACCESS

COVERED PORCH 23' x 4'

BED #3 12' x 12'

Width: 65'-0"
Depth: 45'-10"

SPECIAL FEATURES

2,547 total square feet of living area

Second floor makes economical use of area above garage allowing for three bedrooms and a study/fourth bedroom

First floor study is ideal for a home office

Large pantry is located in the efficient kitchen

2" x 6" exterior walls available, please order plan #533-058D-0092

3 bedrooms, 2 1/2 baths, 2-car garage

Basement foundation

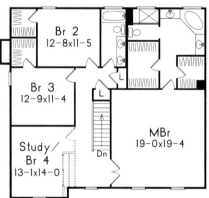

Second Floor
1,464 sq. ft.

Br 2
12-8x11-5

Br 3
12-9x11-4

Study/
Br 4
13-1x14-0

MBr
19-0x19-4

Dn

L

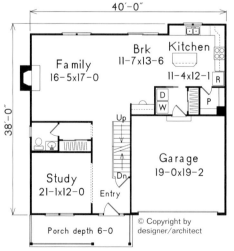

First Floor
1,083 sq. ft.

40'-0"

38'-0"

Family
16-5x17-0

Brk
11-7x13-6

Kitchen
11-4x12-1

D W P R

Up

Study
21-1x12-0

Entry

Dn

Garage
19-0x19-2

© Copyright by
designer/architect

Porch depth 6-0

SPECIAL FEATURES

1,050 total square feet of living area

Master bedroom has its own
private bath and access to the
outdoors onto a private patio

Vaulted ceilings in the living and dining
areas create a feeling of spaciousness

The laundry closet is
convenient to all bedrooms

Efficient U-shaped kitchen

3 bedrooms, 2 baths, 1-car garage

Basement foundation, drawings
also include slab foundation

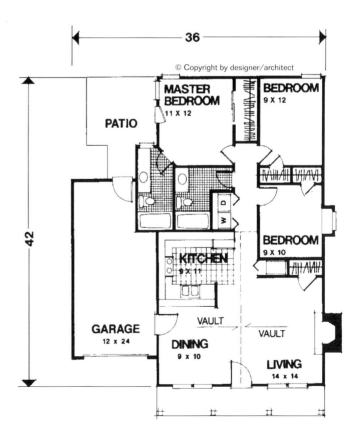

© Copyright by designer/architect

LOWE'S LEGACY SERIES

SPECIAL FEATURES

1,253 total square feet of living area

Sloped ceiling and fireplace in family room add drama

U-shaped kitchen is designed for efficiency

Large walk-in closets are found in all the bedrooms

3 bedrooms, 2 baths, 2-car garage

Crawl space foundation, drawings also include slab foundation

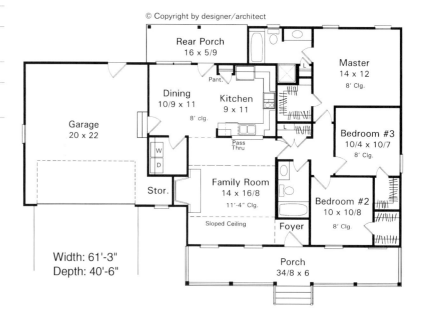

© Copyright by designer/architect

Rear Porch 16 x 5/9

Master 14 x 12 8' Clg.

Dining 10/9 x 11 8' clg.

Kitchen 9 x 11

Pant.

Pass Thru

Garage 20 x 22

W D

Stor.

Bedroom #3 10/4 x 10/7 8' Clg.

Family Room 14 x 16/8 11'-4" Clg.

Bedroom #2 10 x 10/8 8' Clg.

Sloped Ceiling

Foyer

Width: 61'-3"
Depth: 40'-6"

Porch 34/8 x 6

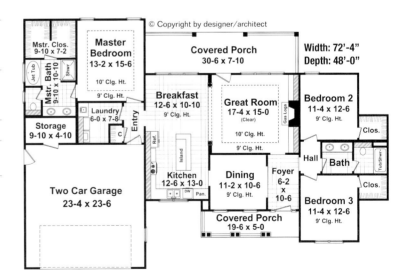

SPECIAL FEATURES

1,800 total square feet of living area

A long narrow island in the kitchen offers plenty of extra workspace when preparing meals

A large walk-in closet and spacious private bath add something special to the master bedroom

Two secondary bedrooms skillfully share a full bath and each have their own walk-in closet

3 bedrooms, 2 baths, 2-car garage

Slab foundation, drawings also include crawl space foundation

© Copyright by designer/architect

Mstr. Clos. 9-10 x 7-2

Master Bedroom 13-2 x 15-6
10' Clg. Ht.
9' Clg. Ht.

Jet Tub

Mstr. Bath 9-10 x 10-10

Shwr

Covered Porch 30-6 x 7-10

Width: 72'-4"
Depth: 48'-0"

Laundry 6-0 x 7-8

Breakfast 12-6 x 10-10
9' Clg. Ht.

Great Room 17-4 x 15-0 (Clear)
10' Clg. Ht.
9' Clg. Ht.

Bedroom 2 11-4 x 12-6
9' Clg. Ht.

Storage 9-10 x 4-10

Entry

Clos.

Kitchen 12-6 x 13-0

Island

Dining 11-2 x 10-6
9' Clg. Ht.

Foyer 6-2 x 10-6

Hall

Bath

Two Car Garage 23-4 x 23-6

DW Pan.

Covered Porch 19-6 x 5-0

Bedroom 3 11-4 x 12-6
9' Clg. Ht.

Clos.

LOWE'S LEGACY SERIES

SPECIAL FEATURES

2,412 total square feet of living area

Energy efficient home with 2" x 6" exterior walls

Coffered ceiling in dining room adds character and spaciousness

Great room is enhanced by a vaulted ceiling and atrium window wall

Spacious and well-planned kitchen includes counterspace dining and overlooks breakfast room and beyond to the deck

Luxurious master bedroom features an enormous walk-in closet, private bath and easy access to the laundry area

4 bedrooms, 2 baths, 3-car side entry garage

Walk-out basement foundation

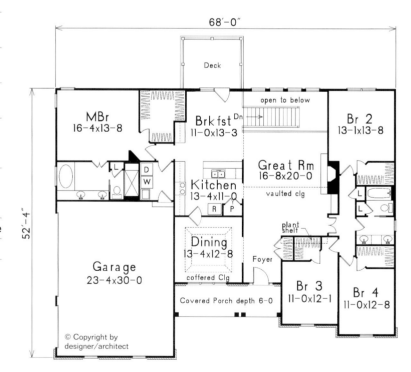

LOWE'S LEGACY SERIES

SPECIAL FEATURES

1,829 total square feet of living area

Entry foyer with coat closet opens to
a large family room with fireplace

Two second floor bedrooms share a full bath

Optional bedroom #4 on the
second floor has an additional
145 square feet of living area

Cozy porch provides a convenient
side entrance into the home

3 bedrooms, 2 1/2 baths,
2-car side entry garage

Partial basement/crawl space foundation

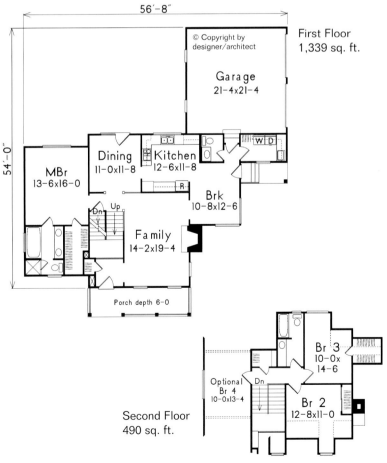

56'-8"

First Floor
1,339 sq. ft.

© Copyright by
designer/architect

Garage
21-4x21-4

54'-0"

MBr
13-6x16-0

Dining
11-0x11-8

Kitchen
12-6x11-8

W D

Brk
10-8x12-6

Dn   Up

Family
14-2x19-4

R

Porch depth 6-0

Second Floor
490 sq. ft.

Br 3
10-0x
14-6

Optional
Br 4
10-0x13-4

Dn

Br 2
12-8x11-0

SPECIAL FEATURES

1,935 total square feet of living area

The living and dining areas combine for an open atmosphere perfect for entertaining

One first floor bedroom offers an abundance of closets, a dressing area and private bath access

The second floor is comprised of a family relaxing room and a large bedroom with private bath access and plenty of storage

3 bedrooms, 2 baths, 2-car garage

Basement foundation

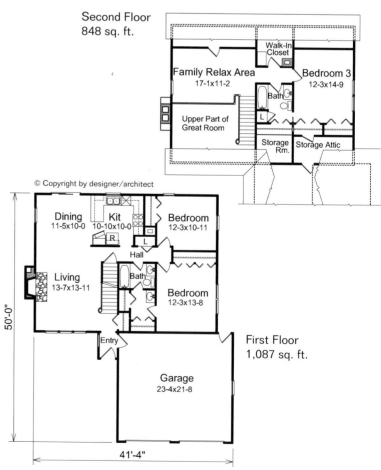

Second Floor
848 sq. ft.

Walk-In Closet

Family Relax Area
17-1x11-2

Bedroom 3
12-3x14-9

Bath

Upper Part of Great Room

Storage Rm.

Storage Attic

© Copyright by designer/architect

Dining
11-5x10-0

Kit
10-10x10-0

Bedroom
12-3x10-11

Hall

Living
13-7x13-11

Bath

Bedroom
12-3x13-8

50'-0"

Entry

First Floor
1,087 sq. ft.

Garage
23-4x21-8

41'-4"

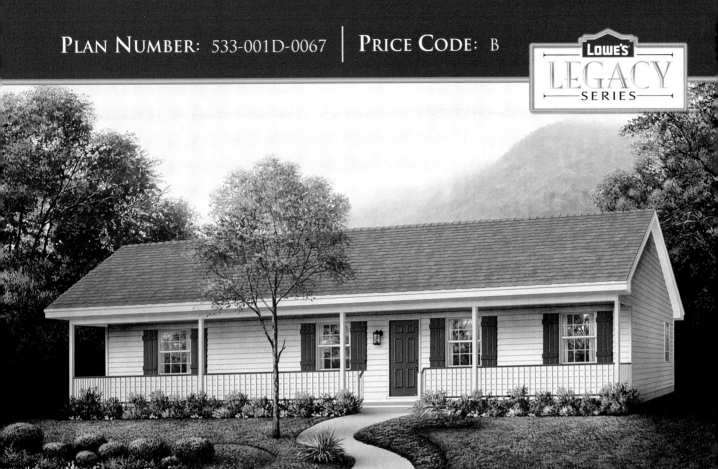

SPECIAL FEATURES

1,285 total square feet of living area

Accommodating home with ranch-style porch

Large storage area on back of home

Master bedroom includes dressing area, private bath and built-in bookcase

Kitchen features pantry, breakfast bar and complete view to the dining room

2" x 6" exterior walls available, please order plan #533-001D-0119

3 bedrooms, 2 baths

Crawl space foundation, drawings also include basement and slab foundations

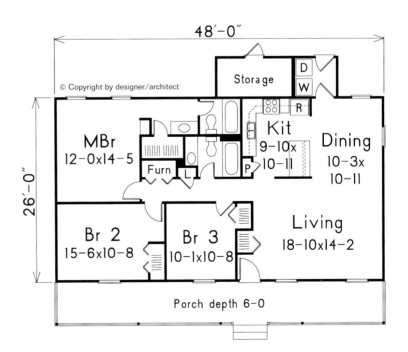

48'-0"

© Copyright by designer/architect

26'-0"

Storage

D
W

MBr
12-0x14-5

Furn

Kit
9-10x
10-11

P

R

Dining
10-3x
10-11

Br 2
15-6x10-8

Br 3
10-1x10-8

Living
18-10x14-2

Porch depth 6-0

LOWE'S
LEGACY
SERIES

SPECIAL FEATURES

1,780 total square feet of living area

Traditional styling with all
the comforts of home

First floor master bedroom has
a walk-in closet and bath

Large kitchen and dining area
opens to the deck

3 bedrooms, 2 1/2 baths, 2-car garage

Basement foundation, drawings also
include crawl space and slab foundations

Second Floor
551 sq. ft.

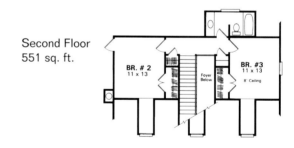

First Floor
1,229 sq. ft.

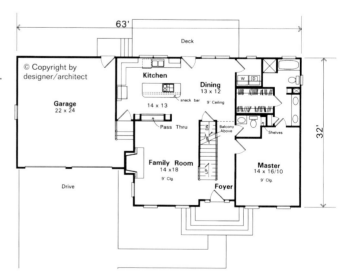

SPECIAL FEATURES

1,855 total square feet of living area

The great room boasts a 12' ceiling and corner fireplace

Bayed breakfast area adjoins the kitchen that features a walk-in pantry

The relaxing master bedroom includes a private bath with walk-in closet and garden tub

Optional second floor has an additional 352 square feet of living area

3 bedrooms, 2 1/2 baths, 2-car side entry garage

Basement foundation, drawings also include crawl space and slab foundations

Optional Second Floor

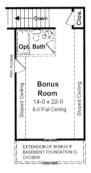

Bonus Room
14-0 x 22-0
8-0 Flat Ceiling

EXTENSION OF BONUS IF BASEMENT FOUNDATION IS CHOSEN.

First Floor
1,855 sq. ft.

Width: 72'-8"
Depth: 51'-0"

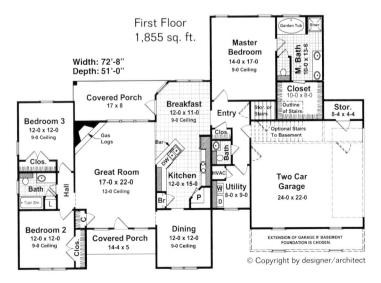

© Copyright by designer/architect

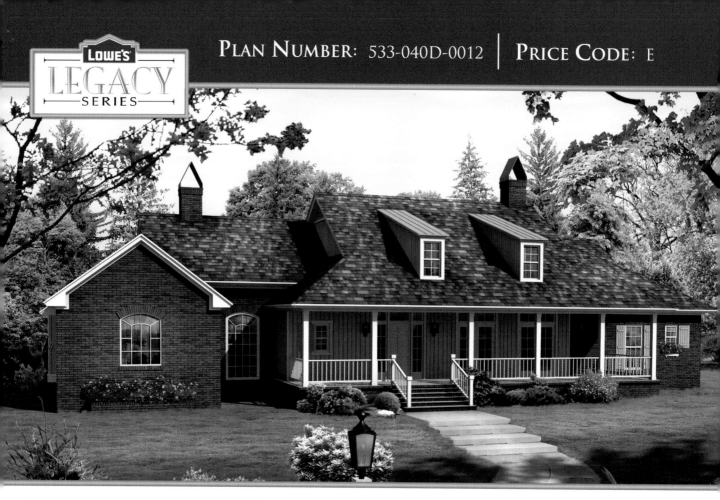

SPECIAL FEATURES

2,988 total square feet of living area

Energy efficient home with
2" x 6" exterior walls

Bedrooms #2 and #3 share a common bath

Rear porch has direct access to the
master bedroom, living and dining rooms

Spacious utility room located
off garage entrance features a
convenient bath with shower

Large L-shaped kitchen has
plenty of workspace

Oversized master bedroom is complete
with a walk-in closet and master bath

3 bedrooms, 3 1/2 baths,
2-car side entry garage

Partial basement/crawl space foundation

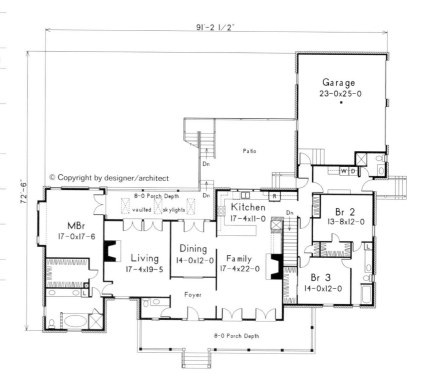

SPECIAL FEATURES

2,645 total square feet of living area

An enormous wrap-around porch surrounds the home with usable outdoor living space and connects the detached garage to the home

Gorgeous features fill this home including a see-through fireplace shared by the great room and dining room, plus these two spaces connect through a barrel vaulted ceiling above

The master bedroom is privately located on the first floor while separate dressing areas and walk-in closets enhance both second floor bedrooms

3 bedrooms, 2 1/2 baths, 2-car side entry garage

Slab foundation

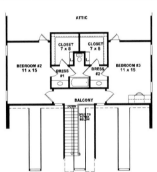

Second Floor
645 sq. ft.

© Copyright by designer/architect

First Floor
2,000 sq. ft.

LOWE'S
LEGACY
SERIES

SPECIAL FEATURES

1,611 total square feet of living area

Sliding doors lead to a delightful screened porch creating a wonderful summer retreat

Master bedroom has a lavishly appointed dressing room and large walk-in closet

The kitchen offers an abundance of cabinets and counterspace with convenient access to the laundry room and garage

3 bedrooms, 2 baths, 2-car side entry garage

Basement foundation

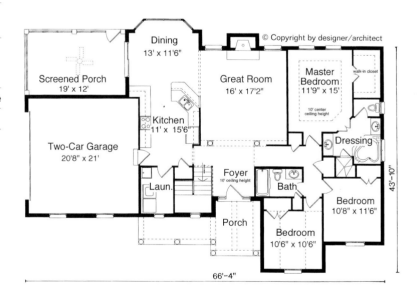

© Copyright by designer/architect

Dining
13' x 11'6"

Screened Porch
19' x 12'

Great Room
16' x 17'2"

Master Bedroom
11'9" x 15'
walk-in closet
10' center ceiling height

Kitchen
11' x 15'6"

Two-Car Garage
20'8" x 21'

Dressing

Laun.

Foyer
10' ceiling height

Bath

Bedroom
10'8" x 11'6"

Porch

Bedroom
10'6" x 10'6"

43'-10"

66'-4"

SPECIAL FEATURES

2,554 total square feet of living area

Dual fireplaces enhance
family and living rooms

All three bedrooms include
spacious walk-in closets

Double-bowl vanity in master
bath for convenience

4 bedrooms, 2 1/2 baths, 2-car garage

Basement foundation, drawings also
include crawl space and slab foundations

Second Floor
1,221 sq. ft.

36'-0"
38'-0"

BEDROOM
12'-10" x 11'

BEDROOM
12'-10" x 11'

c.
c.

HALL
BATH

MASTER BEDROOM
15'-11" x 17'-7"

BEDROOM
13'-3" x 13'-4"

walk in
closet

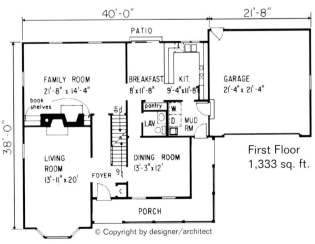

First Floor
1,333 sq. ft.

40'-0"   21'-8"
38'-0"

PATIO

FAMILY ROOM
21'-8" x 14'-4"

BREAKFAST
8' x 11'-8"

KIT.
9'-4" x11'-8"

GARAGE
21'-4" x 21'-4"

book
shelves

pantry

LAV.

W
D.

MUD
RM

LIVING
ROOM
13'-11" x 20'

DINING ROOM
13'-3" x 12'

FOYER

PORCH

© Copyright by designer/architect

SPECIAL FEATURES

2,234 total square feet of living area

Energy efficient home with
2" x 6" exterior walls

The open foyer provides direct access
to the formal dining room and quiet
office set off with French doors

The first floor offers a roomy in-law
suite perfect for guests with a
walk-in closet and nearby full bath

Three main bedrooms are located on the
second floor for extra peace and quiet and
all include walk-in closets for easy organizing

4 bedrooms, 3 baths, 3-car side entry garage

Basement foundation

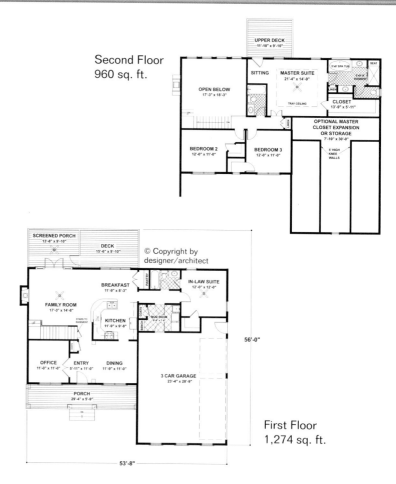

Second Floor
960 sq. ft.

First Floor
1,274 sq. ft.

© Copyright by
designer/architect

SPECIAL FEATURES

2,341 total square feet of living area

The wrap-around covered porch has plenty of space to create an outdoor living area and it also leads to the hearth room through double doors

The bayed breakfast room is an extension of the hearth room and provides a cozy, casual atmosphere

The two-story foyer makes quite a first impression upon entering this home

4 bedrooms, 2 1/2 baths, 2-car garage

Basement foundation

Br2
12-2x11-4

Br3
12-6x11-4

Dn

Plnt
Shv

Open
to Below

Br4
12-6x16-2

Second Floor
770 sq. ft.

60'-0"

© Copyright by designer/architect

47'-0"

Opt.
Door

MBr
15-0x13-0

Kitchen
13-8x11-6

Brkfst
13-8x10-0

Hearth
13-8x14-8

L

D Laun
W

R P

Dn

Family
17-2x16-2

Up

Garage
20-0x19-4

Covered
Porch

First Floor
1,571 sq. ft.

LOWE'S LEGACY SERIES

SPECIAL FEATURES

2,864 total square feet of living area

The large, open kitchen is a chef's dream and features an angled serving bar that opens to the casual dinette and cozy hearth room

Bay windows accentuate the first floor family room and the second floor master suite

French doors off the entry access the quiet study that features handy built-ins for easy organization

4 bedrooms, 2 1/2 baths, 3-car garage

Walk-out basement foundation

Second Floor
1,254 sq. ft.

First Floor
1,610 sq. ft.

© Copyright by designer/architect

SPECIAL FEATURES

2,158 total square feet of living area

Private master suite has a
walk-in closet and bath

Sloped ceiling in family room adds drama

Secondary bedrooms include 9'
ceilings and walk-in closets

Covered porch adds a charming touch

4 bedrooms, 3 baths, 2-car side entry garage

Crawl space foundation, drawings
also include slab foundation

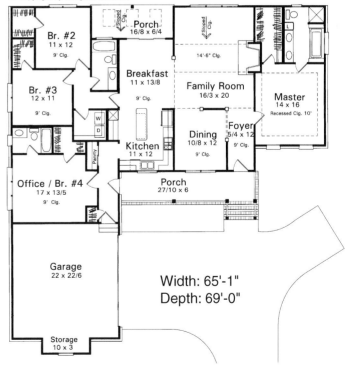

© Copyright by designer/architect

Width: 65'-1"
Depth: 69'-0"

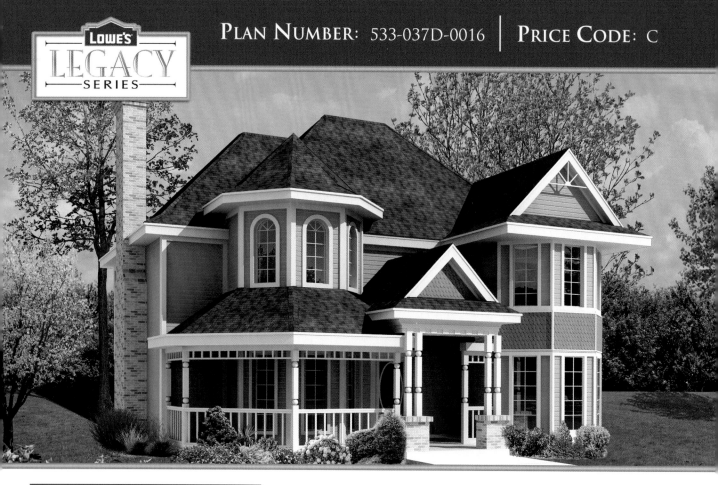

SPECIAL FEATURES

2,066 total square feet of living area

Large master bedroom includes sitting area and private bath

Open living room features a fireplace with built-in bookshelves

Spacious kitchen accesses formal dining area and breakfast room

3 bedrooms, 2 1/2 baths, optional 2-car side entry detached garage

Slab foundation

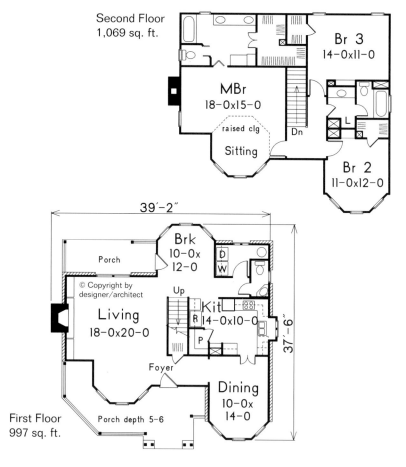

Second Floor
1,069 sq. ft.

Br 3
14-0x11-0

MBr
18-0x15-0

raised clg

Sitting

Dn

Br 2
11-0x12-0

39'-2"

Brk
10-0x
12-0

Porch

© Copyright by
designer/architect

37'-6"

Up

Kit
14-0x10-0

Living
18-0x20-0

P

Foyer

Dining
10-0x
14-0

First Floor
997 sq. ft.

Porch depth 5-6

SPECIAL FEATURES

2,021 total square feet of living area

A corner garden tub in the private master bath becomes the ultimate retreat from the stresses of everyday life

A large eating area extends off the kitchen with center island plus connects to the covered porch with outdoor kitchen

A media/hobby room can be found through double doors in the large great room

The unfinished bonus room has an additional 329 square feet of living area

3 bedrooms, 2 1/2 baths, 2-car side entry garage

Basement foundation, drawings also include crawl space and slab foundations

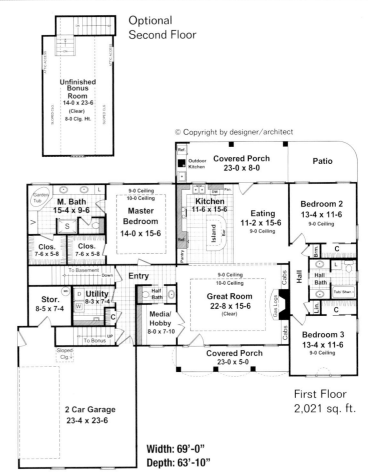

Optional Second Floor

Unfinished Bonus Room
14-0 x 23-6
(Clear)
8-0 Clg. Ht.

© Copyright by designer/architect

Covered Porch 23-0 x 8-0

Patio

M. Bath 15-4 x 9-6

Master Bedroom 14-0 x 15-6
9-0 Ceiling / 10-0 Ceiling

Kitchen 11-6 x 15-6

Eating 11-2 x 15-6
9-0 Ceiling

Bedroom 2 13-4 x 11-6
9-0 Ceiling

Clos. 7-6 x 5-8

Clos. 7-6 x 5-8

Hall Bath

Entry

Great Room 22-8 x 15-6
(Clear)
9-0 Ceiling / 10-0 Ceiling

Stor. 8-5 x 7-4

Utility 8-3 x 7-4

Half Bath

Media/ Hobby 8-0 x 7-10

Bedroom 3 13-4 x 11-6
9-0 Ceiling

Covered Porch 23-0 x 5-0

2 Car Garage 23-4 x 23-6

First Floor 2,021 sq. ft.

Width: 69'-0"
Depth: 63'-10"

LOWE'S LEGACY SERIES

SPECIAL FEATURES

2,685 total square feet of living area

9' ceilings throughout the first floor

Vaulted master bedroom, isolated for privacy, boasts a magnificent bath with garden tub, separate shower and two closets

The laundry area is located near the bedrooms for the ultimate in convenience

Screened porch and morning room are both located off the well-planned kitchen

4 bedrooms, 2 1/2 baths, 3-car garage

Basement foundation

Second Floor
1,325 sq. ft.

MBr
19-8x13-0
vaulted

plant shelf

Br 3
12-8x14-8

open to below

plant shelf

Br 4
11-8x11-4
raised ceiling

Br 2
12-8x13-4
window seat

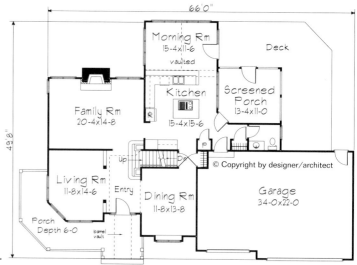

66'0"

49'8"

Morning Rm
15-4x11-6
vaulted

Deck

Family Rm
20-4x14-8

Kitchen
15-4x15-6

Screened Porch
13-4x11-0

© Copyright by designer/architect

Living Rm
11-8x14-6

Up

Entry

Dining Rm
11-8x13-8

Garage
34-0x22-0

Porch Depth 6-0

barrel vault

First Floor
1,360 sq. ft.

SPECIAL FEATURES

2,368 total square feet of living area

This country exterior with its wrap-around porch, impressive stonework and roof dormers is a delight to the eye

A two-story foyer leads to an enormous family room with fireplace and access to the rear patio

The family-sized laundry room with access to a rear covered porch is adjacent to the kitchen

On the second floor, the master bedroom is generous in size and features a vaulted ceiling, two walk-in closets and an elegant private bath

4 bedrooms, 3 1/2 baths, 2-car side entry garage

Basement foundation, drawings also include slab and crawl space foundations

Second Floor
1,154 sq. ft.

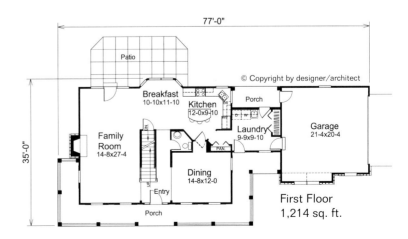

First Floor
1,214 sq. ft.

SPECIAL FEATURES

1,266 total square feet of living area

Energy efficient home with
2" x 6" exterior walls

Narrow frontage is perfect for small lots

Prominent central hall provides a
convenient connection for all main rooms

Design incorporates full-size master
bedroom complete with dressing
room, bath and walk-in closet

Angled kitchen includes handy
laundry facilities and is adjacent
to an oversized storage area

3 bedrooms, 2 baths, 2-car rear entry garage

Crawl space foundation, drawings
also include slab foundation

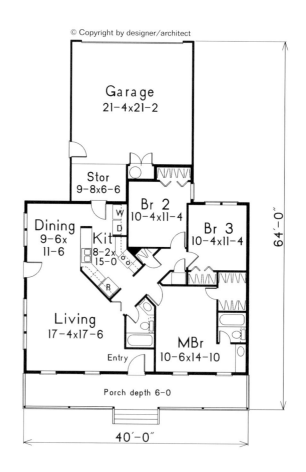

© Copyright by designer/architect

Garage
21-4x21-2

Stor
9-8x6-6

Br 2
10-4x11-4

Br 3
10-4x11-4

Dining
9-6x
11-6

Kit
8-2x
15-0

Living
17-4x17-6

MBr
10-6x14-10

Entry

Porch depth 6-0

64'-0"

40'-0"

SPECIAL FEATURES

1,883 total square feet of living area

Energy efficient home with
2" x 6" exterior walls

Large laundry room located off the
garage has a coat closet and half bath

Large family room with fireplace
and access to the covered porch is
a great central gathering room

U-shaped kitchen has breakfast bar,
large pantry and swing door to dining
room for convenient serving

3 bedrooms, 2 1/2 baths,
2-car side entry garage

Basement foundation

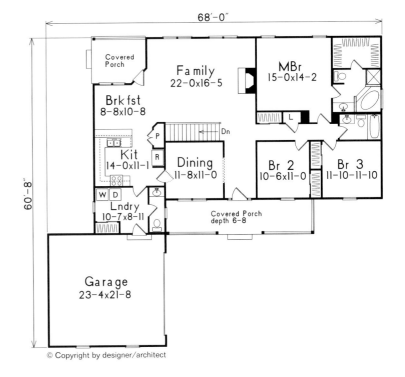

68'-0"

60'-8"

Covered Porch

Family
22-0x16-5

MBr
15-0x14-2

Brkfst
8-8x10-8

Kit
14-0x11-1

P

R

Dn

Dining
11-8x11-0

Br 2
10-6x11-0

Br 3
11-10-11-10

L

W D

Lndry
10-7x8-11

Covered Porch
depth 6-8

Garage
23-4x21-8

© Copyright by designer/architect

SPECIAL FEATURES

1,657 total square feet of living area

Stylish pass-through between living and dining areas

Master bedroom is secluded from the living area for privacy

Large windows in breakfast and dining areas

3 bedrooms, 2 1/2 baths, 2-car drive under garage

Basement foundation

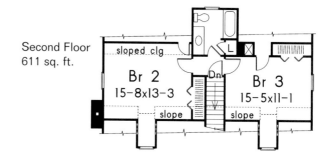

Second Floor
611 sq. ft.

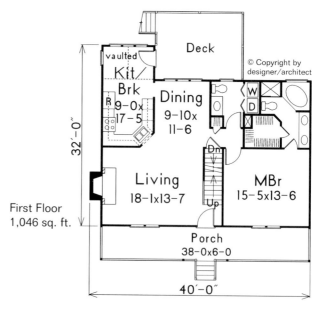

First Floor
1,046 sq. ft.

© Copyright by
designer/architect

SPECIAL FEATURES

2,137 total square feet of living area

Energy efficient home with
2" x 6" exterior walls

Elegant double-door front entry with
large foyer and double coat closets
open into grand size great room

Master bedroom features large
double walk-in closets, dressing
area and private bath

U-shaped kitchen with breakfast
bar and adjacent breakfast nook

Extra large laundry room

3 bedrooms, 2 baths, 2-car side entry garage

Crawl space foundation, drawings also
include basement and slab foundations

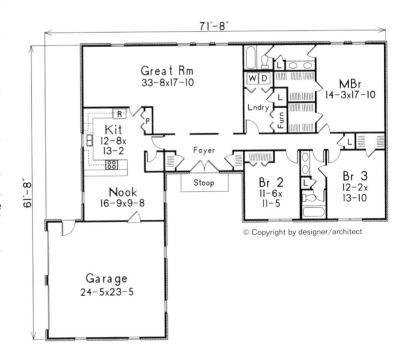

© Copyright by designer/architect

SPECIAL FEATURES

1,197 total square feet of living area

Dining area is adjacent to the living room and is ideal for gathering

Private master bath has a vaulted ceiling, double vanity, separate tub and shower

Plant shelf in family room adds charm

3 bedrooms, 2 baths, 2-car garage

Crawl space foundation, drawings also include slab foundation

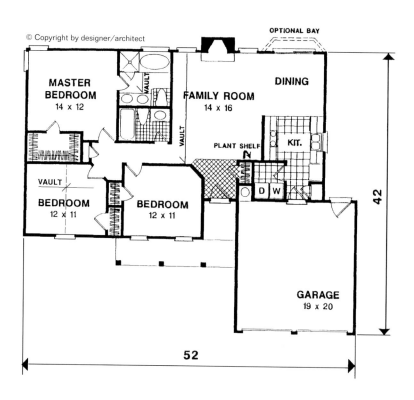

© Copyright by designer/architect

SPECIAL FEATURES

2,266 total square feet of living area

Great room includes a fireplace flanked by built-in bookshelves and dining nook with bay window

Unique media room includes a double-door entrance, walk-in closet and access to a full bath

Master bedroom has a lovely sitting area and private bath with a walk-in closet, step-up tub and double vanity

3 bedrooms, 3 1/2 baths, 2-car side entry garage

Basement foundation, drawings also include crawl space foundation

Second Floor
1,050 sq. ft.

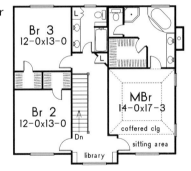

First Floor
1,216 sq. ft.

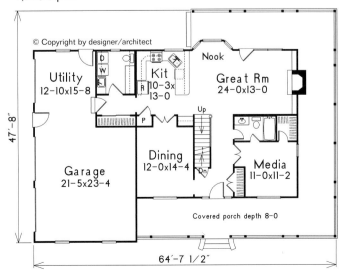

SPECIAL FEATURES

2,458 total square feet of living area

Study in the front of the home makes an ideal home office

Second floor has four bedrooms centered around a bonus room that could easily convert to a family room or fifth bedroom

Private second floor master bedroom is situated above garage

Bonus room on the second floor is included in the square footage

4 bedrooms, 2 1/2 baths, 2-car garage

Basement foundation

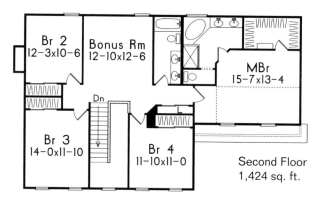

Br 2
12-3x10-6

Bonus Rm
12-10x12-6

MBr
15-7x13-4

Dn

Br 3
14-0x11-10

Br 4
11-10x11-0

Second Floor
1,424 sq. ft.

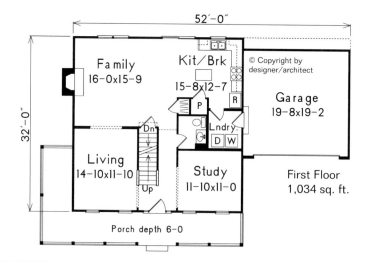

52'-0"

32'-0"

Family
16-0x15-9

Kit/Brk
15-8x12-7

© Copyright by designer/architect

Garage
19-8x19-2

P

R

Dn

Lndry

D   W

Living
14-10x11-10

Up

Study
11-10x11-0

First Floor
1,034 sq. ft.

Porch depth 6-0

LOWE'S LEGACY SERIES

SPECIAL FEATURES

2,531 total square feet of living area

Charming porch with dormers leads
into vaulted great room with atrium

Well-designed kitchen and breakfast bar
adjoin an extra-large laundry/mud room

Double sinks, tub with window above and
plant shelf complete the vaulted master bath

4 bedrooms, 2 1/2 baths,
2-car side entry garage

Walk-out basement foundation

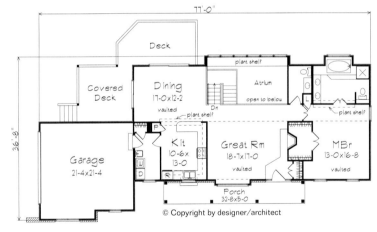

© Copyright by designer/architect

First Floor
1,297 sq. ft.

Rear View

Lower Level
1,234 sq. ft.

Lowe's
LEGACY
SERIES

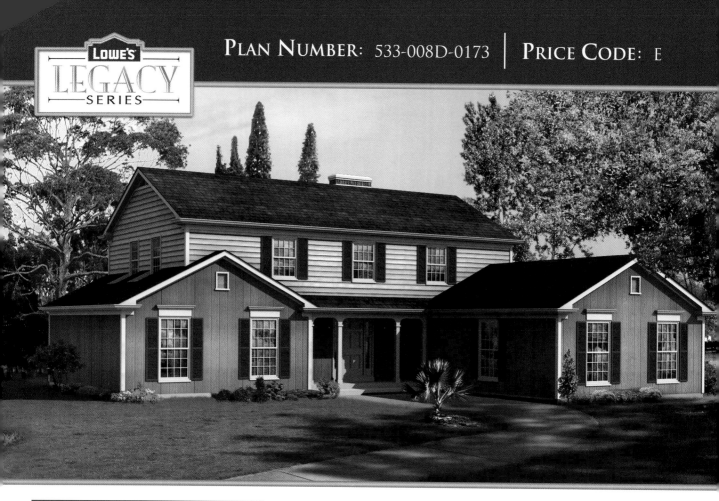

SPECIAL FEATURES

2,760 total square feet of living area

A grand entry includes two guest closets and view of handcrafted stair to second floor

Kitchen is filled with many amenities including a built-in pantry, menu desk and a peninsula which defines the breakfast area

A full bath and two closets accompany the first floor den or office located off the foyer

4 bedrooms, 3 baths, 2-car side entry garage

Basement foundation

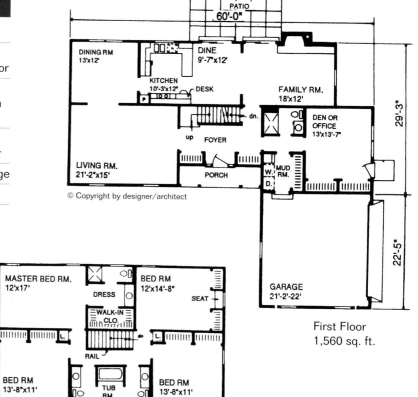

© Copyright by designer/architect

First Floor
1,560 sq. ft.

Second Floor
1,200 sq. ft.

SPECIAL FEATURES

1,437 total square feet of living area

The covered front porch opens into the massive family room

The private master bedroom enjoys a vaulted ceiling, dressing area and bath with walk-in closet

Two secondary bedrooms are located in a separate wing and share a full bath

3 bedrooms, 2 baths

Slab foundation

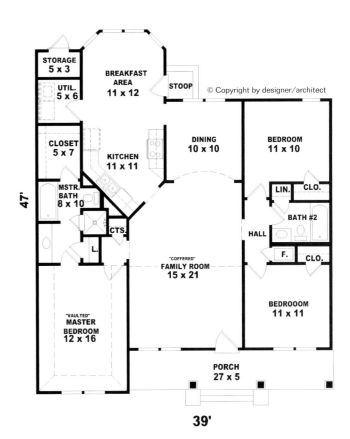

© Copyright by designer/architect

SPECIAL FEATURES

1,483 total square feet of living area

A private bath with double vanities is enjoyed by the master bedroom

Centralized family and dining rooms create an immense amount of space for entertaining and gathering

The garage includes direct porch access

3 bedrooms, 2 baths, 2-car side entry garage

Basement foundation

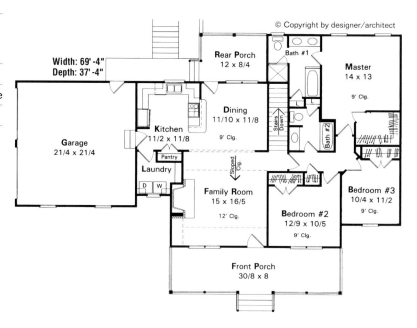

© Copyright by designer/architect

Width: 69'-4"
Depth: 37'-4"

Rear Porch 12 x 8/4
Bath #1
Master 14 x 13
9' Clg.

Dining 11/10 x 11/8
9' Clg.
Stairs Down
Bath #2

Garage 21/4 x 21/4

Kitchen 11/2 x 11/8

Pantry

Laundry

D   W

Sloped Clg.

Family Room 15 x 16/5
12' Clg.

Bedroom #2 12/9 x 10/5
9' Clg.

Bedroom #3 10/4 x 11/2
9' Clg.

Front Porch 30/8 x 8

LOWE'S
LEGACY
SERIES

SPECIAL FEATURES

1,000 total square feet of living area

9' ceilings throughout the
house enhance the space

The open living room offers a gas fireplace
flanked by elegant built-in shelves

The kitchen features a raised bar
on each side for serving food to the
living room or the breakfast area

2 bedrooms, 2 baths

Slab foundation, drawings also
include crawl space foundation

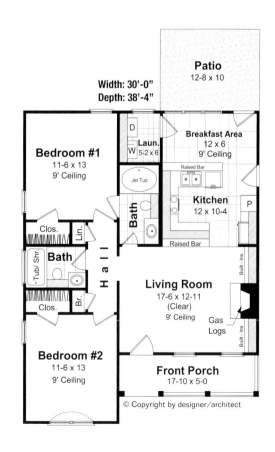

Width: 30'-0"
Depth: 38'-4"

Patio
12-8 x 10

Bedroom #1
11-6 x 13
9' Ceiling

D
Laun.
5-2 x 6
W

Breakfast Area
12 x 6
9' Ceiling

Jet Tub

Raised Bar

Bath

Kitchen
12 x 10-4

P

Clos.

Lin.

Bath
Tub/Shr.

Raised Bar

H a l l

Built - Ins

Clos.

Br.

Living Room
17-6 x 12-11
(Clear)
9' Ceiling

Gas
Logs

Built - Ins

Bedroom #2
11-6 x 13
9' Ceiling

Front Porch
17-10 x 5-0

© Copyright by designer/architect

SPECIAL FEATURES

1,612 total square feet of living area

A private master bedroom offers all the essentials for everyday living

A delightful family room with fireplace is ideally suited for casual family gatherings

Well-planned design enjoys a center island in the kitchen

3 bedrooms, 2 1/2 baths, 2-car garage

Basement foundation

Second Floor
485 sq. ft.

Bedroom #3
11 x 11
8' Clg.

Bath #2

Bedroom #2
13/4 x 12
8' Clg.

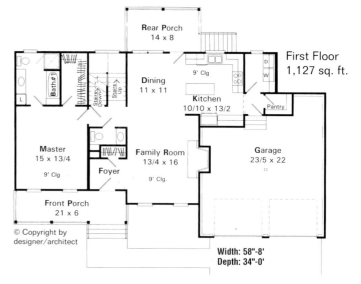

Rear Porch
14 x 8

9' Clg

Dining
11 x 11

Kitchen
10/10 x 13/2

First Floor
1,127 sq. ft.

Pantry

Bath #1

Master
15 x 13/4
9' Clg

Foyer

Family Room
13/4 x 16
9' Clg.

Garage
23/5 x 22

Front Porch
21 x 6

© Copyright by
designer/architect

Width: 58"-8'
Depth: 34'-0'

SPECIAL FEATURES

2,438 total square feet of living area

Energy efficient home with
2" x 6" exterior walls

Three second floor bedrooms surround
the balcony overlooking the great room

Laundry/mud room located between
kitchen and garage is convenient

First floor master bedroom includes
lots of closetspace and a luxury bath

4 bedrooms, 2 1/2 baths, 2-car garage

Basement foundation

Second Floor
760 sq. ft.

open to below

Br 2
13-0x13-0

Br 4
12-5x13-10

Br 3
13-0x13-4

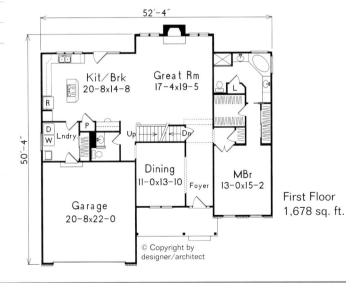

52'-4"

50'-4"

Kit/Brk
20-8x14-8

Great Rm
17-4x19-5

Lndry.

Dining
11-0x13-10

Foyer

MBr
13-0x15-2

Garage
20-8x22-0

First Floor
1,678 sq. ft.

© Copyright by
designer/architect

SPECIAL FEATURES

1,144 total square feet of living area

A large laundry room connects the home to the garage and contains a sink for ease with household chores

Vaulted spaces including the kitchen, dining and sitting rooms provide an open atmosphere homeowners crave

Two bedrooms share a centrally located full bath

2 bedrooms, 1 bath, 2-car garage

Crawl space foundation

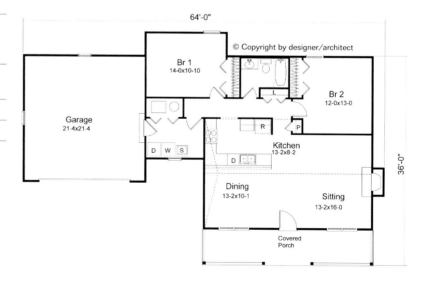

64'-0"

© Copyright by designer/architect

Br 1
14-0x10-10

Br 2
12-0x13-0

Garage
21-4x21-4

D W S

Kitchen
13-2x8-2

D

36'-0"

Dining
13-2x10-1

Sitting
13-2x16-0

Covered
Porch

LOWE'S LEGACY SERIES

SPECIAL FEATURES

1,827 total square feet of living area

Energy efficient home with
2" x 6" exterior walls

Two large bedrooms on the second
floor for extra privacy, plus two
bedrooms on the first floor

L-shaped kitchen is adjacent
to the family room

Ample closet space in all bedrooms

4 bedrooms, 2 baths, 2-car garage

Crawl space foundation, drawings also
include basement and slab foundations

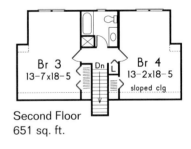

Br 3
13-7x18-5

Dn

Br 4
13-2x18-5
sloped clg

Second Floor
651 sq. ft.

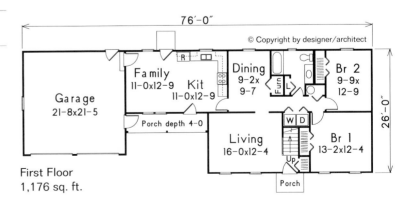

76'-0"

© Copyright by designer/architect

Garage
21-8x21-5

Family
11-0x12-9

Kit
11-0x12-9

Dining
9-2x 9-7

Br 2
9-9x 12-9

Furn

Porch depth 4-0

Living
16-0x12-4

W D

Br 1
13-2x12-4

Up

Porch

26'-0"

First Floor
1,176 sq. ft.

SPECIAL FEATURES

2,420 total square feet of living area

The huge great room has a fireplace with flanking shelves, a wide bay window and dining area surrounded with windows

Many excellent features adorn the kitchen including a corner window sink, island snack bar, walk-in pantry and breakfast area with adjoining covered patio

The apartment with its own exterior entrance and entry with coat closet accesses the dining and great rooms of the primary residence

1,014 square feet of optional living area on the lower level includes a large family room with fireplace and home theater room with walk-in bar and half bath

4 bedrooms, 3 1/2 baths,
2-car side entry garage

Basement foundation

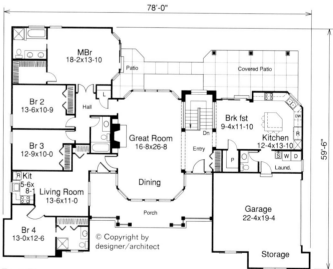

First Floor
2,420 sq. ft.

© Copyright by designer/architect

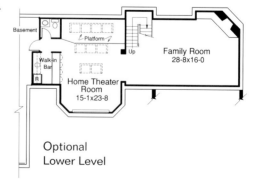

Optional
Lower Level

LOWE'S
LEGACY
SERIES

SPECIAL FEATURES

1,668 total square feet of living area

Large bay windows grace the breakfast area, master bedroom and dining room

Extensive walk-in closets and storage spaces are located throughout the home

Handy covered entry porch

Large living room has a fireplace, built-in bookshelves and a sloped ceiling

3 bedrooms, 2 baths, 2-car drive under garage

Basement foundation

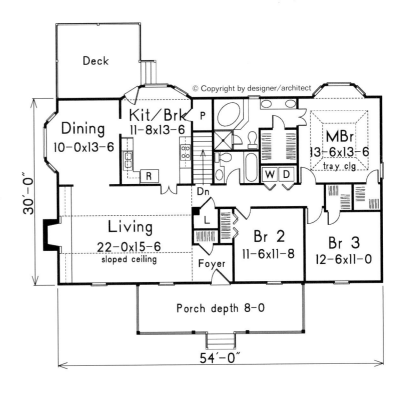

© Copyright by designer/architect

Deck

Dining
10-0x13-6

Kit/Brk
11-8x13-6

P

MBr
13-6x13-6
tray clg

R

Dn

W D

Living
22-0x15-6
sloped ceiling

L

Br 2
11-6x11-8

Br 3
12-6x11-0

Foyer

30'-0"

Porch depth 8-0

54'-0"

SPECIAL FEATURES

1,694 total square feet of living area

A beautiful box window in the living room and bay window in the dining room flood these spaces with an abundance of light

The open kitchen enjoys a snack bar counter connecting to the dining room, a built-in desk, and pantry

A double-door entry leads into the relaxing master bedroom complete with a built-in desk, walk-in closet and private bath

3 bedrooms, 2 baths, 2-car garage

Basement foundation, drawings also include slab and crawl space foundations

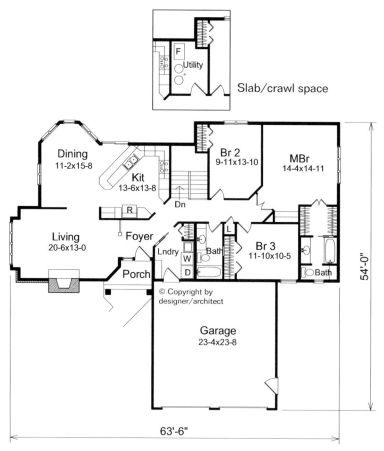

Slab/crawl space

© Copyright by designer/architect

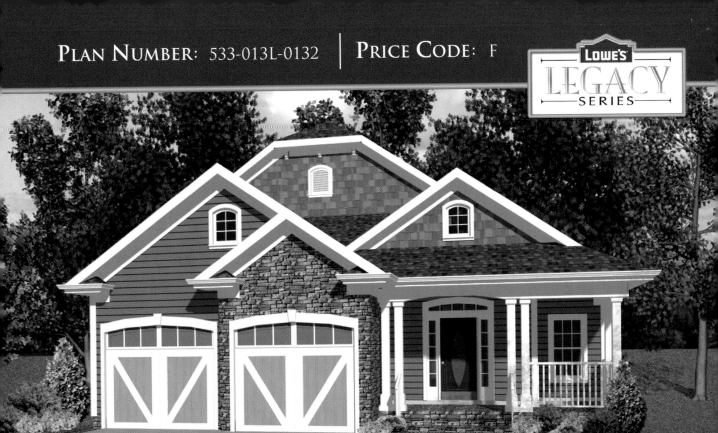

LOWE'S LEGACY SERIES

SPECIAL FEATURES

2,296 total square feet of living area

The highly functional kitchen offers double snack bars, a pantry and an adjacent breakfast nook

Located off the breakfast nook is an oversized laundry room with plenty of space for a washer and dryer as well as a laundry sink and upright freezer

The spacious master suite, with its bowed window, tray ceiling, sitting area, luxurious bath and abundant closet, is truly an owner's retreat

The second floor features two secondary bedroom suites, each featuring a walk-in closet and private bath

3 bedrooms, 3 1/2 baths, 2-car garage

Crawl space foundation

First Floor
1,636 sq. ft.

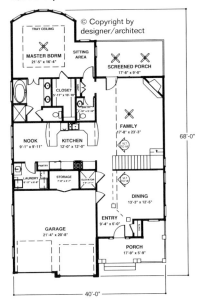

© Copyright by designer/architect

Second Floor
660 sq. ft.

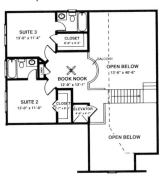

SPECIAL FEATURES

1,362 total square feet of living area

Large living room joins dining area creating an open living atmosphere

Master bedroom includes a private bath

Cozy family room accesses the outdoors and the garage

Handy storage area is located in the garage

3 bedrooms, 2 baths, 2-car garage

Crawl space foundation, drawings also include basement and slab foundations

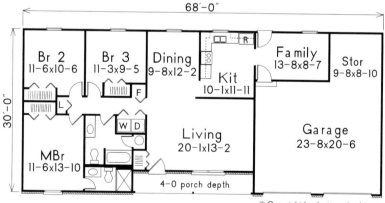

68'-0"

30'-0"

Br 2
11-6x10-6

Br 3
11-3x9-5

Dining
9-8x12-2

Kit
10-1x11-11

Family
13-8x8-7

Stor
9-8x8-10

MBr
11-6x13-10

Living
20-1x13-2

Garage
23-8x20-6

4-0 porch depth

© Copyright by designer/architect

SPECIAL FEATURES

- 2,659 total square feet of living area
- 9' ceilings throughout the first floor
- Balcony overlooks the large family room
- Private first floor master bedroom features two walk-in closets, a sloped ceiling and a luxury bath
- Double French doors in the dining room open onto the porch
- 4 bedrooms, 3 1/2 baths, 2-car garage
- Basement foundation

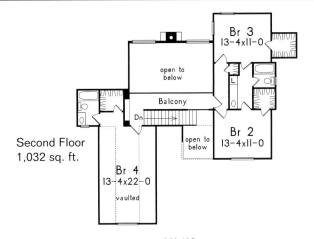

Second Floor
1,032 sq. ft.

Br 3
13-4x11-0

Balcony

Br 2
13-4x11-0

Br 4
13-4x22-0
vaulted

open to below

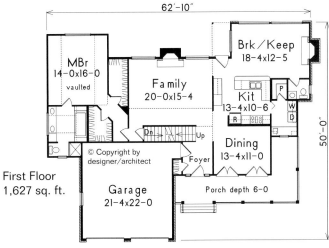

First Floor
1,627 sq. ft.

62'-10"

50'-0"

MBr
14-0x16-0
vaulted

Family
20-0x15-4

Brk/Keep
18-4x12-5

Kit
13-4x10-6

Dining
13-4x11-0

Foyer

Garage
21-4x22-0

Porch depth 6-0

© Copyright by designer/architect

SPECIAL FEATURES

1,900 total square feet of living area

The breakfast area enjoys views of the large fireplace located in the great room

The master bedroom is separated from the other bedrooms for privacy and features a luxury bath and two walk-in closets

The dining/office is a versatile space that can adapt to your needs

The bonus room above the garage has an additional 348 square feet of living area

3 bedrooms, 2 1/2 baths, 2-car side entry garage

Slab foundation, drawings also include crawl space foundation

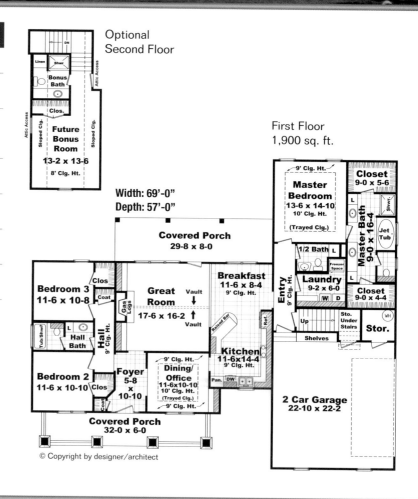

Optional Second Floor

First Floor
1,900 sq. ft.

Width: 69'-0"
Depth: 57'-0"

© Copyright by designer/architect

LOWE'S
LEGACY
SERIES

SPECIAL FEATURES

1,333 total square feet of living area

Country charm with a covered front porch

Dining area looks into the
family room with fireplace

Master suite has a walk-in
closet and private bath

3 bedrooms, 2 baths, 2-car carport

Slab foundation, drawings also
include crawl space foundation

Width: 55'-6"
Depth: 64'-3"

© Copyright by designer/architect

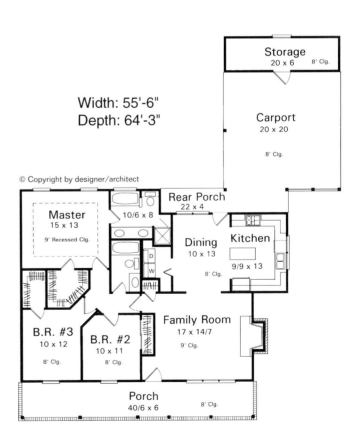

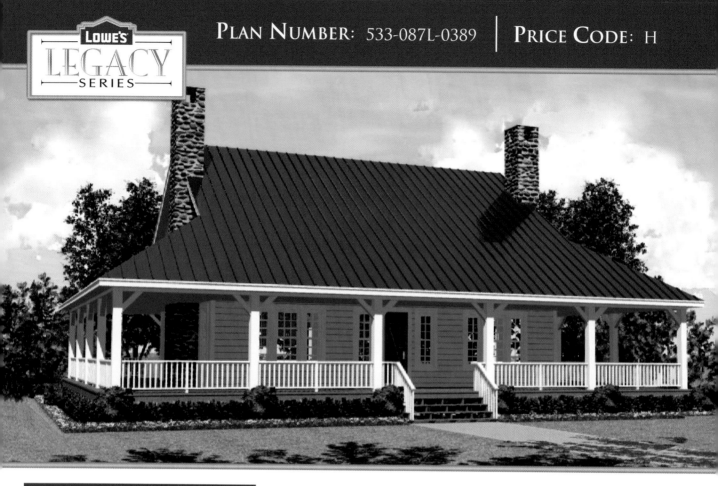

SPECIAL FEATURES

2,373 total square feet of living area

A screen porch connects with the wrap-around porch and is accessed by the dining room

The master bedroom remains private and enjoys a fireplace, two walk-in closets and a deluxe bath

A massive utility room is conveniently accessed from the master bedroom and two porches

3 bedrooms, 2 1/2 baths

Crawl space foundation, drawings also include basement foundation

Second Floor
741 sq. ft.

First Floor
1,632 sq. ft.

© Copyright by designer/architect

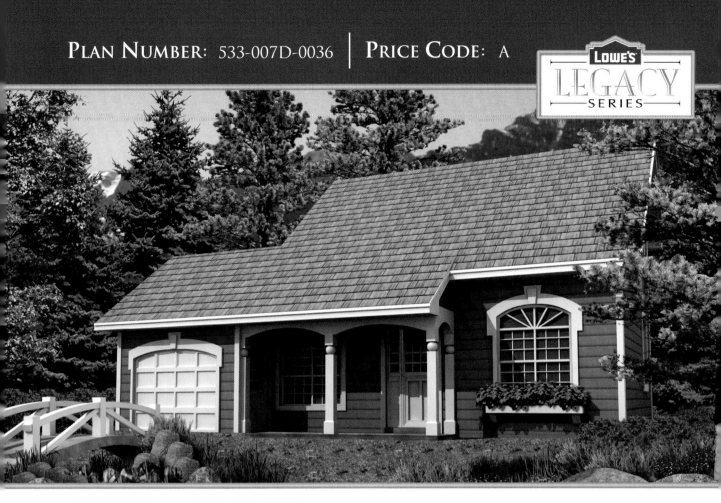

SPECIAL FEATURES

1,330 total square feet of living area

Vaulted living room is open to the bayed dining room and kitchen creating an ideal space for entertaining

Two bedrooms, a bath and linen closet complete the first floor and are easily accessible

The second floor offers two bedrooms with walk-in closets, a very large storage room and an opening with louvered doors which overlooks the living room

4 bedrooms, 2 baths, 1-car garage

Basement foundation

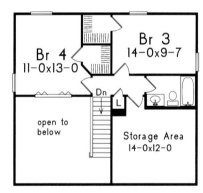

Br 4
11-0x13-0

Br 3
14-0x9-7

Dn
L

open to
below

Storage Area
14-0x12-0

Second Floor
446 sq. ft.

© Copyright by designer/architect

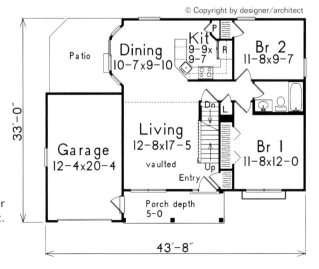

Patio

Dining
10-7x9-10

Kit
9-9x
9-7

P
R

Br 2
11-8x9-7

33'-0"

Garage
12-4x20-4

Living
12-8x17-5

vaulted

Dn
L

Up

Entry

Br 1
11-8x12-0

First Floor
884 sq. ft.

Porch depth
5-0

43'-8"

SPECIAL FEATURES

1,997 total square feet of living area

A grand wrap-around porch greets guests and offers a relaxing space to enjoy the outdoors

The efficient kitchen is designed with a center island, pantry, built-in desk and adjoining breakfast nook with access to the backyard

The bedrooms enjoy the peace and quiet of the second floor

3 bedrooms, 2 1/2 baths, 2-car garage

Basement foundation

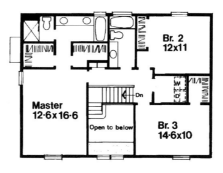

Second Floor
933 sq. ft.

Br. 2
12x11

Master
12·6x16·6

Open to below

Br. 3
14·6x10

First Floor
1,064 sq. ft.

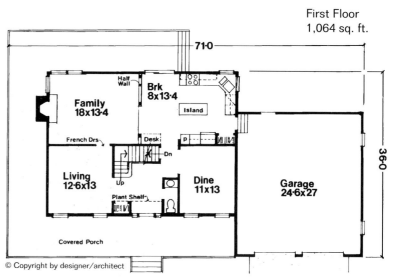

71-0

Half Wall

Brk
8x13·4

Family
18x13·4

Island

French Drs

Desk

P

Living
12·6x13

Up

Dn

36-0

Dine
11x13

Garage
24·6x27

Plant Shelf

Covered Porch

© Copyright by designer/architect

LOWE'S
LEGACY
SERIES

SPECIAL FEATURES

2,751 total square feet of living area

Large palladian window in foyer welcomes the sun

Spacious living room dominates design with sunken floor, sloped ceiling and see-through fireplace

State-of-the-art kitchen features a peninsula and built-in pantry

Dramatic in size and design, the master bedroom boasts a balcony overlook of the living room below

4 bedrooms, 2 1/2 baths, 2-car garage

Partial basement/crawl space foundation, drawings also include crawl space foundation

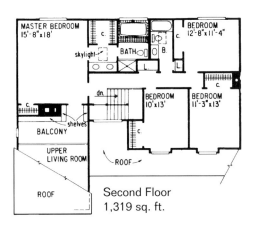

Second Floor
1,319 sq. ft.

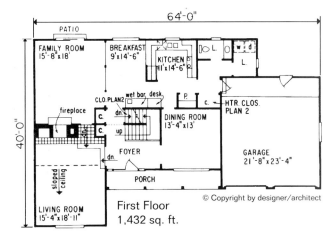

First Floor
1,432 sq. ft.

© Copyright by designer/architect

SPECIAL FEATURES

1,501 total square feet of living area

The friendly covered porch with arched openings invites guests inside and adds stunning curb appeal

The exquisite great room offers a vaulted ceiling and grand fireplace flanked by built-in cabinets

The beautiful master bedroom features a trayed ceiling, two walk-in closets and a plush bath with garden tub

3 bedrooms, 2 baths, 2-car garage

Slab foundation, drawings also include basement and crawl space foundations

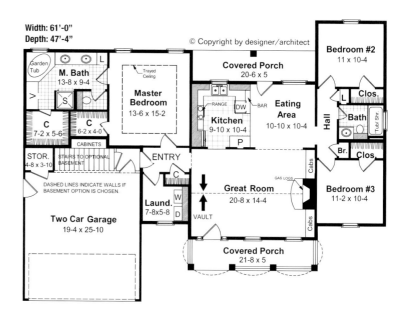

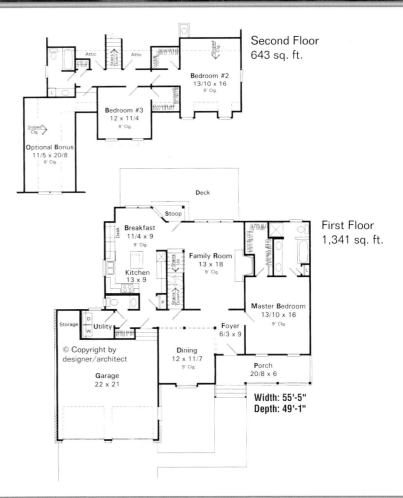

SPECIAL FEATURES

1,984 total square feet of living area

Decorative columns define
the formal dining room

All bedrooms have spacious walk-in closets
allowing the bedrooms to remain tidy

Optional bonus room has an additional
236 square feet of living area

3 bedrooms, 2 1/2 baths, 2-car garage

Basement foundation

Second Floor
643 sq. ft.

Attic   Attic

Bedroom #2
13/10 x 16
8' Clg.

Bedroom #3
12 x 11/4
8' Clg.

Sloped
Clg.

Optional Bonus
11/5 x 20/8
8' Clg.

First Floor
1,341 sq. ft.

Deck

Stoop

Breakfast
11/4 x 9
9' Clg.

Family Room
13 x 18
9' Clg.

Kitchen
13 x 9

Master Bedroom
13/10 x 16
9' Clg.

Storage

Utility

© Copyright by
designer/architect

Foyer
6/3 x 9

Dining
12 x 11/7
9' Clg.

Garage
22 x 21

Porch
20/8 x 6

Width: 55'-5"
Depth: 49'-1"

LOWE'S LEGACY SERIES

SPECIAL FEATURES

1,850 total square feet of living area

Large living room with fireplace is illuminated by three second story skylights

Living and dining rooms are separated by a low wall while the dining room and kitchen are separated by a snack bar creating a spacious atmosphere

Master bedroom has a huge bath with double vanity and large walk-in closet

Two second floor bedrooms share a uniquely designed bath with skylight

3 bedrooms, 2 1/2 baths, 2-car garage

Basement foundation

Second Floor
630 sq. ft.

Bedrm 2
10-0x14-8

Bedrm 3
12-0x14-7

Open To Below

Open To Below

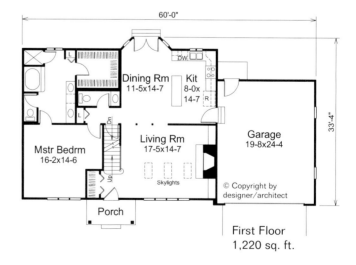

60'-0"

33'-4"

Dining Rm
11-5x14-7

Kit
8-0x
14-7

Garage
19-8x24-4

Mstr Bedrm
16-2x14-6

Living Rm
17-5x14-7

Skylights

© Copyright by
designer/architect

Porch

First Floor
1,220 sq. ft.

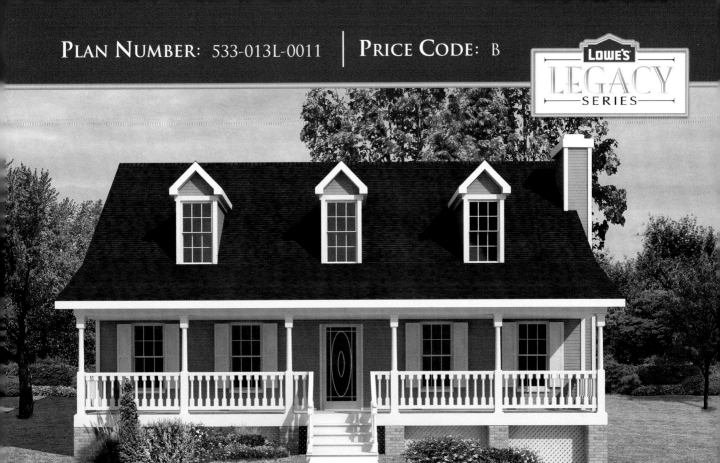

SPECIAL FEATURES

1,643 total square feet of living area

First floor master bedroom has a private bath, walk-in closet and easy access to the laundry closet

Comfortable family room features a vaulted ceiling and a cozy fireplace

Two bedrooms on the second floor share a bath

3 bedrooms, 2 1/2 baths, 2-car drive under garage

Basement foundation, drawings also include crawl space foundation

Second Floor
579 sq. ft.

First Floor
1,064 sq. ft.

© Copyright by designer/architect

Lowe's LEGACY SERIES

SPECIAL FEATURES

1,148 total square feet of living area

The large wrap-around porch is ideal for early morning breakfast or for late evening lounging

A separate entry, full masonry fireplace and balcony/dining area that overlooks the two-story atrium with floor-to-ceiling window wall are some of the many amenities of the vaulted great room

The spacious kitchen features an angled snack bar and enjoys easy access to the laundry and garage

The atrium is open to 462 square feet of optional living area below

2 bedrooms, 1 bath, 1-car side entry garage

Walk-out basement foundation

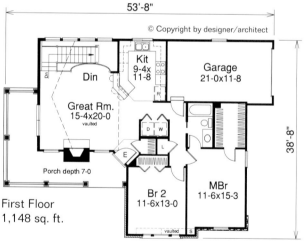

53'-8"

© Copyright by designer/architect

Kit 9-4x 11-8

Din

Garage 21-0x11-8

Great Rm. 15-4x20-0 vaulted

D W L

E

38'-8"

Porch depth 7-0

MBr 11-6x15-3

Br 2 11-6x13-0

vaulted S

First Floor 1,148 sq. ft.

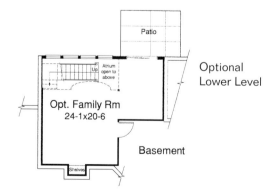

Patio

Up Atrium open to above

Optional Lower Level

Opt. Family Rm 24-1x20-6

Shelves

Basement

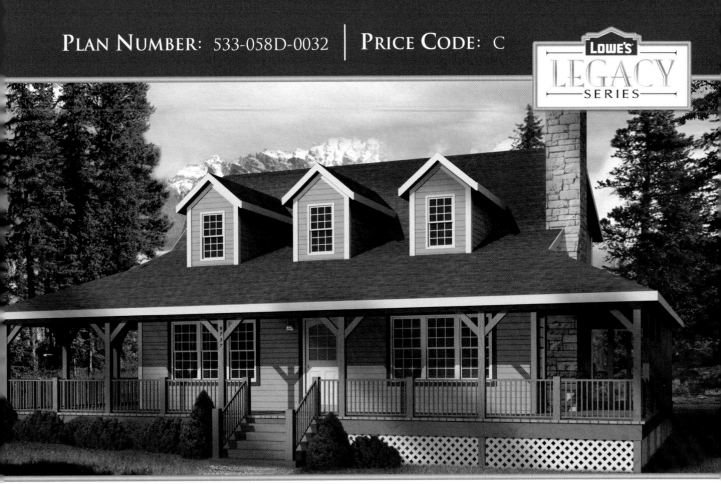

LOWE'S
LEGACY
SERIES

SPECIAL FEATURES

1,879 total square feet of living area

Open floor plan on both floors
makes home appear larger

Loft area overlooks great room or can
become an optional fourth bedroom

Large storage in rear of home
has access from exterior

3 bedrooms, 2 baths

Crawl space foundation

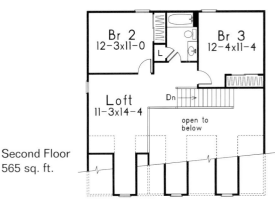

Br 2
12-3x11-0

Br 3
12-4x11-4

Loft
11-3x14-4

Dn

open to
below

Second Floor
565 sq. ft.

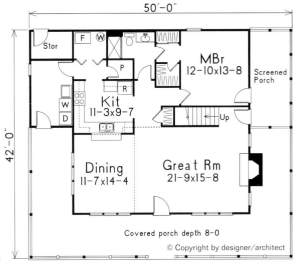

50'-0"

42'-0"

Stor

F | W

MBr
12-10x13-8

Screened
Porch

P

R

Kit
11-3x9-7

W
D

Up

Dining
11-7x14-4

Great Rm
21-9x15-8

Covered porch depth 8-0

First Floor
1,314 sq. ft.

© Copyright by designer/architect

SPECIAL FEATURES

1,999 total square feet of living area

Delightful dormers and an inviting porch greet guests and add superb curb appeal

Inside, the vaulted living room ceiling soars to 17' increasing spaciousness and a handy media center adds great organization

An elegant three-sided fireplace adjoins both the living and dining rooms, adding grand style

3 bedrooms, 2 1/2 baths, 2-car side entry garage

Basement foundation

Second Floor
672 sq. ft.

First Floor
1,327 sq. ft.

LOWE'S LEGACY SERIES

SPECIAL FEATURES

3,050 total square feet of living area

Sunny garden room and two-way fireplace create a bright, airy living room

Front porch is enhanced by arched transom windows and bold columns

Sitting alcove, French door access to side patio, walk-in closets and abundant storage enhance the master bedroom

4 bedrooms, 3 1/2 baths, 2-car detached garage

Slab foundation, drawings also include crawl space foundation

Second Floor
787 sq. ft.

Br 4
12-4x14-8

Br 2
11-3x12-0

Br 3
11-4x12-0

First Floor
2,263 sq. ft.

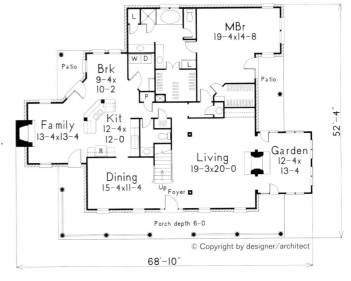

MBr
19-4x14-8

Patio

Brk
9-4x
10-2

Family
13-4x13-4

Kit
12-4x
12-0

Dining
15-4x11-4

Living
19-3x20-0

Garden
12-4x
13-4

Patio

Foyer

Up

Porch depth 6-0

52'-4"

68'-10"

SPECIAL FEATURES

2,292 total square feet of living area

Wood-crafted staircase ascends
into dramatic two-story foyer
with second floor overlook

Entertaining family will be delightful
in the large family room with fireplace
and views to the outdoors

Open kitchen center island cabinet
illustrates a carefully planned design

Second floor master bedroom enjoys
a luxury bath and walk-in closet

4 bedrooms, 2 1/2 baths, 2-car garage

Basement foundation

Second Floor
1,092 sq. ft.

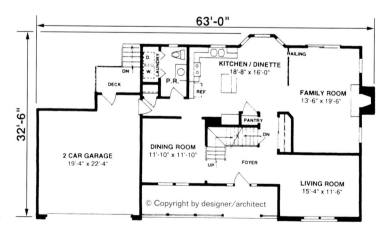

First Floor
1,200 sq. ft.

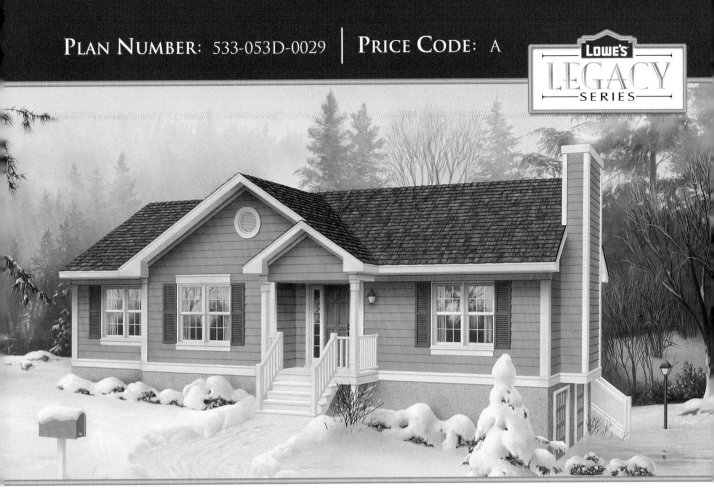

LOWE'S
LEGACY
SERIES

SPECIAL FEATURES

1,220 total square feet of living area

A vaulted ceiling adds luxury
to the living room and master bedroom

Spacious living room is accented
with a large fireplace and hearth

Gracious dining area is adjacent to the
convenient wrap-around kitchen

Washer and dryer are handy
to the bedrooms

Covered porch entry adds appeal

Rear deck adjoins dining area

3 bedrooms, 2 baths, 2-car
drive under garage

Basement foundation

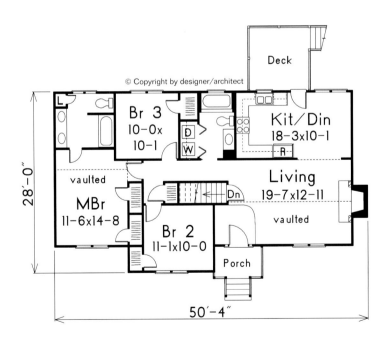

Deck

© Copyright by designer/architect

Br 3
10-0x
10-1

Kit/Din
18-3x10-1

MBr
11-6x14-8

Living
19-7x12-11

vaulted

vaulted

Br 2
11-1x10-0

Dn

Porch

28'-0"

50'-4"

SPECIAL FEATURES

1,832 total square feet of living area

Energy efficient home with
2" x 6" exterior walls

Distinctive master bedroom enhanced
by skylights, garden tub, separate
shower and walk-in closet

U-shaped kitchen features a
convenient pantry, laundry area
and full view to breakfast room

Foyer opens into spacious living room

Large front porch creates
enjoyable outdoor living

3 bedrooms, 2 baths

Crawl space foundation, drawings also
include basement and slab foundations

© Copyright by designer/architect

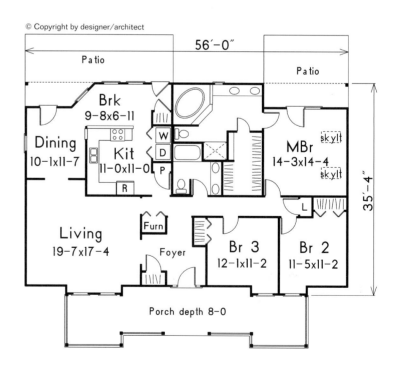

LOWE'S
LEGACY
SERIES

SPECIAL FEATURES

1,608 total square feet of living area

Easily relax in this spacious living room that features a unique soffit ceiling and a handsome fireplace

The efficiently designed kitchen opens to the dining room and enjoys a nearby pantry for storage

A walk-in closet and deluxe private bath enhance the master bedroom suite

2 bedrooms, 2 baths, 2-car garage

Basement foundation

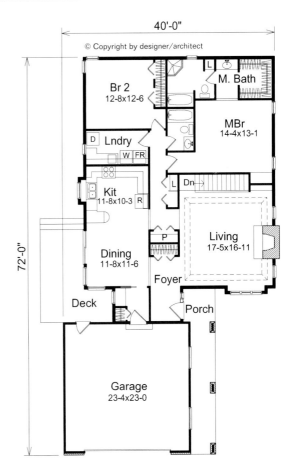

40'-0"

72'-0"

© Copyright by designer/architect

Br 2
12-8x12-6

M. Bath

Lndry

MBr
14-4x13-1

Kit
11-8x10-3

Dn

Living
17-5x16-11

Dining
11-8x11-6

Foyer

Deck

Porch

Garage
23-4x23-0

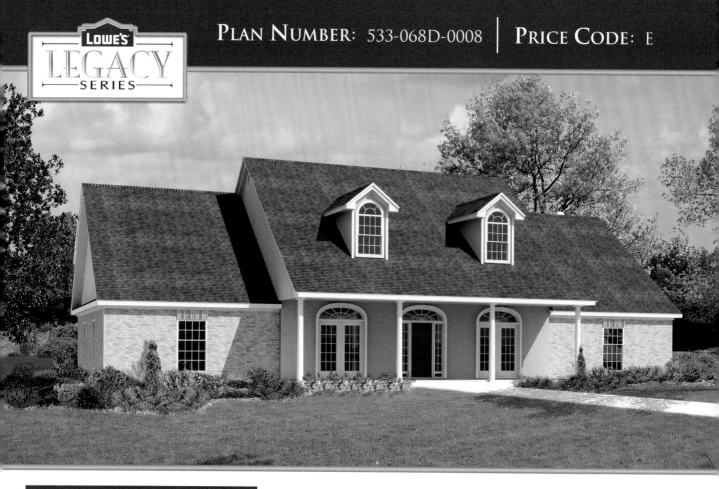

SPECIAL FEATURES

2,651 total square feet of living area

Vaulted family room has a corner fireplace and access to the breakfast room and outdoor patio

Dining room has a double-door entry from the covered front porch and a beautiful built-in corner display area

Master bedroom has a 10' tray ceiling, private bath and two walk-in closets

Kitchen has an enormous amount of counterspace with plenty of eating area and overlooks a cheerful breakfast room

3 bedrooms, 2 baths, 2-car side entry garage

Basement foundation, drawings also include crawl space and slab foundations

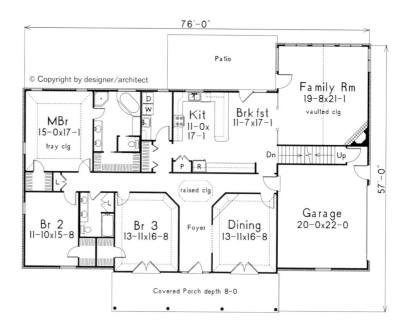

© Copyright by designer/architect

SPECIAL FEATURES

2,758 total square feet of living area

Vaulted great room excels with fireplace, wet bar, plant shelves and skylights

Fabulous master bedroom enjoys a fireplace, large bath, walk-in closet and vaulted ceiling

Trendsetting kitchen and breakfast area adjoin the spacious screened porch

Convenient office near kitchen is perfect for a computer room, hobby enthusiast or fifth bedroom

4 bedrooms, 2 1/2 baths, 3-car side entry garage

Basement foundation

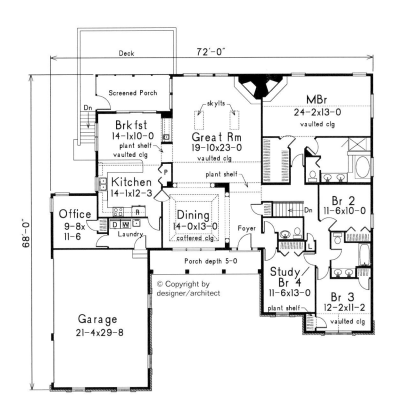

SPECIAL FEATURES

1,792 total square feet of living area

A massive family room with fireplace and access onto the porch is the perfect place to relax or entertain

The spacious kitchen and dining area includes a cooktop island and walk-in pantry

All the bedrooms are located on the second floor for extra peace and quiet

3 bedrooms, 2 1/2 baths

Slab foundation

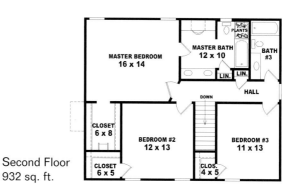

Second Floor
932 sq. ft.

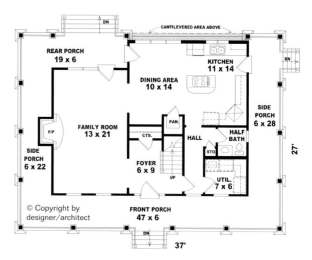

First Floor
860 sq. ft.

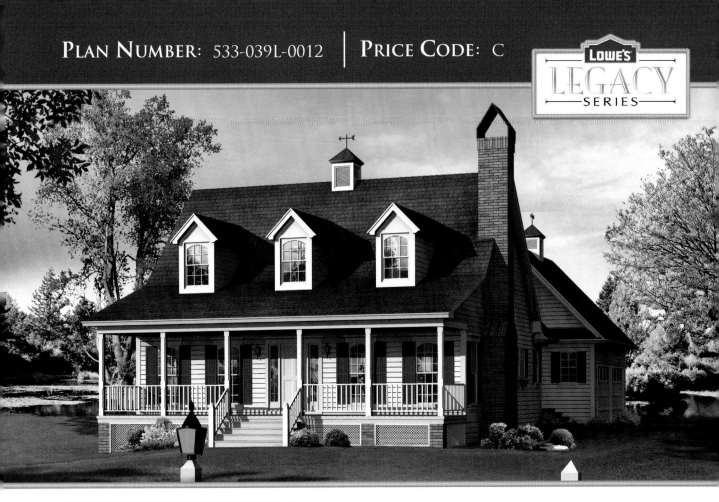

SPECIAL FEATURES

1,815 total square feet of living area

Second floor has a built-in desk in the hall that is ideal as a computer work station or mini office area

Two doors into the laundry area make it handy from the master bedroom and the rest of the home

Inviting covered porch

The kitchen provides an abundance of counterspace and cabinetry

3 bedrooms, 2 1/2 baths, 2-car side entry garage

Basement foundation

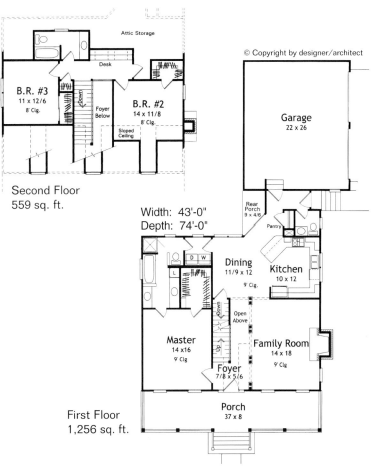

Second Floor
559 sq. ft.

Width: 43'-0"
Depth: 74'-0"

First Floor
1,256 sq. ft.

© Copyright by designer/architect

SPECIAL FEATURES

2,067 total square feet of living area

An enormous master bath has separate vanities, a whirlpool tub and a walk-in closet on each end

The flex space would make an excellent formal dining room or home office space

The rear covered porch is a fantastic outdoor retreat and leads onto the open patio

The unfinished bonus room has an additional 379 square feet of living area

3 bedrooms, 2 1/2 baths, 2-car garage

Slab foundation, drawings also include crawl space foundation

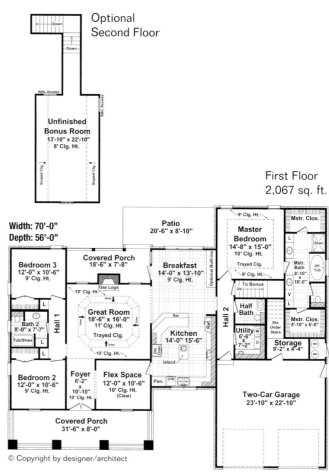

Optional Second Floor

First Floor
2,067 sq. ft.

© Copyright by designer/architect

SPECIAL FEATURES

1,334 total square feet of living area

This welcoming design is ideal for a vacation, starter or empty-nester home

Relax on cozy front and rear porches that are large enough for rocking chairs

The spacious first floor master suite features a walk-in closet, sitting area and private bath

The second floor features two bedrooms that share a full bath

3 bedrooms, 2 1/2 baths

Crawl space foundation

Second Floor
381 sq. ft.

First Floor
953 sq. ft.

SPECIAL FEATURES

2,694 total square feet of living area

Inviting great room with fireplace and flanking windows is open to the kitchen and breakfast room

The kitchen features a snack bar and adjacent breakfast room with bay window, large walk-in pantry and spacious laundry room

The master bedroom includes a sumptuous bath, huge walk-in closet and nearby room ideal for a study or nursery

A large two-story entry staircase leads to the second floor family and game room area, two bedrooms and a hall bath

4 bedrooms, 2 1/2 baths, 2-car side entry garage

Basement foundation

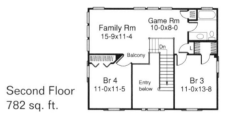

Second Floor
782 sq. ft.

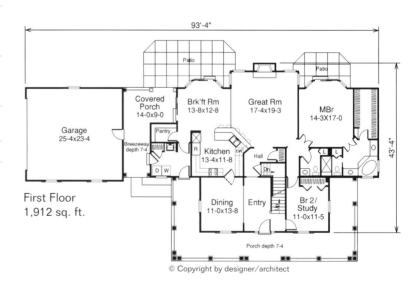

First Floor
1,912 sq. ft.

© Copyright by designer/architect

SPECIAL FEATURES

2,186 total square feet of living area

A see-through fireplace is the focal point in the family and living areas

Columns grace the entrance into the living room

Large laundry room has an adjoining half bath

Ideal second floor bath includes a separate vanity with double sinks

3 bedrooms, 2 1/2 baths, 2-car garage

Basement foundation

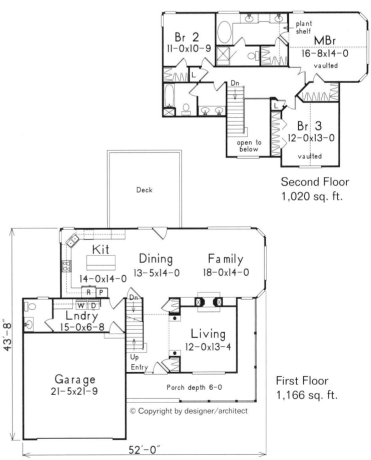

Br 2
11-0x10-9

plant shelf

MBr
16-8x14-0
vaulted

Dn

Br 3
12-0x13-0
vaulted

open to below

Second Floor
1,020 sq. ft.

Deck

Kit
14-0x14-0

Dining
13-5x14-0

Family
18-0x14-0

R P

W D

Lndry
15-0x6-8

Dn

Living
12-0x13-4

Up
Entry

Garage
21-5x21-9

Porch depth 6-0

43'-8"

© Copyright by designer/architect

52'-0"

First Floor
1,166 sq. ft.

LOWE'S LEGACY SERIES

SPECIAL FEATURES

2,772 total square feet of living area

10' ceilings on the first floor and 9' ceilings on the second floor create a spacious atmosphere

Large bay windows accent the study and master bath

Breakfast room features a dramatic curved wall with direct view and access onto porch

4 bedrooms, 3 1/2 baths, 2-car side entry garage

Slab foundation

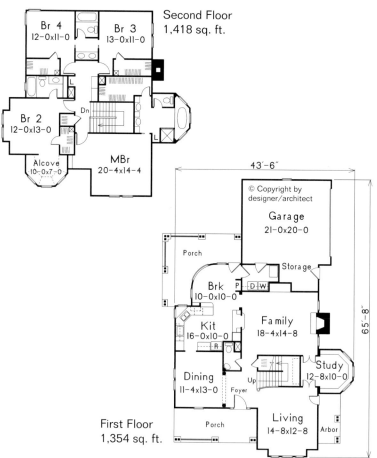

Second Floor 1,418 sq. ft.

Br 4 12-0x11-0

Br 3 13-0x11-0

Br 2 12-0x13-0

Dn

Alcove 10-0x7-0

MBr 20-4x14-4

43'-6"

© Copyright by designer/architect

Garage 21-0x20-0

65'-8"

Porch

Storage

Brk 10-0x10-0

P D W

Kit 16-0x10-0

R

Family 18-4x14-8

Dining 11-4x13-0

Up

Study 12-8x10-0

Foyer

Living 14-8x12-8

Porch

Arbor

First Floor 1,354 sq. ft.

SPECIAL FEATURES

1,897 total square feet of living area

Energy efficient home with
2" x 6" exterior walls

The kitchen/breakfast room is spacious
enough for plenty of family to relax
and dine without feeling crowded

A corner whirlpool tub and large
walk-in closet are great additions
to the master bedroom

A large open loft area on the second
floor offers casual gathering space
perfect for a children's playroom

The bonus room above the garage has an
additional 241 square feet of living area

3 bedrooms, 2 1/2 baths, 2-car garage

Basement foundation

Second Floor
626 sq. ft.

Bonus Room 10-4x23-4

Br3 11-11x12-6

Loft Area 12-0x12-6

Open to Below

Br2 12-4x10-3

Dn   P

First Floor
1,271 sq. ft.

74'-0"

38'-0"

Garage 21-4x23-4

W   D

P

Kitchen/Brkfst 24-4x12-6

R

Covered Porch

Family 16-9x15-2

Dn

Up

MBr 12-4x15-2

Covered Porch

© Copyright by designer/architect

SPECIAL FEATURES

2,215 total square feet of living area

The stunning great room is topped with an inverted vaulted ceiling and shares a see-through stone surround fireplace with the cheerful vaulted hearth room

The pampering master bedroom features a coffered ceiling for an elegant feel along with a large private bath and walk-in closet

The open and spacious kitchen is outfitted with a large wrap-around counter with enough casual dining space for five people

3 bedrooms, 2 1/2 baths, 2-car garage

Basement foundation

SPECIAL FEATURES

1,704 total square feet of living area

Sensational large front porch for summer evenings and rear breezeway for enjoying the outdoors

Entry leads to dining/living area featuring a sloped ceiling and second floor balcony overlook

Sophisticated master bedroom is complemented by a luxury bath with separate shower and toilet area

Two good-sized bedrooms on the second floor share a centrally located bath

3 bedrooms, 2 1/2 baths, 2-car rear entry garage

Basement foundation, drawings also include slab foundation

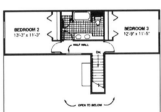

Second Floor
480 sq. ft.

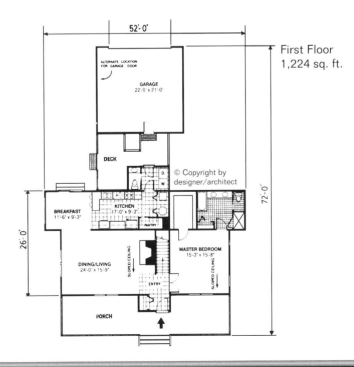

First Floor
1,224 sq. ft.

© Copyright by designer/architect

SPECIAL FEATURES

2,327 total square feet of living area

9' ceilings throughout

Covered porches on both floors
create outdoor living space

Secondary bedrooms share a full bath

L-shaped kitchen features an island
cooktop and convenient laundry room

3 bedrooms, 2 1/2 baths,
2-car side entry garage

Basement foundation

Second Floor
1,011 sq. ft.

MBr
14-9x15-11
raised clg.

Br 3
12-0x11-0

Br 2
12-0x13-3

Porch

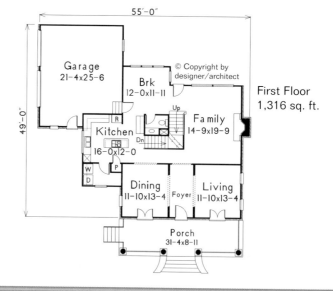

55'-0"

Garage
21-4x25-6

Brk
12-0x11-11

© Copyright by
designer/architect

49'-0"

Kitchen
16-0x12-0

Family
14-9x19-9

First Floor
1,316 sq. ft.

Dining
11-10x13-4

Foyer

Living
11-10x13-4

Porch
31-4x8-11

SPECIAL FEATURES

1,791 total square feet of living area

Vaulted great room and octagon-shaped dining area enjoy a spectacular view of the covered patio

Kitchen features a pass-through to the dining area, center island, large walk-in pantry and breakfast room with large bay window

Master bedroom is vaulted with sitting area

The garage includes extra storage space

2" x 6" exterior walls available, please order plan #533-007E-0049

4 bedrooms, 2 baths, 2-car garage with storage

Basement foundation, drawings also include crawl space and slab foundations

© Copyright by designer/architect

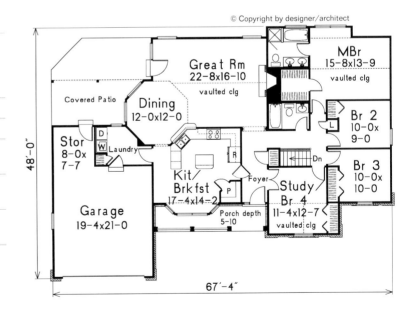

LOWE'S LEGACY SERIES

SPECIAL FEATURES

2,249 total square feet of living area

An L-shaped front porch and private master bedroom porch offer grand outdoor living spaces

Open living areas, including a family room with fireplace, an efficient kitchen with breakfast area and formal living and dining rooms complete the first floor

Two additional bedrooms share a bath on the second floor

3 bedrooms, 2 1/2 baths, 2-car garage

Basement foundation

Second Floor
550 sq. ft.

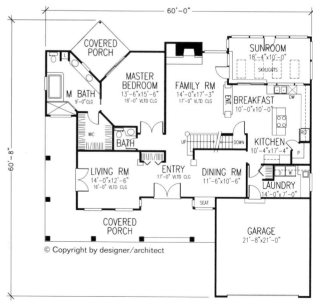

© Copyright by designer/architect

First Floor
1,699 sq. ft.

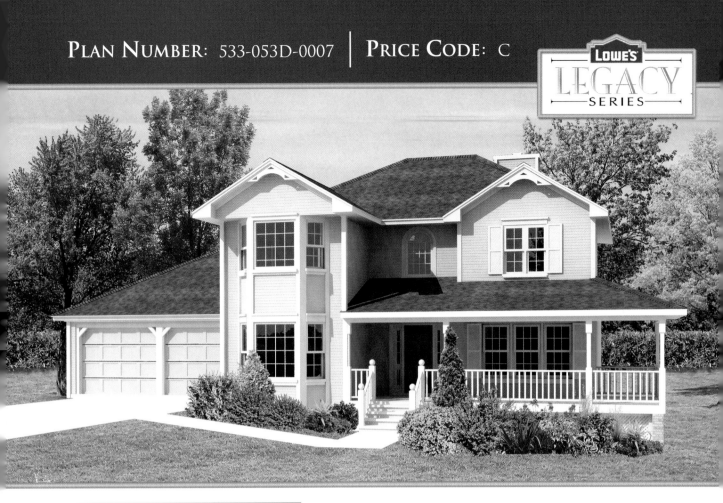

SPECIAL FEATURES

1,922 total square feet of living area

Varied front elevation features numerous accents

Master bedroom suite is well-secluded with double-door entry and private bath

Formal living and dining rooms located off the entry

3 bedrooms, 2 1/2 baths, 2-car garage

Basement foundation

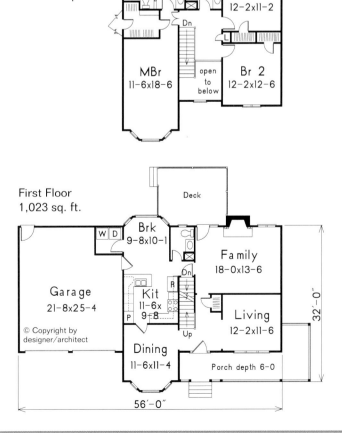

Second Floor
899 sq. ft.

Br 3
12-2x11-2

MBr
11-6x18-6

open to below

Br 2
12-2x12-6

First Floor
1,023 sq. ft.

Deck

Brk
9-8x10-1

Family
18-0x13-6

Garage
21-8x25-4

Kit
11-6x 9-8

Living
12-2x11-6

© Copyright by designer/architect

Dining
11-6x11-4

Porch depth 6-0

32'-0"

56'-0"

SPECIAL FEATURES

2,050 total square feet of living area

Large kitchen and dining area have access to garage and porch

Master bedroom features a unique turret design, private bath and large walk-in closet

Laundry facilities are conveniently located near the bedrooms

2" x6" exterior walls available, please order plan #533-001D-0112

3 bedrooms, 2 1/2 baths, 2-car side entry garage

Basement foundation, drawings also include crawl space and slab foundations

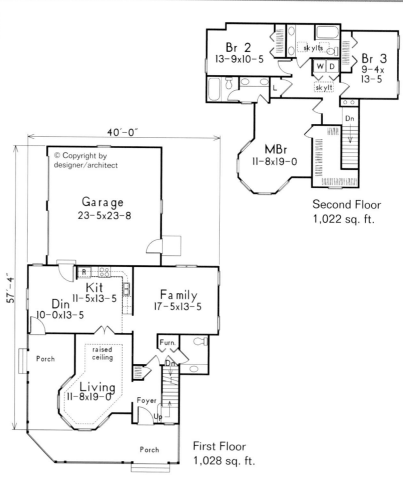

Br 2
13-9x10-5

Br 3
9-4x
13-5

W D

skylts

skylt

L

Dn

MBr
11-8x19-0

Second Floor
1,022 sq. ft.

40'-0"

© Copyright by
designer/architect

Garage
23-5x23-8

57'-4"

Kit
11-5x13-5

Din
10-0x13-5

Family
17-5x13-5

Furn.

raised
ceiling

Dn

Living
11-8x19-0

Porch

Foyer

Up

Porch

First Floor
1,028 sq. ft.

LOWE'S LEGACY SERIES

SPECIAL FEATURES

1,707 total square feet of living area

The great room and dining area combine for an open atmosphere that makes this home feel much larger than its actual size

The snack bar at the kitchen adds additional dining space and a sliding glass door to the covered porch expands the living space to the outdoors

The second floor master bedroom offers comfort and luxury to the homeowner while additional bedrooms and a bonus study complete this family plan

The bonus bedroom above the garage provides an additional 282 square feet of living area

3 bedrooms, 2 1/2 baths, 2-car garage

Basement foundation

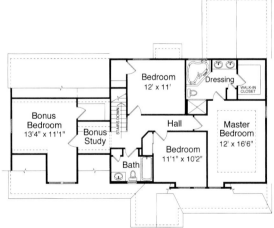

Second Floor
799 sq. ft.

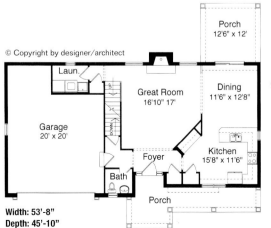

First Floor
908 sq. ft.

© Copyright by designer/architect

Width: 53'-8"
Depth: 45'-10"

SPECIAL FEATURES

1,143 total square feet of living area

Energy efficient home with
2" x 6" exterior walls

Enormous stone fireplace in the family
room adds warmth and character

Spacious kitchen with breakfast
bar overlooks the family room

Separate dining area is great for entertaining

Vaulted family room and kitchen
create an open atmosphere

2 bedrooms, 1 bath

Crawl space foundation

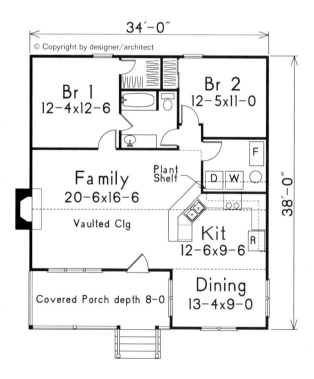

34'-0"

© Copyright by designer/architect

Br 1
12-4x12-6

Br 2
12-5x11-0

38'-0"

Family
20-6x16-6

Plant Shelf

Vaulted Clg

D W

F

Kit
12-6x9-6

R

Covered Porch depth 8-0

Dining
13-4x9-0

SPECIAL FEATURES

1,406 total square feet of living area

Master bedroom has a sloped ceiling

Kitchen and dining area merge becoming a gathering place

Enter the family room from the charming covered front porch to find a fireplace and lots of windows

3 bedrooms, 2 baths, 2-car detached garage

Slab foundation, drawings also include crawl space foundation

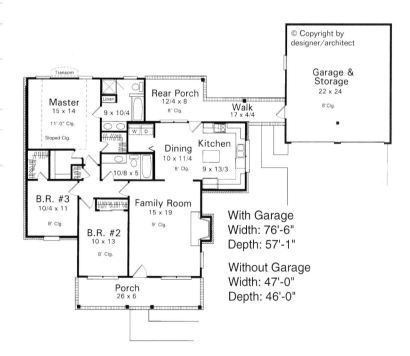

With Garage
Width: 76'-6"
Depth: 57'-1"

Without Garage
Width: 47'-0"
Depth: 46'-0"

SPECIAL FEATURES

1,428 total square feet of living area

Large vaulted family room opens to dining area and kitchen with breakfast bar

First floor master bedroom offers large bath, walk-in closet and nearby laundry facilities

A spacious loft/bedroom #3 overlooking the family room and an additional bedroom and bath complement the second floor

3 bedrooms, 2 baths

Basement foundation

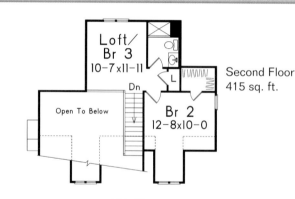

Loft/
Br 3
10-7x11-11

Second Floor
415 sq. ft.

Open To Below

Dn

Br 2
12-8x10-0

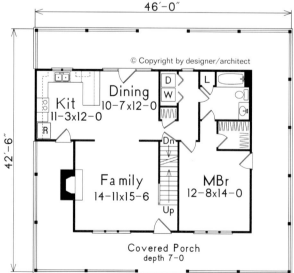

46'-0"

First Floor
1,013 sq. ft.

© Copyright by designer/architect

42'-6"

Dining
10-7x12-0

Kit
11-3x12-0

Family
14-11x15-6

MBr
12-8x14-0

Dn

Up

Covered Porch
depth 7-0

SPECIAL FEATURES

1,647 total square feet of living area

Enormous great room boasts
a vaulted ceiling

Located in the great room is an open
kitchen with an island and breakfast bar

Stunning loft overlooks the great room

2 bedrooms, 1 bath

Slab foundation, drawings also
include basement foundation

Second Floor
359 sq. ft.

First Floor
1,288 sq. ft.

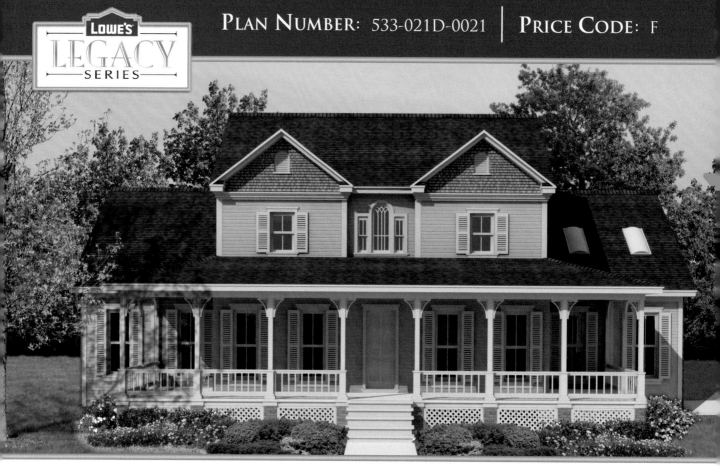

SPECIAL FEATURES

3,153 total square feet of living area

Energy efficient home with
2" x 6" exterior walls

Master bedroom has full amenities

Covered breezeway and front and rear
porches add quality outdoor living areas

Full-sized workshop and storage with
garage below is a unique combination

4 bedrooms, 2 full baths,
2 half baths, 2-car drive under garage

Basement foundation, drawings also
include crawl space and slab foundations

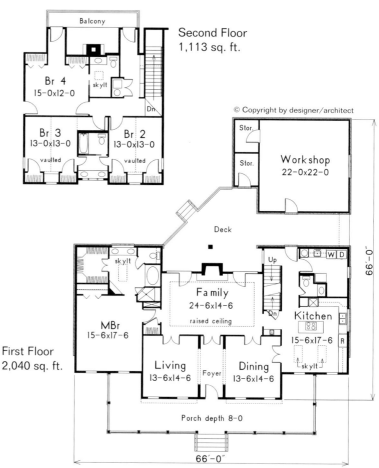

Second Floor
1,113 sq. ft.

Balcony

Br 4
15-0x12-0
skylt

Br 3
13-0x13-0
vaulted

Br 2
13-0x13-0
vaulted

Dn

© Copyright by designer/architect

Stor.
Stor.

Workshop
22-0x22-0

Deck

First Floor
2,040 sq. ft.

skylt

MBr
15-6x17-6

Family
24-6x14-6
raised ceiling

Up
Dn

W D

Kitchen
15-6x17-6

skylt

R

Living
13-6x14-6

Foyer

Dining
13-6x14-6

Porch depth 8-0

66'-0"

66'-0"

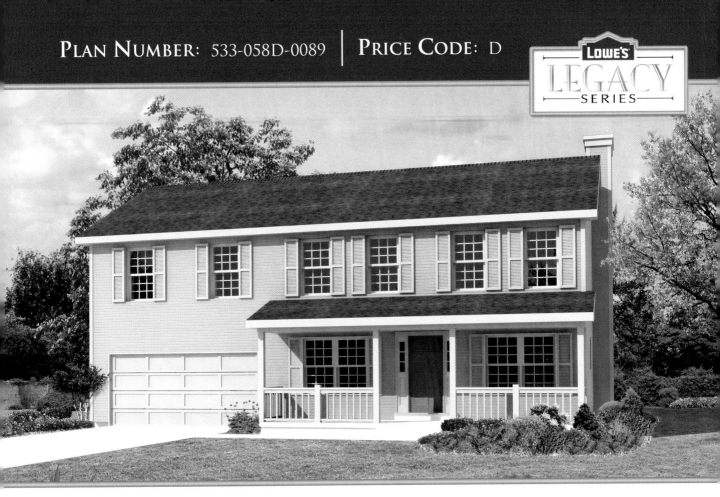

LOWE'S LEGACY SERIES

SPECIAL FEATURES

2,240 total square feet of living area

Energy efficient home with
2" x 6" exterior walls

Floor plan makes good use of space
above garage allowing for four bedrooms
and a bonus room on the second floor

Formal dining room is easily
accessible to the kitchen

Cozy family room features a
fireplace and sunny bay window

Bonus room on the second floor is
included in the square footage

4 bedrooms, 2 1/2 baths, 2-car garage

Basement foundation

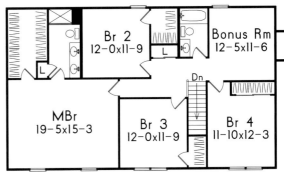

Br 2
12-0x11-9

Bonus Rm
12-5x11-6

MBr
19-5x15-3

Br 3
12-0x11-9

Br 4
11-10x12-3

Dn

Second Floor
1,344 sq. ft.

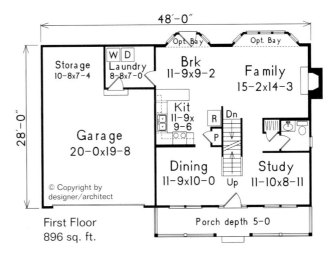

48'-0"

28'-0"

Storage
10-8x7-4

W D
Laundry
8-8x7-0

Brk
11-9x9-2

Family
15-2x14-3

Kit
11-9x
9-6

R
P
Dn

Garage
20-0x19-8

Dining
11-9x10-0

Up

Study
11-10x8-11

© Copyright by
designer/architect

First Floor
896 sq. ft.

Porch depth 5-0

SPECIAL FEATURES

2,322 total square feet of living area

Cedar shake siding, French style shutters and a multi-gabled roof line add warmth and character to the exterior

The enormous great room offers a vaulted ceiling and fireplace flanked by patio doors

A vaulted kitchen and breakfast room enjoy a large bay window and state-of-the-art design

The vaulted master bedroom includes a large walk-in closet, luxury bath and five windows to embrace the sun

4 bedrooms, 3 baths, 3-car garage

Basement foundation, drawings also include slab and crawl space foundations

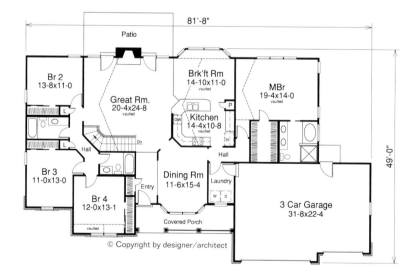

SPECIAL FEATURES

1,787 total square feet of living area

A vaulted ceiling with dormers above highlight the spacious living room that also features a handsome fireplace

The central kitchen/breakfast nook easily serves the formal dining room and opens to the large family room

A curved staircase leads to the second floor where three bedrooms can be found, including the master suite that offers a private bath and walk-in closet

3 bedrooms, 2 1/2 baths, 2-car garage

Basement foundation

Second Floor
805 sq. ft.

MBR 13'4x14 13'-6" VAULT
BR 3 10x10'8 8' CEILING
BR 2 12x14 8' CEILING

DN
OPEN TO BELOW
DORMER SKYLIGHTS ABOVE

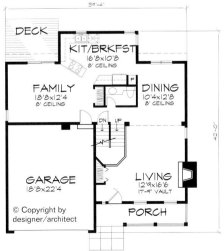

First Floor
982 sq. ft.

DECK
KIT/BRKFST 16'8x10'8 8' CEILING
FAMILY 18'8x12'4 8' CEILING
DINING 10'4x12'8 8' CEILING
DN UP
GARAGE 18'8x22'4
LIVING 12'9x16'6 17'-9" VAULT
PORCH

© Copyright by designer/architect

LOWE'S LEGACY SERIES

SPECIAL FEATURES

1,852 total square feet of living area

The stately great room features a vaulted ceiling and a corner gas fireplace

The covered or screened-in porch is a great place to relax and enjoy the outdoors

The future bonus room on the second floor has an additional 352 square feet of living space

3 bedrooms, 2 1/2 baths, 2-car garage

Basement foundation, drawings also include crawl space and slab foundations

Optional Second Floor

FUTURE HALF BATH

FUTURE BONUS ROOM 14-8 x 24

SLOPED CEILING

First Floor
1,852 sq. ft.

© Copyright by designer/architect

Bed Room 12-2 X 11-10

Covered or Screened-in Porch 16 x 8

Gas Logs

Dining 12-0 X 17-4

Jet Tub

Master Bedroom 14-4 X 13-6

Her Closet

OPTIONAL
Office, Shop, Bonus, Porch, or Storage 11-6 X 12-6

Clos.

Hall Bath

Hall

Great Room 16-0 X 26-0 Vaulted Clg.

Raised Bar

M. Bath

Shr.

His Closet

Storage

Clos.

Bed Room 12-0 X 11-4

DW

Kitchen 13-4 X 12-8

ISLD

Hall

Half Bath

To Basement

To Bonus Room

Outline Of Stairs

Foyer

Laundry 7-10 X 5-10

D W S

OPTIONAL Side Entrance Garage

Covered Porch 41-6 x 6

2 Car Garage 24-0 X 24-0

Width: 78'-0"
Depth: 49'-6"

Rear View

SPECIAL FEATURES

1,787 total square feet of living area

Skylights brighten the screen
porch which connects to the family
room and deck outdoors

Master bedroom features a comfortable
sitting area, large private bath and
direct access to the screen porch

Kitchen has a serving bar which
extends dining into the family room

3 bedrooms, 2 baths, 2-car side entry garage

Basement foundation, drawings also
include crawl space and slab foundations

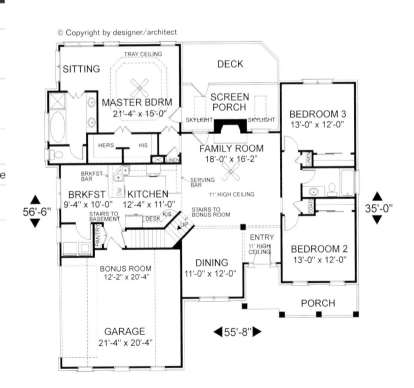

© Copyright by designer/architect

SPECIAL FEATURES

1,875 total square feet of living area

Energy efficient home with
2" x 6" exterior walls

Country style exterior with
wrap-around porch and dormers

Large second floor bedrooms share
a dressing area and bath

Master bedroom includes bay window,
walk-in closet, dressing area and bath

3 bedrooms, 2 baths, 2-car side entry garage

Crawl space foundation, drawings also
include basement and slab foundations

Second Floor
820 sq. ft.

Br 2
13-9x17-2

Br 3
13-6x17-2

Dn

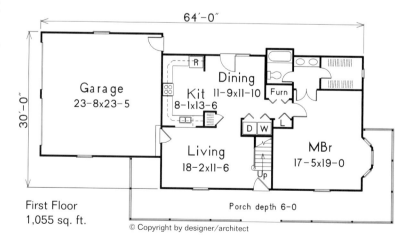

First Floor
1,055 sq. ft.

64'-0"

30'-0"

Garage
23-8x23-5

Dining
Kit 11-9x11-10
8-1x13-6

Furn

Living
18-2x11-6

MBr
17-5x19-0

Porch depth 6-0

© Copyright by designer/architect

SPECIAL FEATURES

2,685 total square feet of living area

Vaulted great room has a large fireplace and a wet bar

Sunny breakfast room has a large bay window and access outdoors

All secondary bedrooms are on the second floor for privacy

4 bedrooms, 3 1/2 baths, 2-car side entry garage

Basement foundation

Second Floor
945 sq. ft.

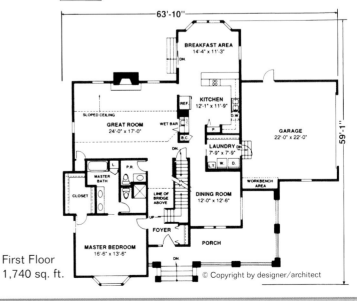

First Floor
1,740 sq. ft.

© Copyright by designer/architect

SPECIAL FEATURES

2,828 total square feet of living area

Multiple gables and wrap-around porch create a classic country exterior

The spacious entry features a see-through stone fireplace and provides access to the study, guest bedroom and bath, dining room and staircase

A well-designed kitchen has an island snack bar, built-in pantry and access to porch

The two-story dining room includes a stone fireplace, master bedroom balcony overlook and 17' high window wall that accesses rear patio

4 bedrooms, 2 1/2 baths, 1-car and a 2-car rear entry garage

Basement foundation

Second Floor
1,256 sq. ft.

First Floor
1,572 sq. ft.

© Copyright by designer/architect

SPECIAL FEATURES

1,798 total square feet of living area

French doors lead into the home with a view of the vaulted great room

A coffered ceiling tops the formal dining room providing an elegant atmosphere

The cozy breakfast area has access to the rear patio easily extending dining opportunities to the outdoors

3 bedrooms, 2 baths, 2-car side entry garage

Slab foundation

© Copyright by designer/architect

SPECIAL FEATURES

3,072 total square feet of living area

The grand, two-story foyer features a view of the impressive circular staircase

The formal living and dining rooms combine, and offer stunning bow windows and a pass-through to the kitchen

A handsome fireplace warms the expansive family room that also includes a bay window and opens to the breakfast area

4 bedrooms, 2 full baths, 3 half baths, 2-car side entry garage

Basement foundation, drawings also include slab foundation

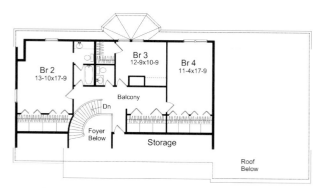

Second Floor
1,152 sq. ft.

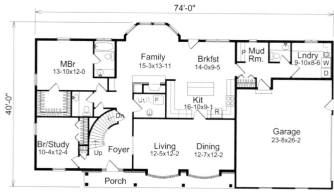

First Floor
1,920 sq. ft.

© Copyright by designer/architect

LOWE'S
LEGACY
SERIES

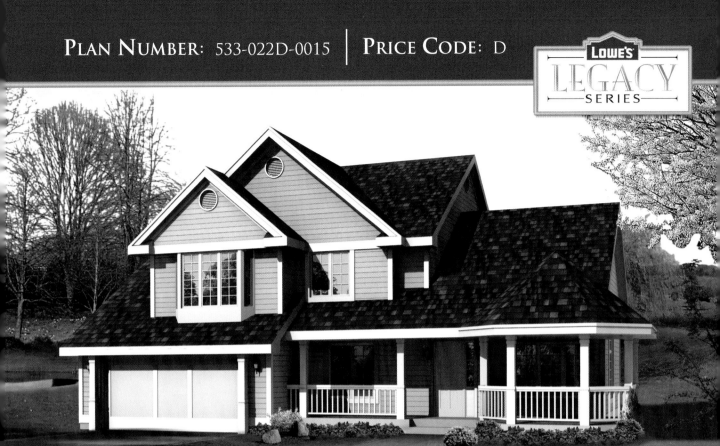

SPECIAL FEATURES

2,361 total square feet of living area

Octagon-shaped front porch is the focal point of this facade

Large living room with a vaulted ceiling couples the front porch with the rear patio for open entertaining

Family room with fireplace and kitchen with ample breakfast bar are situated in a secluded corner

Master bedroom boasts a vaulted ceiling and an oversized bay window

4 bedrooms, 2 1/2 baths, 2-car garage

Basement foundation

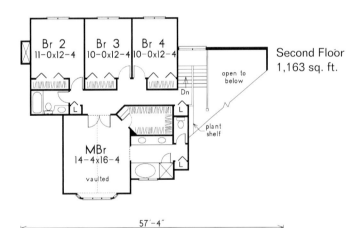

Second Floor
1,163 sq. ft.

Br 2
11-0x12-4

Br 3
10-0x12-4

Br 4
10-0x12-4

open to below

Dn

plant shelf

MBr
14-4x16-4
vaulted

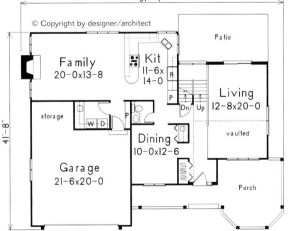

First Floor
1,198 sq. ft.

© Copyright by designer/architect

57'-4"

41'-8"

Family
20-0x13-8

Kit
11-6x 14-0

Patio

storage

W D

Dn   Up

Living
12-8x20-0

vaulted

Dining
10-0x12-6

Garage
21-6x20-0

Porch

SPECIAL FEATURES

1,769 total square feet of living area

Energy efficient home with
2" x 6" exterior walls

Living room boasts an elegant
cathedral ceiling and fireplace

U-shaped kitchen and dining
area combine for easy living

Secondary bedrooms include double closets

Secluded master bedroom with sloped
ceiling, large walk-in closet and private bath

3 bedrooms, 2 baths

Basement foundation, drawings also
include crawl space and slab foundations

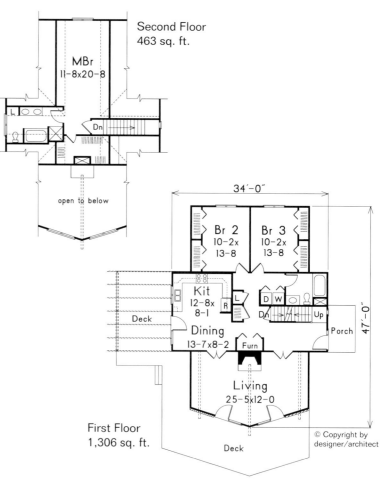

Second Floor
463 sq. ft.

MBr
11-8x20-8

Dn

open to below

First Floor
1,306 sq. ft.

34'-0"

Br 2
10-2x
13-8

Br 3
10-2x
13-8

Kit
12-8x
8-1

Dining
13-7x8-2

Living
25-5x12-0

Deck

Porch

Furn

Up

Deck

47'-0"

© Copyright by
designer/architect

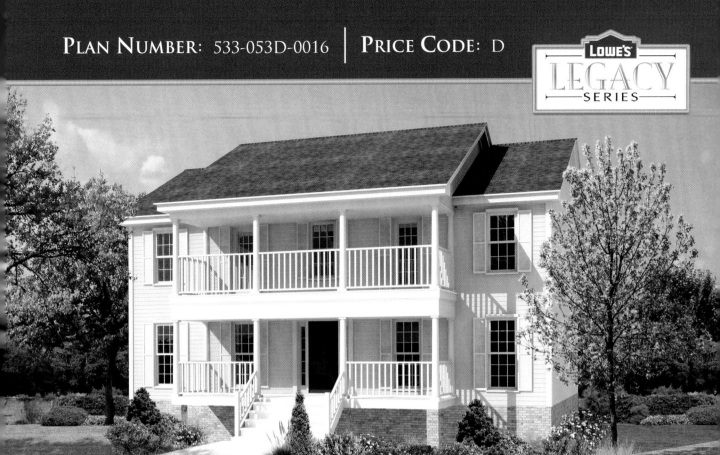

SPECIAL FEATURES

2,216 total square feet of living area

Luxury master bedroom suite features full-windowed bathtub bay, double walk-in closets and access to the front balcony

Spacious kitchen has enough space for dining

Second floor laundry facility is centrally located

4 bedrooms, 2 1/2 baths, 2-car drive under garage

Basement foundation

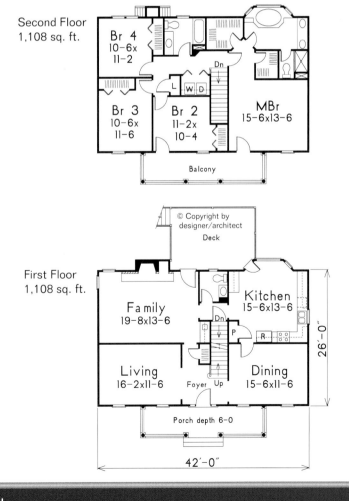

Second Floor 1,108 sq. ft.

Br 4 10-6x 11-2

Br 3 10-6x 11-6

Br 2 11-2x 10-4

MBr 15-6x13-6

Dn

L W D

Balcony

© Copyright by designer/architect

Deck

First Floor 1,108 sq. ft.

Family 19-8x13-6

Kitchen 15-6x13-6

Dn

P

R

Living 16-2x11-6

Foyer Up

Dining 15-6x11-6

26'-0"

Porch depth 6-0

42'-0"

SPECIAL FEATURES

1,800 total square feet of living area

A large flex space can easily convert to a home office or formal dining room depending on your needs

A large and spacious kitchen has a center island with eating bar and an attached breakfast room with bay window

The corner jet tub in the master bath pampers the homeowners in their private retreat

The unfinished bonus room has an additional 326 square feet of living area

3 bedrooms, 2 baths, 2-car garage

Slab foundation, drawings also include crawl space foundation

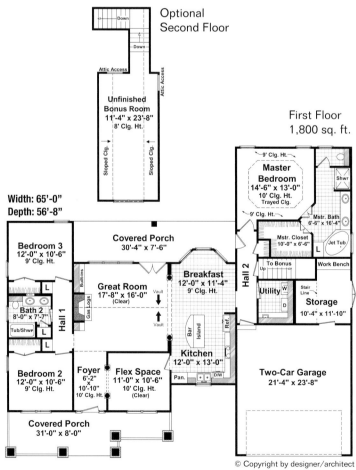

Optional Second Floor

Unfinished Bonus Room
11'-4" x 23'-8"
8' Clg. Ht.

Attic Access

First Floor
1,800 sq. ft.

Width: 65'-0"
Depth: 56'-8"

Master Bedroom
14'-6" x 13'-0"
10' Clg. Ht.
Trayed Clg.

Mstr. Bath
6'-6" x 16'-4"

Mstr. Closet
10'-0" x 6'-6"

Jet Tub

Bedroom 3
12'-0" x 10'-6"
9' Clg. Ht.

Covered Porch
30'-4" x 7'-6"

Breakfast
12'-0" x 11'-4"
9' Clg. Ht.

Great Room
17'-8" x 16'-0"
(Clear)

Hall 2

To Bonus

Utility

Work Bench

Bath 2
8'-0" x 7'-7"

Hall 1

Storage
10'-4" x 11'-10"

Kitchen
12'-0" x 13'-0"

Bedroom 2
12'-0" x 10'-6"
9' Clg. Ht.

Foyer
6'-2" x 10'-10"
10' Clg. Ht.

Flex Space
11'-0" x 10'-6"
10' Clg. Ht.
(Clear)

Two-Car Garage
21'-4" x 23'-8"

Covered Porch
31'-0" x 8'-0"

© Copyright by designer/architect

Lowe's LEGACY SERIES

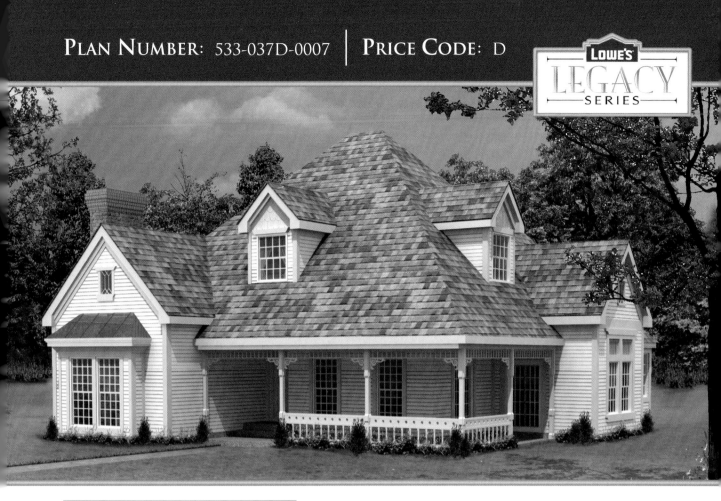

SPECIAL FEATURES

2,282 total square feet of living area

Living and dining rooms combine to create a large, convenient entertaining area that includes a fireplace

Comfortable covered porch allows access from secondary bedrooms

Second floor game room overlooks the foyer and includes a full bath

Kitchen and breakfast areas are surrounded by mullioned windows

3 bedrooms, 3 baths, 2-car detached garage

Slab foundation, drawings also include crawl space foundation

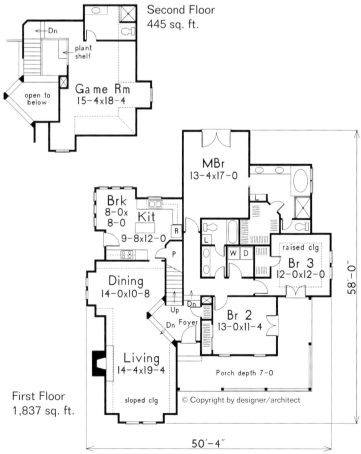

Second Floor
445 sq. ft.

Dn

plant shelf

open to below

Game Rm
15-4x18-4

MBr
13-4x17-0

Brk
8-0x8-0

Kit
9-8x12-0

raised clg

Br 3
12-0x12-0

Dining
14-0x10-8

Up

Dn Foyer

Dn

Br 2
13-0x11-4

Living
14-4x19-4

Porch depth 7-0

sloped clg

© Copyright by designer/architect

First Floor
1,837 sq. ft.

58'-0"

50'-4"

LOWE'S LEGACY SERIES

SPECIAL FEATURES

1,217 total square feet of living area

The covered porch welcomes guests into this lovely cottage

Inside, the massive living area includes the combined kitchen/breakfast room and family room, all warmed by a grand fireplace

The master bedroom enjoys a walk-in closet and private bath

2 bedrooms, 2 baths

Basement foundation

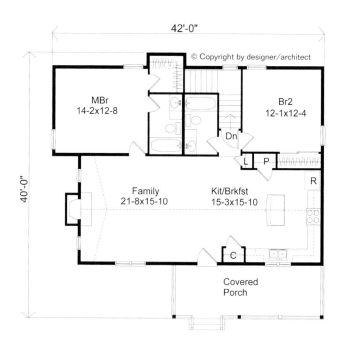

42'-0"

40'-0"

© Copyright by designer/architect

MBr
14-2x12-8

Br2
12-1x12-4

Dn

L   P

R

Family
21-8x15-10

Kit/Brkfst
15-3x15-10

C

Covered
Porch

LOWE'S
LEGACY
SERIES

SPECIAL FEATURES

1,197 total square feet of living area

Energy efficient home with
2" x 6" exterior walls

U-shaped kitchen includes ample
workspace, breakfast bar, laundry area
and direct access to the outdoors

Large living room has a
convenient coat closet

Master bedroom features
a large walk-in closet

3 bedrooms, 1 bath

Crawl space foundation, drawings also
include basement and slab foundations

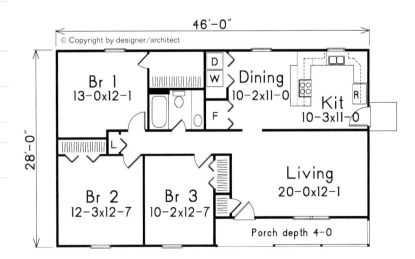

© Copyright by designer/architect

46'-0"

28'-0"

Br 1
13-0x12-1

Dining
10-2x11-0

Kit
10-3x11-0

D
W
F

L

Br 2
12-3x12-7

Br 3
10-2x12-7

Living
20-0x12-1

Porch depth 4-0

SPECIAL FEATURES

2,001 total square feet of living area

Energy efficient home with
2" x 6" exterior walls

Arched openings on the front porch
create a welcoming entrance

The sunroom/breakfast area
features an abundance of windows
for a cheerful atmosphere

The kitchen offers a raised bar opening
to the sunroom/breakfast area which
makes serving food an easy task

3 bedrooms, 2 baths, 2-car side entry garage

Slab foundation

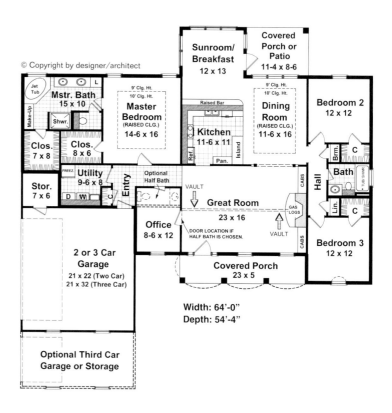

© Copyright by designer/architect

Sunroom/
Breakfast
12 x 13

Covered
Porch or
Patio
11-4 x 8-6

9' Clg. Ht.
10' Clg. Ht.
Master
Bedroom
(RAISED CLG.)
14-6 x 16

Jet
Tub
Mstr. Bath
15 x 10

Make-Up

Shwr.

Raised Bar

Kitchen
11-6 x 11

9' Clg. Ht.
10' Clg. Ht.
Dining
Room
(RAISED CLG.)
11-6 x 16

Bedroom 2
12 x 12

Clos.
7 x 8

Clos.
8 x 6

Ref.

Pan.

Island

Brm.

C

Bath

FREEZ.

Utility
9-6 x 8

Optional
Half Bath

CABS

Hall

TUB SHWR.

Stor.
7 x 6

D W

Entry

VAULT

Great Room
23 x 16

GAS
LOGS

Lin.

C

2 or 3 Car
Garage
21 x 22 (Two Car)
21 x 32 (Three Car)

Office
8-6 x 12

DOOR LOCATION IF
HALF BATH IS CHOSEN.

VAULT

CABS

Bedroom 3
12 x 12

Covered Porch
23 x 5

Width: 64'-0"
Depth: 54'-4"

Optional Third Car
Garage or Storage

LOWE'S LEGACY SERIES

SPECIAL FEATURES

2,967 total square feet of living area

The charming exterior is graced
with a country porch and multiple
arched projected box windows

Dining area is oversized and adjoins a fully
equipped kitchen with walk-in pantry

Two bay windows light up the enormous
informal living area to the rear

4 bedrooms, 3 1/2 baths,
3-car side entry garage

Basement foundation

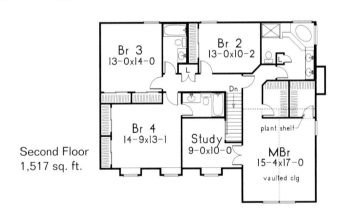

Second Floor
1,517 sq. ft.

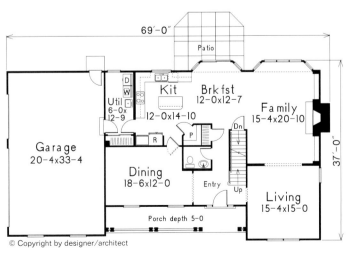

First Floor
1,450 sq. ft.

© Copyright by designer/architect

SPECIAL FEATURES

2,370 total square feet of living area

Open living areas create a spacious, airy feeling

The two-story foyer is an unusual touch to this home's interior

Master bedroom includes sitting area, sizable master bath and double walk-in closets

3 bedrooms, 2 1/2 baths, optional 2-car garage

Basement foundation

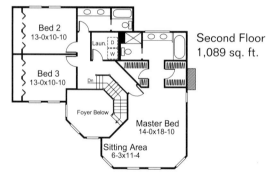

Second Floor
1,089 sq. ft.

Bed 2
13-0x10-10

Bed 3
13-0x10-10

Laun.

Foyer Below

Master Bed
14-0x18-10

Sitting Area
6-3x11-4

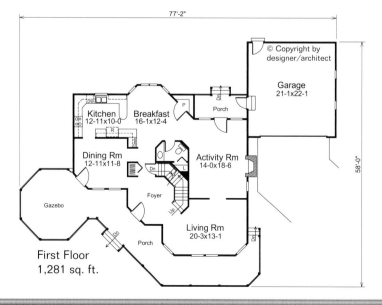

77'-2"

© Copyright by designer/architect

Garage
21-1x22-1

Porch

Kitchen
12-11x10-0

Breakfast
16-1x12-4

Dining Rm
12-11x11-8

Activity Rm
14-0x18-6

Foyer

Gazebo

Living Rm
20-3x13-1

Porch

58'-0"

First Floor
1,281 sq. ft.

SPECIAL FEATURES

1,525 total square feet of living area

This appealing home features plenty of amenities and fits beautifully on a narrow lot

The warm kitchen with a sunny breakfast nook is well designed to serve as the busiest room in the home

Three bedrooms are located on the second floor for extra peace and quiet

3 bedrooms, 2 1/2 baths, 2-car garage

Basement foundation

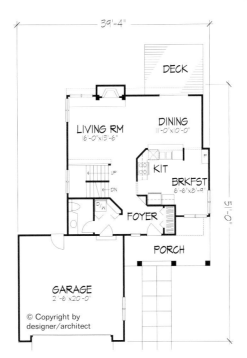

First Floor
765 sq. ft.

Second Floor
760 sq. ft.

SPECIAL FEATURES

2,098 total square feet of living area

Energy efficient home
with 2" x 6" exterior walls

Covered porch wraps around the
entire house, leading to the deck
and screened porch in the back

Spacious kitchen has plenty of cabinet
space as well as counterspace

Convenient laundry chute is located
near the second floor bathroom

3 bedrooms, 2 1/2 baths, 3-car
side entry detached garage

Crawl space foundation, drawings
also include basement foundation

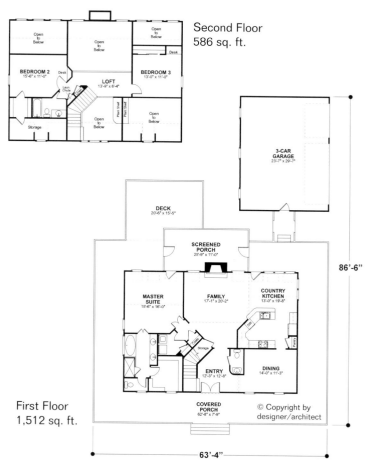

Second Floor
586 sq. ft.

First Floor
1,512 sq. ft.

© Copyright by
designer/architect

SPECIAL FEATURES

2,440 total square feet of living area

The two-story great room is sure to be an attention getter with an entire wall of windows and a stately fireplace

The corner whirlpool tub in the master bath is flanked by a vanity on each side adding a sense of symmetry to the space

A substantial desk space can be found in the breakfast room

4 bedrooms, 4 baths, 2-car side entry garage

Basement foundation

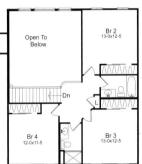

Second Floor
766 sq. ft.

© Copyright by designer/architect

First Floor
1,674 sq. ft.

SPECIAL FEATURES

1,646 total square feet of living area

Attractive cottage features two large porch areas

The great room includes a corner fireplace and beautiful views provided by ten windows and doors

A U-shaped kitchen with snack counter is open to the breakfast room and enjoys access to both the side and rear porch

The master bedroom has a luxury bath with corner tub, double vanities with make-up counter and a huge walk-in closet

2 bedrooms, 2 baths, 2-car side entry garage

Basement foundation, drawings also include slab and crawl space foundations

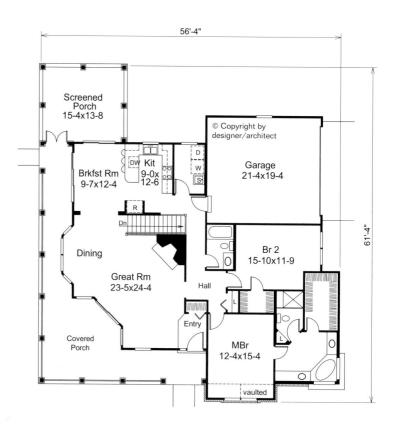

56'-4"

61'-4"

Screened Porch 15-4x13-8

© Copyright by designer/architect

Kit 9-0x 12-6

Brkfst Rm 9-7x12-4

Garage 21-4x19-4

Dining

Br 2 15-10x11-9

Great Rm 23-5x24-4

Hall

Covered Porch

Entry

MBr 12-4x15-4

vaulted

SPECIAL FEATURES

1,784 total square feet of living area

Spacious living area with corner fireplace offers a cheerful atmosphere with large windows

The large second floor gathering room is great for a children's play area

Secluded master bedroom has separate porch entrances and a large master bath with walk-in closet

3 bedrooms, 2 1/2 baths, 1-car garage

Basement foundation, drawings also include crawl space foundation

Second Floor
672 sq. ft.

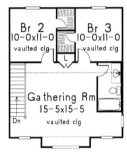

Br 2
10-0x11-0
vaulted clg

Br 3
10-0x11-0
vaulted clg

Gathering Rm
15-5x15-5
vaulted clg

Dn

First Floor
1,112 sq. ft.

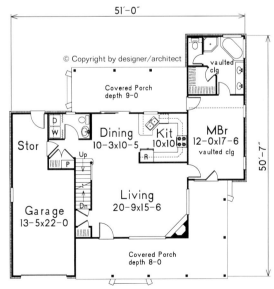

51'-0"

© Copyright by designer/architect

Covered Porch
depth 9-0

vaulted clg

Stor

Dining
10-3x10-5

Kit
10x10

MBr
12-0x17-6
vaulted clg

Up

Living
20-9x15-6

Garage
13-5x22-0

Dn

50'-7"

Covered Porch
depth 8-0

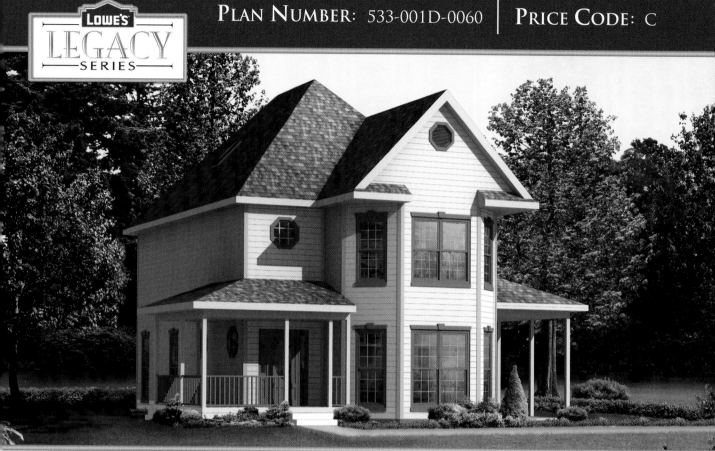

LOWE'S LEGACY SERIES

SPECIAL FEATURES

1,818 total square feet of living area

Spacious living and dining rooms

Master bedroom has a walk-in closet, dressing area and bath

Convenient carport and storage area

2" x 6" exterior walls available, please order plan #533-001D-0113

3 bedrooms, 2 1/2 baths, 1-car carport

Crawl space foundation, drawings also include basement and slab foundations

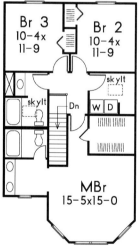

Second Floor
890 sq. ft.

Br 3
10-4x 11-9

Br 2
10-4x 11-9

skylt

skylt Dn W D

MBr
15-5x15-0

© Copyright by designer/architect

Patio

Living
23-5x15-8
raised ceiling

Storage

Carport

L Furn

Kit
12-3x 12-2

42'-0"

Foyer Up

Dining
15-5x13-0

First Floor
928 sq. ft.

Porch depth 6-0

36'-0"

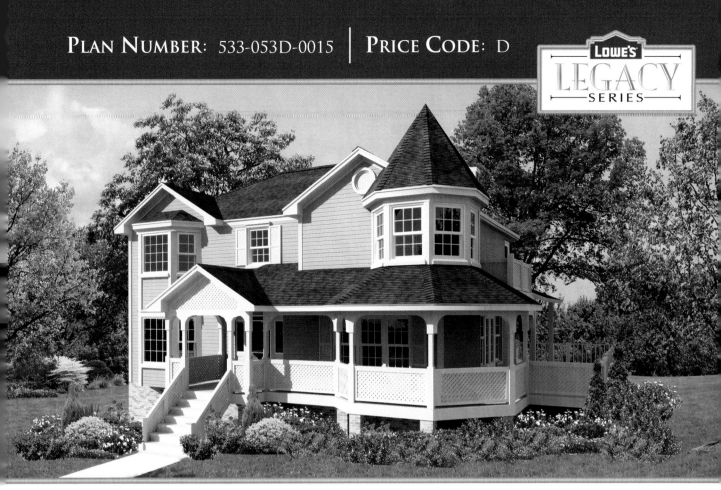

LOWE'S
LEGACY
SERIES

SPECIAL FEATURES

2,214 total square feet of living area

Victorian accents dominate facade

Covered porches and decks fan out
to connect front and rear entries
and add to outdoor living space

Elegant master bedroom suite features a
five-sided windowed alcove and private deck

Corner kitchen has a sink-top peninsula

4 bedrooms, 2 1/2 baths,
2-car drive under garage

Basement foundation

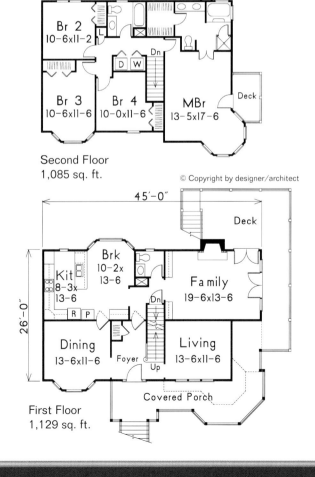

Second Floor
1,085 sq. ft.

© Copyright by designer/architect

First Floor
1,129 sq. ft.

SPECIAL FEATURES

4,166 total square feet of living area

An amazing master bedroom features a coffered sitting area, a cozy fireplace and a plush bath with a step-up whirlpool tub as the focal point

The second floor features a large recreation room with a half bath and utility room within its walls

Bedroom #2 would make a great guest room with a built-in desk and direct access to a full bath

4 bedrooms, 4 1/2 baths, 3-car garage

Slab foundation

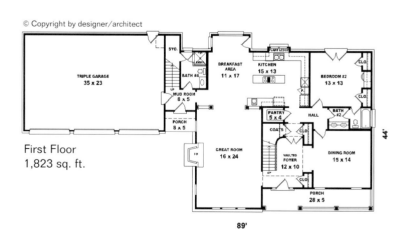

Second Floor
2,343 sq. ft.

© Copyright by designer/architect

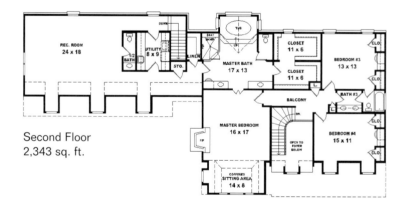

First Floor
1,823 sq. ft.

SPECIAL FEATURES

1,735 total square feet of living area

9' ceilings throughout the first floor

A U-shaped kitchen opens into the dining room with deck access

Optional bonus room on the second floor has an additional 295 square feet of living area

3 bedrooms, 2 1/2 baths, 2-car side entry garage

Crawl space foundation

First Floor
1,189 sq. ft.

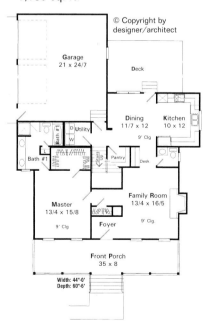

Second Floor
546 sq. ft.

LOWE'S LEGACY SERIES

SPECIAL FEATURES

2,250 total square feet of living area

The kitchen easily serves the casual bayed breakfast room or the formal dining room

The master bedroom enjoys a luxurious bath, two walk-in closets, porch access and a nearby office/nursery

A large laundry room complete with a sink and counterspace adds simplicity to the household chore

The unfinished bonus room has an additional 310 square feet of living area

4 bedrooms, 3 baths, 2-car side entry garage

Slab foundation, drawings also include crawl space foundation

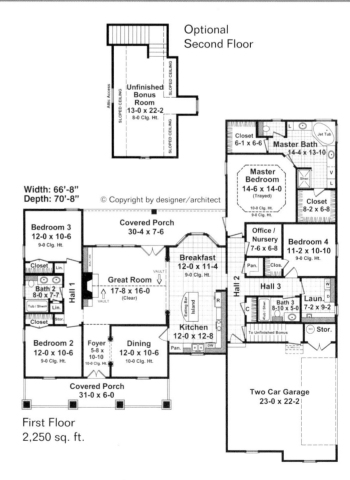

Optional Second Floor

Attic Access

Unfinished Bonus Room
13-0 x 22-2
8-0 Clg. Ht.

SLOPED CEILING

Width: 66'-8"
Depth: 70'-8"

© Copyright by designer/architect

Closet 6-1 x 6-6

Master Bath 14-4 x 13-10

Jet Tub

Master Bedroom 14-6 x 14-0
(Trayed)
10-0 Clg. Ht.
9-0 Clg. Ht.

Closet 8-2 x 6-8

Office / Nursery 7-6 x 6-8

Bedroom 4 11-2 x 10-10
9-0 Clg. Ht.

Bedroom 3 12-0 x 10-6
9-0 Clg. Ht.

Covered Porch 30-4 x 7-6

Closet Lin.

Breakfast 12-0 x 11-4
9-0 Clg. Ht.

Hall 1

Bath 2 8-0 x 7-7

Great Room 17-8 x 16-0
(Clear)
VAULT

Hall 2

Hall 3

Laun. 7-2 x 9-2

Bath 3 8-10 x 5-0

Eating Bar Island

Kitchen 12-0 x 12-8

To Unfinished Bonus

Stor.

Bedroom 2 12-0 x 10-6
9-0 Clg. Ht.

Foyer 5-8 x 10-10

Dining 12-0 x 10-6
10-0 Clg. Ht.

Covered Porch 31-0 x 6-0

Two Car Garage 23-0 x 22-2

First Floor
2,250 sq. ft.

SPECIAL FEATURES

1,542 total square feet of living area

Varied ceiling heights throughout help create a distinctive interior

The master suite encourages privacy and contains a full bath and walk-in closet

The kitchen island incorporates the cooktop creating more counterspace

3 bedrooms, 2 baths, 2-car garage

Crawl space foundation, drawings also include slab foundation

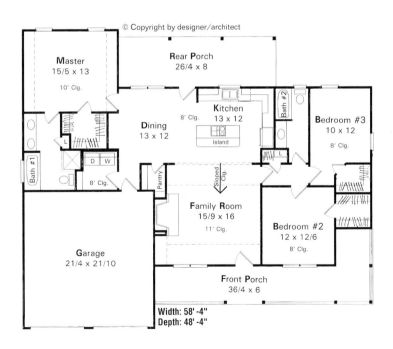

© Copyright by designer/architect

Master
15/5 x 13
10' Clg.

Rear Porch
26/4 x 8

Kitchen
13 x 12
8' Clg.

Bedroom #3
10 x 12
8' Clg.

Dining
13 x 12

Island

Bath #2

Bath #1
8' Clg.

D W

Pantry

Sloped Clg.

Family Room
15/9 x 16
11' Clg.

Bedroom #2
12 x 12/6
8' Clg.

Garage
21/4 x 21/10

Front Porch
36/4 x 6

Width: 58'-4"
Depth: 48'-4"

SPECIAL FEATURES

1,761 total square feet of living area

Exterior window dressing, roof dormers and planter boxes provide visual warmth and charm

Great room boasts a vaulted ceiling, fireplace and opens to a pass-through kitchen

The vaulted master bedroom includes a luxury bath and walk-in closet

Home features eight separate closets with an abundance of storage

4 bedrooms, 2 baths, 2-car side entry garage

Basement foundation

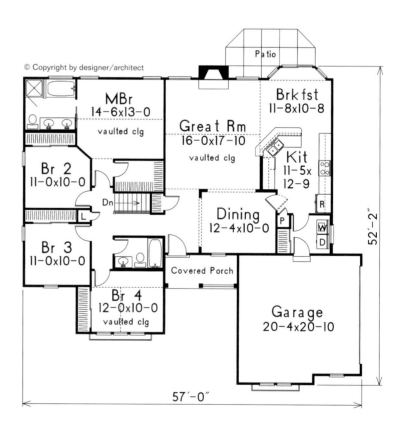

© Copyright by designer/architect

LOWE'S
LEGACY
SERIES

SPECIAL FEATURES

1,977 total square feet of living area

An enormous entry with adjacent dining area and powder room leads to a splendid two-story family room with fireplace

Kitchen features an abundance of cabinets, built-in pantry and breakfast room with menu desk and bay window

A spacious vaulted master bedroom, two secondary bedrooms with bath and loft area adorn the second floor

3 bedrooms, 2 1/2 baths, 2-car garage with storage area

Basement foundation

Second Floor
1,000 sq. ft.

First Floor
977 sq. ft.

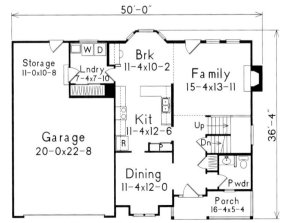

© Copyright by designer/architect

SPECIAL FEATURES

1,695 total square feet of living area

Facade features a cozy wrap-around porch, projected living room window and repeating front gables

Balcony overlooks to the entry below

Kitchen has a full-view corner window with adjacent eating space that opens to the screened porch

Vaulted master bedroom enjoys double closets and a private bath

3 bedrooms, 2 1/2 baths, 2-car garage

Basement foundation

Second Floor
825 sq. ft.

Br 3
11-6x11-6

MBr
15-10x12-8
vaulted

Dn

open to
below

Br 2
12-4x11-0

raised ceiling

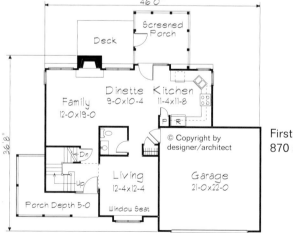

46'0"

Deck

Screened Porch

Family
12-0x19-0

Dinette
9-0x10-4

Kitchen
11-4x11-8

36'8"

Dn

© Copyright by designer/architect

First Floor
870 sq. ft.

Up

Living
12-4x12-4

Garage
21-0x22-0

Porch Depth 5-0

Window Seat

LOWE'S
LEGACY
SERIES

SPECIAL FEATURES

1,474 total square feet of living area

Kitchen and dining area include center
eat-in island and large pantry

Laundry facilities and hall bath are roomy

Both secondary bedrooms
have walk-in closets

3 bedrooms, 2 baths, 2-car detached garage

Slab foundation, drawings also
include crawl space foundation

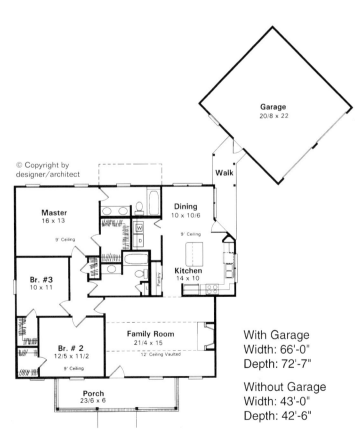

© Copyright by
designer/architect

Garage
20/8 x 22

Walk

Master
16 x 13

9' Ceiling

Dining
10 x 10/6

9' Ceiling

W
D

Kitchen
14 x 10

Pantry

Br. #3
10 x 11

Family Room
21/4 x 15

12' Ceiling Vaulted

Br. # 2
12/5 x 11/2

9' Ceiling

Porch
23/6 x 6

With Garage
Width: 66'-0"
Depth: 72'-7"

Without Garage
Width: 43'-0"
Depth: 42'-6"

SPECIAL FEATURES

1,888 total square feet of living area

The flex space has a half bath nearby and could easily convert to an ideal guest room

The kitchen eating bar/island has dining space and workspace for food preparation

The great room with fireplace is the focal point of this home

The optional second floor has an additional 272 square feet of living space

3 bedrooms, 2 1/2 baths, 2-car side entry garage

Slab foundation, drawings also include crawl space foundation

Rear View

Optional Second Floor

Bonus Room
12-2 x 22-4
8-0 CLG. HT.

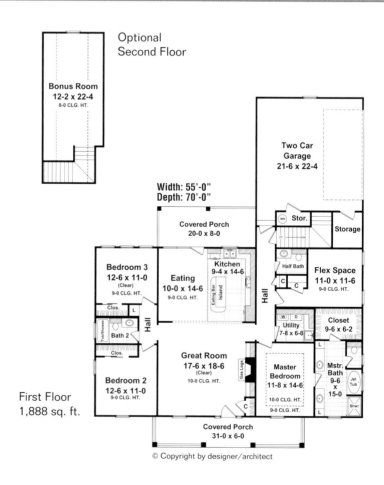

Width: 55'-0"
Depth: 70'-0"

Two Car Garage
21-6 x 22-4

Covered Porch
20-0 x 8-0

WH Stor.

Storage

Kitchen
9-4 x 14-6

Half Bath

Flex Space
11-0 x 11-6
9-0 CLG. HT.

Bedroom 3
12-6 x 11-0
(Clear)
9-0 CLG. HT.

Eating
10-0 x 14-6
9-0 CLG. HT.

Clos.

Hall

Bath 2

Clos.

W D
Utility
7-8 x 6-8

Closet
9-6 x 6-2

Bedroom 2
12-6 x 11-0
9-0 CLG. HT.

Great Room
17-6 x 18-6
(Clear)
10-0 CLG. HT.

Gas Logs

Master Bedroom
11-8 x 14-6
10-0 CLG. HT.
9-0 CLG. HT.

Mstr. Bath
9-6 x 15-0
Jet Tub
Shwr.

First Floor
1,888 sq. ft.

Covered Porch
31-0 x 6-0

© Copyright by designer/architect

SPECIAL FEATURES

- 1,985 total square feet of living area

- Cozy family room features a fireplace and double French doors opening onto the porch

- The open kitchen includes a convenient island

- The extraordinary master bedroom has a tray ceiling and a large walk-in closet

- Lovely bayed breakfast area has easy access to the deck

- 3 bedrooms, 2 1/2 baths

- Partial basement/crawl space foundation

© Copyright by designer/architect

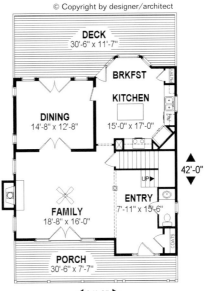

DECK
30'-6" x 11'-7"

BRKFST

KITCHEN
15'-0" x 17'-0"

DINING
14'-8" x 12'-8"

UP

42'-0"

ENTRY
7'-11" x 15'-6"

FAMILY
18'-8" x 16'-0"

COATS

PORCH
30'-6" x 7'-7"

◄ 31'-2" ►

First Floor
1,009 sq. ft.

TRAY CEILING

MASTER BDRM
16'-4" x 15'-0"

D W

DN

BEDROOM 2
12'-0" x 12'-8"

BEDROOM 3
12'-8" x 12'-0"

WINDOW SEAT

Second Floor
976 sq. ft.

SPECIAL FEATURES

1,874 total square feet of living area

9' ceilings throughout the first floor

Two-story foyer opens into the large family room with fireplace

First floor master bedroom includes a private bath with tub and shower

4 bedrooms, 2 1/2 baths, 2-car garage

Basement foundation, drawings also include slab foundation

Second Floor
633 sq. ft.

First Floor
1,241 sq. ft.

© Copyright by designer/architect

SPECIAL FEATURES

2,112 total square feet of living area

Kitchen efficiently connects to
the formal dining area

Nook located between the family room and
kitchen creates an ideal breakfast area

Both baths on the second
floor feature skylights

3 bedrooms, 3 baths

Basement foundation, drawings also
include crawl space foundation

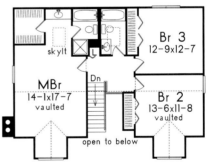

Second Floor
896 sq. ft.

Br 3
12-9x12-7

MBr
14-1x17-7
vaulted

Dn

Br 2
13-6x11-8
vaulted

skylt

open to below

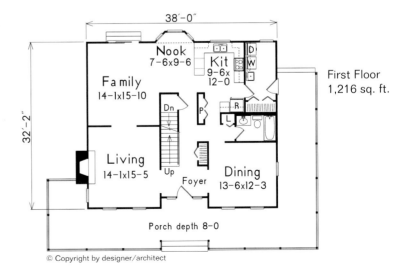

38'-0"

Nook
7-6x9-6

Kit
9-6x
12-0

Family
14-1x15-10

Dn

Living
14-1x15-5

Up

Foyer

Dining
13-6x12-3

32'-2"

First Floor
1,216 sq. ft.

Porch depth 8-0

© Copyright by designer/architect

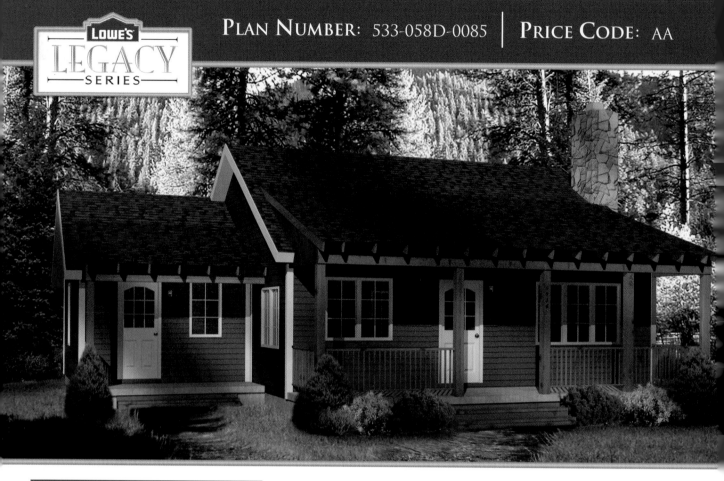

SPECIAL FEATURES

1,000 total square feet of living area

Energy efficient home with
2" x 6" exterior walls

Large mud room has a separate
covered porch entrance

Full-length covered front porch

Bedrooms are on opposite sides
of the home for privacy

Vaulted ceiling creates an open
and spacious feeling

2 bedrooms, 1 bath

Crawl space foundation

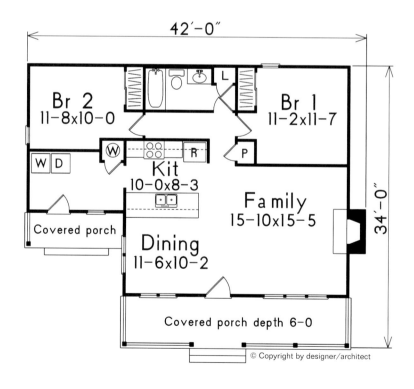

LOWE'S
LEGACY
SERIES

SPECIAL FEATURES

1,285 total square feet of living area

Energy efficient home with
2" x 6" exterior walls

Accommodating home with ranch style porch

Large storage area on back of home

Master bedroom includes dressing area,
private bath and built-in bookcase

Kitchen features pantry, breakfast bar
and complete view to dining room

3 bedrooms, 2 baths

Crawl space foundation, drawings also
include basement and slab foundations

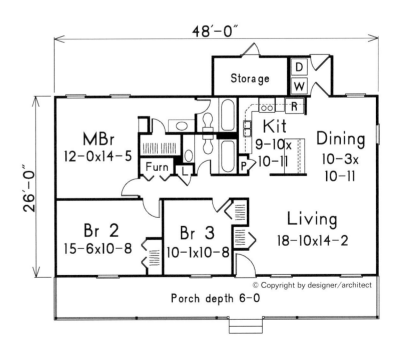

48'-0"

Storage

D
W
R

26'-0"

MBr
12-0x14-5

Furn

Kit
9-10x
10-11

Dining
10-3x
10-11

P

Br 2
15-6x10-8

Br 3
10-1x10-8

Living
18-10x14-2

© Copyright by designer/architect

Porch depth 6-0

LOWE'S
LEGACY
SERIES

SPECIAL FEATURES

1,591 total square feet of living area

Spacious porch and patio
provide outdoor enjoyment

Large entry foyer leads to a cheery kitchen
and breakfast room which welcomes the
sun through a wide array of windows

The great room features a vaulted
ceiling, corner fireplace, wet bar
and access to the rear patio

Double walk-in closets, private porch
and a luxury bath are special highlights
of the vaulted master bedroom suite

3 bedrooms, 2 baths, 2-car side entry garage

Basement foundation

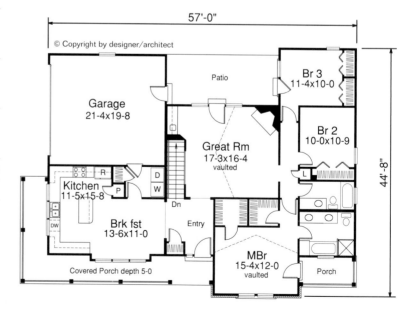

SPECIAL FEATURES

2,636 total square feet of living area

Master bedroom has a generous
walk-in closet, luxurious bath
and a vaulted sitting area

Spacious kitchen has an island cooktop
and vaulted breakfast nook

Bonus room above garage has an
additional 389 square feet of living area

4 bedrooms, 3 1/2 baths, 2-car side
entry garage, 1-car drive under garage

Basement foundation

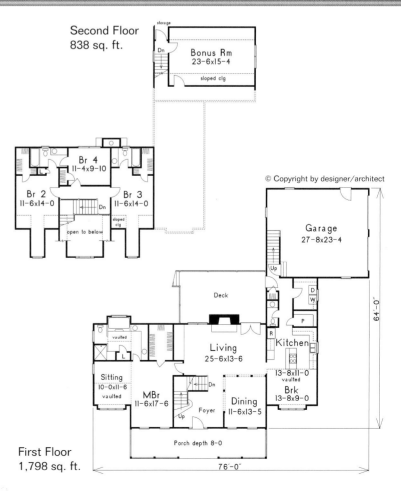

Second Floor
838 sq. ft.

storage

Dn | Bonus Rm
23-6x15-4
sloped clg

© Copyright by designer/architect

Br 4
11-4x9-10

Br 2
11-6x14-0

Br 3
11-6x14-0

open to below | sloped clg

Garage
27-8x23-4

64-0

Deck

Living
25-6x13-6

Kitchen

13-8x11-0
vaulted

Brk
13-8x9-0

vaulted

Sitting
10-0x11-6
vaulted

MBr
11-6x17-6

Foyer

Dn

Up

Dining
11-6x13-5

Porch depth 8-0

First Floor
1,798 sq. ft.

76'-0"

SPECIAL FEATURES

2,361 total square feet of living area

Enormous breakfast area and kitchen create a perfect gathering place

Family room is enhanced with a wall of windows and a large fireplace

Office/gameroom is easily accessible through a separate side entrance

3 bedrooms, 3 baths, 2-car side entry garage

Basement foundation

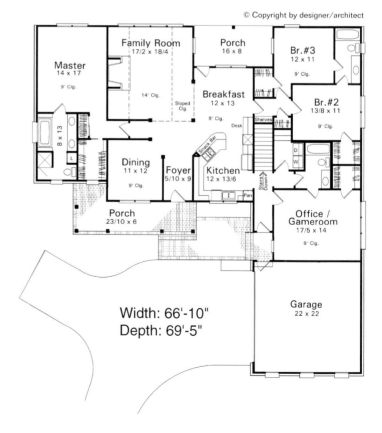

© Copyright by designer/architect

Width: 66'-10"
Depth: 69'-5"

SPECIAL FEATURES

1,757 total square feet of living area

An enormous oval-shaped tub graces the master bath with tranquil luxury

The two second floor bedrooms skillfully share the full bath between them

A large utility room provides extra storage space

The second floor future expansion offers an additional 287 square feet of living space

3 bedrooms, 2 1/2 baths, 2-car garage

Slab foundation

Second Floor
642 sq. ft.

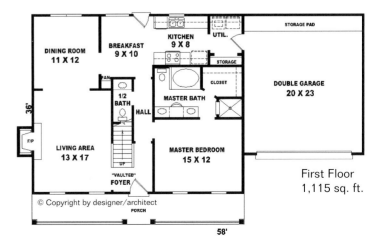

© Copyright by designer/architect

First Floor
1,115 sq. ft.

SPECIAL FEATURES

1,056 total square feet of living area

A welcoming porch opens to find the spacious living room featuring a coat closet, fireplace and sloped ceiling

The centrally located kitchen easily serves the dining area and offers a snack bar counter for quick and casual meals

The full bath includes a linen closet for extra storage

2 bedrooms, 1 bath, 2-car garage

Basement foundation

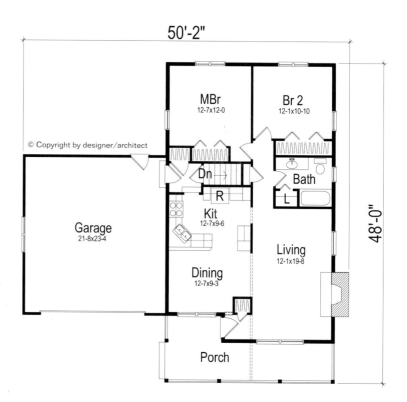

SPECIAL FEATURES

1,550 total square feet of living area

Wrap-around front porch is an ideal gathering place

Handy snack bar is positioned so the kitchen flows into the family room

Master bedroom has many amenities

3 bedrooms, 2 baths, 2-car detached side entry garage

Slab foundation, drawings also include crawl space foundation

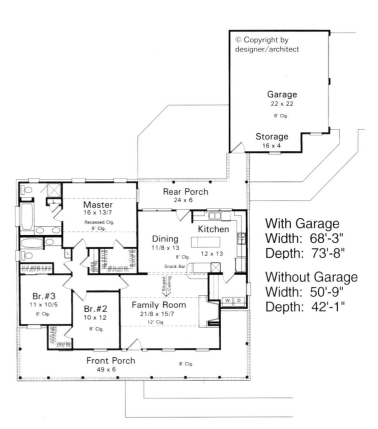

With Garage
Width: 68'-3"
Depth: 73'-8"

Without Garage
Width: 50'-9"
Depth: 42'-1"

SPECIAL FEATURES

3,498 total square feet of living area

Both bedrooms on the second floor feature spacious sitting areas

The dining area and kitchen are topped with handsome beamed ceilings that are sure to attract attention

The second floor loft could easily be converted to a secluded home office

The future apartment above the garage has an additional 470 square feet of living area

3 bedrooms, 2 1/2 baths, 3-car side entry garage

Slab foundation

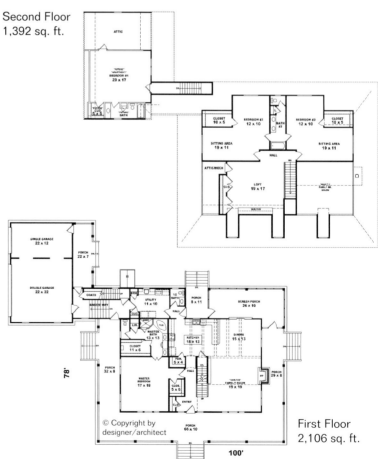

Second Floor
1,392 sq. ft.

First Floor
2,106 sq. ft.

© Copyright by designer/architect

SPECIAL FEATURES

1,684 total square feet of living area

Delightful wrap-around porch is anchored by a full masonry fireplace

The vaulted great room includes a large bay window, fireplace, dining balcony and atrium window wall

Double walk-in closets, large luxury bath and sliding doors to an exterior balcony are a few fantastic features of the master bedroom

Atrium opens to 611 square feet of optional living area on the lower level

3 bedrooms, 2 baths, 2-car drive under rear entry garage

Walk-out basement foundation

Rear View

First Floor
1,684 sq. ft.

55'-8"

46'-4"

Balcony

MBr
18-4x13-0

Kit
10-2x
11-9

Dining

Dn

Great Rm
16-0x21-4
vaulted

Entry

Porch depth 6-0

Br 2
12-8x14-0

Br 3
11-4x12-6

© Copyright by
designer/architect

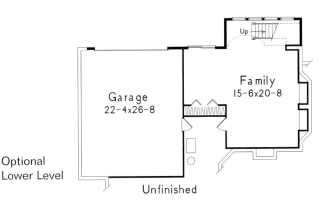

Up

Garage
22-4x26-8

Family
15-6x20-8

Optional
Lower Level

Unfinished

SPECIAL FEATURES

1,694 total square feet of living area

The vaulted great room, dining and kitchen borrow space and natural light from the atrium to create spacious living in a small home

A vaulted ceiling, double entry doors, luxurious bath and large walk-in closet are features of the master bedroom that are rarely found in a home of this size

The lower level consists of a family room/atrium, two secondary bedrooms, full bath, mechanical closet/laundry and a two-car rear garage perfect for boat storage and lake access

3 bedrooms, 2 1/2 baths, 2-car drive under rear entry garage

Walk-out basement foundation

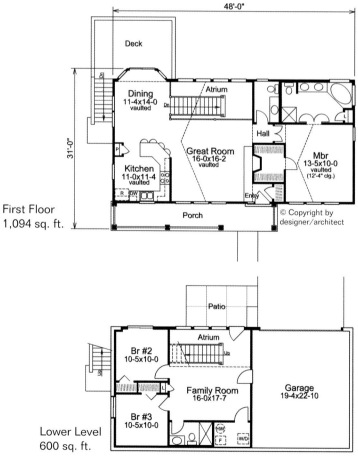

First Floor
1,094 sq. ft.

Lower Level
600 sq. ft.

© Copyright by designer/architect

SPECIAL FEATURES

1,897 total square feet of living area

No doors between the main rooms on the first floor allows easy flow between spaces

Family room has large windows and a fireplace, perfect for summer or winter living

Master bedroom has a generous walk-in closet

Distinctive bayed bedrooms are flooded with warm, natural light

4 bedrooms, 3 baths, 3-car side entry garage

Basement foundation

Second Floor
902 sq. ft.

SITTING

MASTER SUITE
20' x 15'
Tray Ceiling

Tray Ceiling

Opt. Door

OPTIONAL
PLAYROOM / MEDIAROOM
21'-3" x 11'-6"
263 Sq. Ft.

BEDROOM 3
11' x 13'

BEDROOM 2
14' x 11'

© Copyright by designer/architect

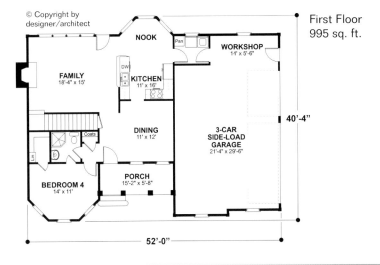

First Floor
995 sq. ft.

NOOK

Pan.

WORKSHOP
14' x 5'-6"

FAMILY
18'-4" x 15'

DW

KITCHEN
11' x 16'

DINING
11' x 12'

3-CAR
SIDE-LOAD
GARAGE
21'-4" x 29'-6"

40'-4"

BEDROOM 4
14' x 11'

Coats

PORCH
15'-2" x 5'-8"

52'-0"

SPECIAL FEATURES

2,440 total square feet of living area

The garage enters the home to find a convenient laundry area and mud room

The open kitchen/breakfast area includes an island, pantry and space for casual dining

The master bedroom is secluded on the first floor with a private bath and three bedrooms and two baths on the second floor round out this family home

4 bedrooms, 4 baths, 2-car side entry garage

Basement foundation

Second Floor
766 sq. ft.

Br 2
13-0x12-5

Open To Below

Dn

Br 3
13-0x12-5

Br 4
12-0x11-5

58'-8"

First Floor
1,674 sq. ft.

Great Room
17-3x17-5

Kit/Brkfst
20-8x15-3

L

Dn

Up

P

R

Laun

50'-10"

MBr
13-0x15-6

Dining
12-0x13-8

W   D

Covered Porched

Garage
20-8x24-6

© Copyright by designer/architect

SPECIAL FEATURES

2,213 total square feet of living area

Master bedroom features a full bath with separate vanities, large walk-in closet and access to the covered porch

Living room is enhanced by a fireplace, bay window and columns framing the gallery

9' ceilings throughout home add to the open feeling

4 bedrooms, 2 1/2 baths, 2-car side entry garage

Slab foundation

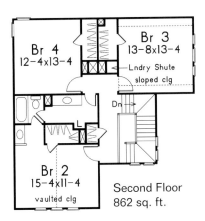

Br 4
12-4x13-4

Br 3
13-8x13-4

Lndry Shute
sloped clg

Dn

Br 2
15-4x11-4
vaulted clg

Second Floor
862 sq. ft.

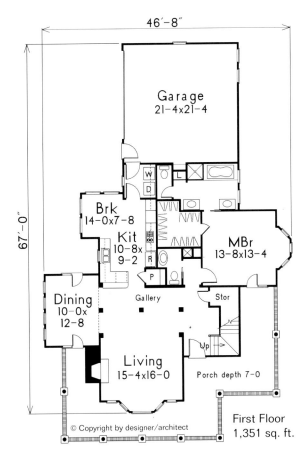

46'-8"

67'-0"

Garage
21-4x21-4

W
D

Brk
14-0x7-8

Kit
10-8x
9-2

MBr
13-8x13-4

Dining
10-0x
12-8

Gallery

Stor

R
P

Up

Living
15-4x16-0

Porch depth 7-0

© Copyright by designer/architect

First Floor
1,351 sq. ft.

SPECIAL FEATURES

2,140 total square feet of living area

Relaxing covered porch provides four entrances into home

The kitchen includes a cooktop island, pantry and connects to the eating bar

The spacious family/dining room features a grand fireplace and three double-door entrances to the outdoors

The master bedroom enjoys a private bath with separate vanities, a whirlpool tub and massive walk-in closet

3 bedrooms, 2 1/2 baths, 2-car garage

Basement foundation

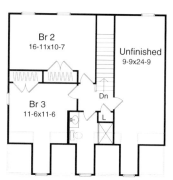

Second Floor
536 sq. ft.

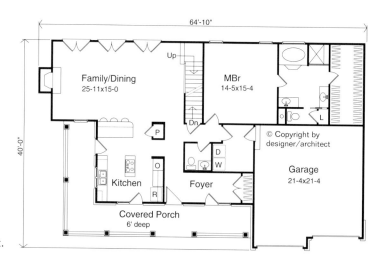

First Floor
1,604 sq. ft.

LOWE'S
LEGACY
SERIES

SPECIAL FEATURES

2,511 total square feet of living area

Kitchen, breakfast and living
rooms feature tray ceilings

Various architectural elements combine
to create an impressive exterior

Master bedroom includes large
walk-in closet, oversized bay window
and private bath with shower and tub

Large utility room has a
convenient workspace

4 bedrooms, 2 1/2 baths,
3-car side entry garage

Basement foundation, drawings also
include crawl space and slab foundations

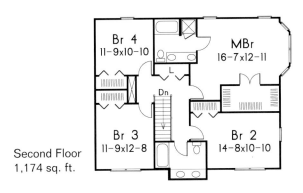

Second Floor
1,174 sq. ft.

Br 4
11-9x10-10

MBr
16-7x12-11

Br 3
11-9x12-8

Br 2
14-8x10-10

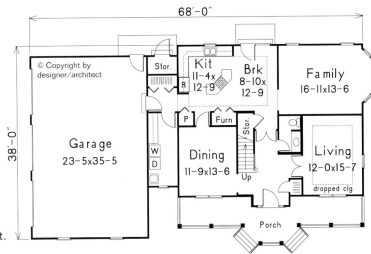

68'-0"

38'-0"

© Copyright by
designer/architect

Stor.

Kit
11-4x
12-9

Brk
8-10x
12-9

Family
16-11x13-6

Garage
23-5x35-5

Dining
11-9x13-6

Living
12-0x15-7
dropped clg

Porch

First Floor
1,337 sq. ft.

LOWE'S LEGACY SERIES

SPECIAL FEATURES

1,649 total square feet of living area

The central great room offers a vaulted ceiling, gorgeous fireplace, built-in media center and French doors leading to the back deck

Windows surround the cheerful breakfast area that features built-in shelves and easily connects with the kitchen

The first floor master suite features a 14' vaulted ceiling, private bath, and large walk-in closet

3 bedrooms, 2 1/2 baths, 2-car garage

Basement foundation, drawings also include walk-out basement foundation

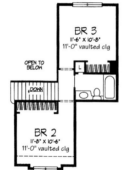

Second Floor
407 sq. ft.

BR 3
11'-6" X 10'-8"
11'-0" vaulted clg

OPEN TO BELOW

DOWN

BR 2
11'-8" X 10'-6"
11'-0" vaulted clg

First Floor
1,242 sq. ft.

55'-0"

DECK
55'-0" X 11'-0"

MASTER SUITE
13'-8" X 16'-0"
14'-0" vaulted clg

GREAT ROOM
13'-6" X 16'-8"
16'-8" vaulted clg

media center

KITCHEN
23'-4" X 11'-0"

island

BREAKFAST
12'-0" vaulted clg

shelves

desk

PANTRY

LAUNDRY
8'-0" X 6'-0"

W.I.C.

MASTER BATH

ENTRY

DINING
11'-6" X 10'-2"

PORCH

GARAGE
20'-0" X 21'-0"

43'-0"

© Copyright by designer/architect

LOWE'S
LEGACY
SERIES

SPECIAL FEATURES

1,568 total square feet of living area

Multiple entrances from three porches help to bring the outdoors in

The lodge-like great room features a vaulted ceiling, stone fireplace, step-up entrance foyer and opens to a huge screened porch

The kitchen has an island and peninsula, a convenient laundry room and adjoins a spacious dining area which leads to a screened porch and rear patio

The master bedroom has two walk-in closets, a luxury bath and access to the screened porch and patio

2 bedrooms, 2 baths, 3-car side entry garage

Crawl space foundation

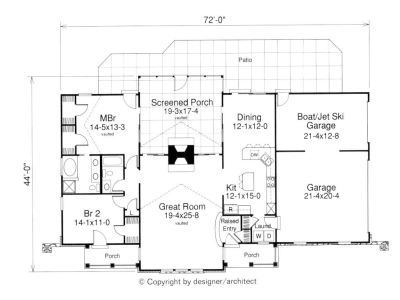

© Copyright by designer/architect

SPECIAL FEATURES

2,253 total square feet of living area

Great room is joined by the
rear covered porch

Secluded parlor provides area for
peace and quiet or a private office

Sloped ceiling adds drama to
the master bedroom

Great room, kitchen and breakfast area
combine for a large open living area

3 bedrooms, 2 1/2 baths, 2-car garage

Basement foundation

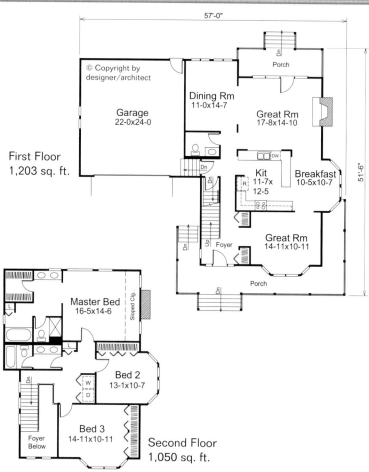

57'-0"

© Copyright by
designer/architect

Porch

Dining Rm
11-0x14-7

Garage
22-0x24-0

Great Rm
17-8x14-10

First Floor
1,203 sq. ft.

Kit
11-7x
12-5

Breakfast
10-5x10-7

Foyer

Great Rm
14-11x10-11

Porch

51'-6"

Master Bed
16-5x14-6

Sloped Clg.

Bed 2
13-1x10-7

Foyer
Below

Bed 3
14-11x10-11

Second Floor
1,050 sq. ft.

SPECIAL FEATURES

2,562 total square feet of living area

Large, open foyer creates a grand entrance

Convenient open breakfast area includes peninsula counter, bay window and easy access to the deck

Dining and living rooms flow together for expanded entertaining space

Bonus room above the garage is included in the square footage

3 bedrooms, 2 1/2 baths, 2-car side entry garage

Basement foundation, drawings also include slab and crawl space foundations

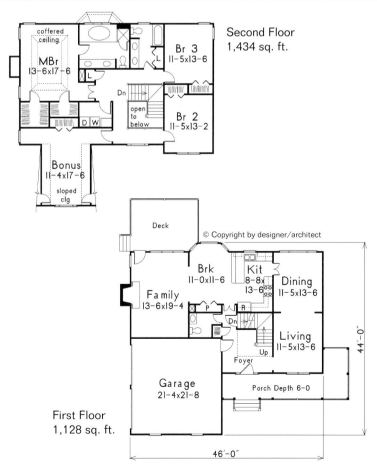

Second Floor
1,434 sq. ft.

coffered ceiling
MBr
13-6x17-6
Br 3
11-5x13-6
Dn
open to below
Br 2
11-5x13-2
D W
Bonus
11-4x17-6
sloped clg

© Copyright by designer/architect

Deck
Brk
11-0x11-6
Kit
8-8x 13-6
Dining
11-5x13-6
Family
13-6x19-4
Dn
Living
11-5x13-6
Up
Foyer
Garage
21-4x21-8
Porch Depth 6-0
44'-0"
46'-0"

First Floor
1,128 sq. ft.

SPECIAL FEATURES

1,966 total square feet of living area

Private dining room remains the focal point when entering the home

Kitchen and breakfast room join to create a functional area

Lots of closet space in the second floor bedrooms

3 bedrooms, 2 1/2 baths, 2-car side entry garage

Basement foundation

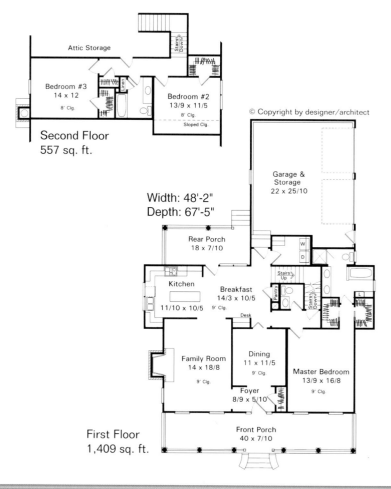

Attic Storage

Bedroom #3
14 x 12
8' Clg.

Bedroom #2
13/9 x 11/5
8' Clg.
Sloped Clg.

Second Floor
557 sq. ft.

© Copyright by designer/architect

Garage & Storage
22 x 25/10

Width: 48'-2"
Depth: 67'-5"

Rear Porch
18 x 7/10

Stairs Up

Stairs Down

Kitchen
11/10 x 10/5

Breakfast
14/3 x 10/5
9' Clg.

Desk

Family Room
14 x 18/8
9' Clg.

Dining
11 x 11/5
9' Clg.

Master Bedroom
13/9 x 16/8
9' Clg.

Foyer
8/9 x 5/10

First Floor
1,409 sq. ft.

Front Porch
40 x 7/10

SPECIAL FEATURES

2,593 total square feet of living area

Central family room becomes a gathering place

Second floor recreation room is a great game room for children

First floor master bedroom is secluded from main living areas

3 bedrooms, 2 1/2 baths, 2-car side entry garage

Basement foundation, drawings also include crawl space and slab foundations

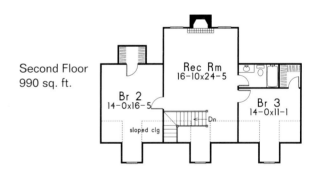

Second Floor
990 sq. ft.

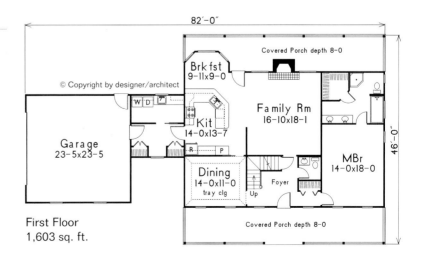

First Floor
1,603 sq. ft.

LOWE'S LEGACY SERIES

SPECIAL FEATURES

1,488 total square feet of living area

The covered porch spills into the open living area comprised of the adjoining great room, kitchen and dining area

French doors lead from the dining area to the rear patio, extending the living space to the outdoors

The split-bedroom design allows for extra privacy for the master suite that features two separate baths and walk-in closets

3 bedrooms, 3 baths, 2-car garage

Basement foundation

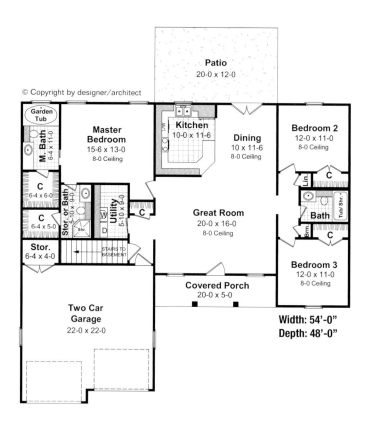

© Copyright by designer/architect

Patio
20-0 x 12-0

Garden Tub

M. Bath
6-4 x 11-0

Master Bedroom
15-6 x 13-0
8-0 Ceiling

Kitchen
10-0 x 11-6

Dining
10 x 11-6
8-0 Ceiling

Bedroom 2
12-0 x 11-0
8-0 Ceiling

C
6-4 x 6-0

Stor. or Bath
5-10 x 9-0

Utility
5-10 x 9-0

C

Lin.

C

C
6-4 x 5-0

W
D

Shr.

Great Room
20-0 x 16-0
8-0 Ceiling

Bath

Tub/Shr.

C

Stor.
6-4 x 4-0

STAIRS TO BASEMENT

Covered Porch
20-0 x 5-0

Bedroom 3
12-0 x 11-0
8-0 Ceiling

Two Car Garage
22-0 x 22-0

Width: 54'-0"
Depth: 48'-0"

SPECIAL FEATURES

1,685 total square feet of living area

9' ceilings on the first floor

A large center island in the kitchen encourages proper preparation

Triple windows in the dining room offer ample light and warmth

3 bedrooms, 2 1/2 baths, 2-car garage

Basement foundation

Second Floor
464 sq. ft.

First Floor
1,221 sq. ft.

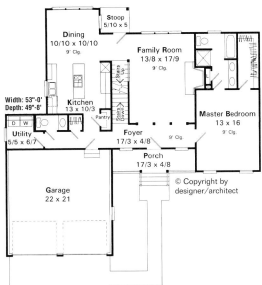

© Copyright by designer/architect

SPECIAL FEATURES

2,665 total square feet of living area

9' ceilings on the first floor

Spacious kitchen features many cabinets, a center island cooktop and bayed breakfast area adjacent to the laundry room

Second floor bedrooms boast walk-in closets, dressing areas and share a bath

Twin patio doors and fireplace grace living room

4 bedrooms, 3 baths, 2-car rear entry garage

Slab foundation, drawings also include crawl space foundation

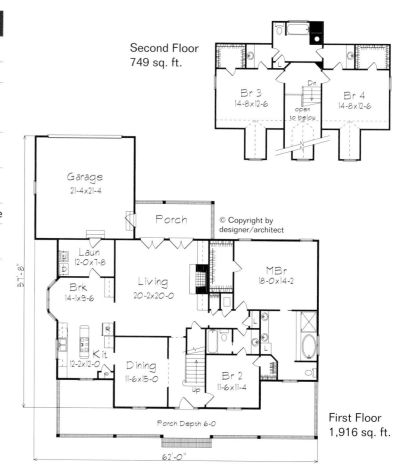

Second Floor
749 sq. ft.

© Copyright by designer/architect

First Floor
1,916 sq. ft.

LOWE'S LEGACY SERIES

SPECIAL FEATURES

3,500 total square feet of living area

An interesting side sunroom connects to the living area, rear porch and wrap-around front porch

The large rear porch will be ideal for outdoor dining or relaxation

The spacious bayed recreation room provides a casual place for the entire family to relax

The second floor future media room has an additional 234 square feet of living space

4 bedrooms, 3 1/2 baths, 3-car side entry garage

Slab foundation

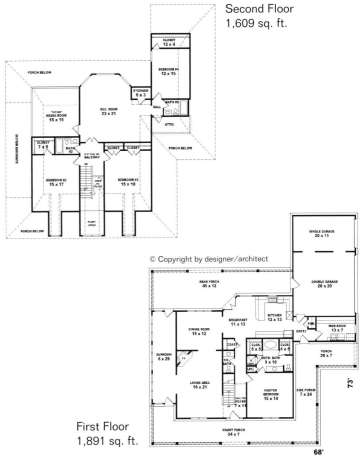

Second Floor
1,609 sq. ft.

© Copyright by designer/architect

First Floor
1,891 sq. ft.

SPECIAL FEATURES

2,002 total square feet of living area

Energy efficient home with
2" x 6" exterior walls

High ceilings throughout the house
give it a feeling of spaciousness

The gas fireplace warms the great room
and is flanked by built-in cabinets

The covered porch or patio is
connected to the breakfast area,
perfect for bringing meals outside

3 bedrooms, 2 baths, 2-car side entry garage

Slab foundation, drawings also include
crawl space and basement foundations

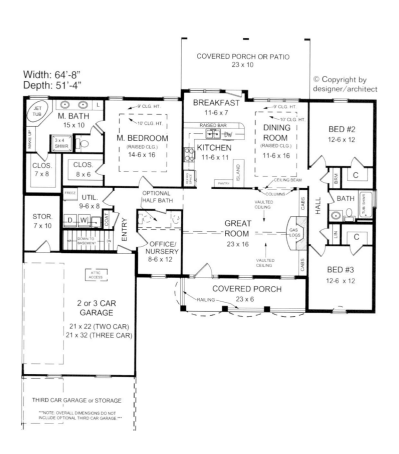

SPECIAL FEATURES

1,977 total square feet of living area

Classic traditional exterior is always in style

Spacious great room boasts a vaulted ceiling, dining area, atrium with elegant staircase and feature windows

Atrium opens to 1,416 square feet of optional living area below which consists of a family room, two bedrooms, two baths and a study

4 bedrooms, 2 1/2 baths, 3-car side entry garage

Walk-out basement foundation

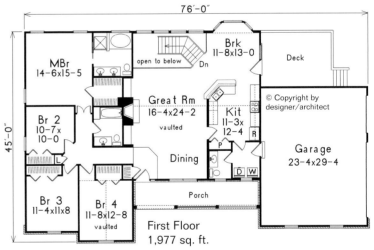

76'-0"

MBr
14-6x15-5

Br 2
10-7x
10-0

Br 3
11-4x11x8

Br 4
11-8x12-8
vaulted

open to below

Great Rm
16-4x24-2
vaulted

Dining

Porch

Brk
11-8x13-0

Deck

© Copyright by
designer/architect

Kit
11-3x
12-4

Garage
23-4x29-4

45'-0"

First Floor
1,977 sq. ft.

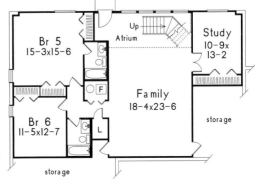

Br 5
15-3x15-6

Up
Atrium

Study
10-9x
13-2

Family
18-4x23-6

storage

Br 6
11-5x12-7

Optional
Lower Level

storage

SPECIAL FEATURES

1,339 total square feet of living area

Full-length covered porch
enhances front facade

Vaulted ceiling and stone fireplace
add drama to the family room

Walk-in closets in the bedrooms
provide ample storage space

Combined kitchen/dining area
adjoins the family room for the
perfect entertaining space

2" x 6" exterior walls available,
please order plan #533-058D-0072

3 bedrooms, 2 1/2 baths

Crawl space foundation

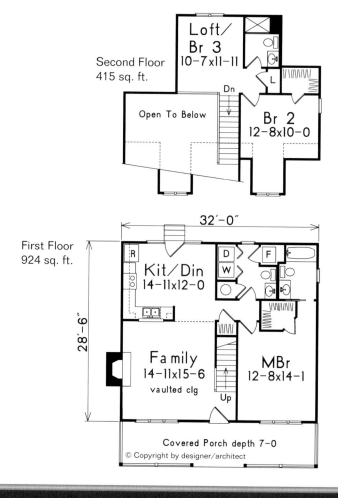

Second Floor 415 sq. ft.

Loft/Br 3 10-7x11-11

Br 2 12-8x10-0

Open To Below

First Floor 924 sq. ft.

32'-0"

28'-6"

Kit/Din 14-11x12-0

Family 14-11x15-6 vaulted clg

MBr 12-8x14-1

Covered Porch depth 7-0

© Copyright by designer/architect

SPECIAL FEATURES

- 2,244 total square feet of living area

- Energy efficient home with
  2" x 6" exterior walls

- Exposed beams and fireplace add
  rustic look to family room

- Large laundry room with
  walk-in storage closet

- Master bedroom features private bath,
  oversized walk-in closet and dressing table

- 4 bedrooms, 2 1/2 baths, 2-car garage

- Crawl space foundation, drawings also
  include basement and slab foundations

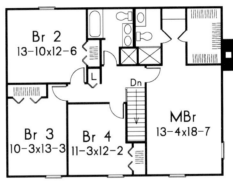

Br 2
13-10x12-6

Dn

MBr
13-4x18-7

Br 3
10-3x13-3

Br 4
11-3x12-2

Second Floor
1,114 sq. ft.

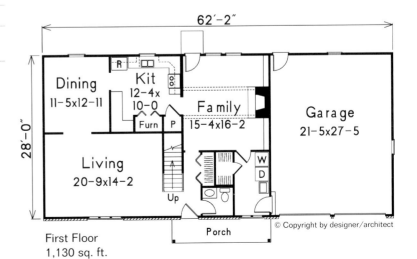

62'-2"

28'-0"

Dining
11-5x12-11

Kit
12-4x
10-0

Family
15-4x16-2

Garage
21-5x27-5

Furn P

Living
20-9x14-2

W
D

Up

Porch

© Copyright by designer/architect

First Floor
1,130 sq. ft.

SPECIAL FEATURES

1,100 total square feet of living area

The two bedrooms are larger than you would expect for a house of this size, and one includes a private bath with a whirlpool tub

A separate laundry room, pantry, linen and hall closet add convenient storage and workspace to this design

Relax with friends and family on either the front or rear covered porches

2 bedrooms, 2 baths

Slab foundation

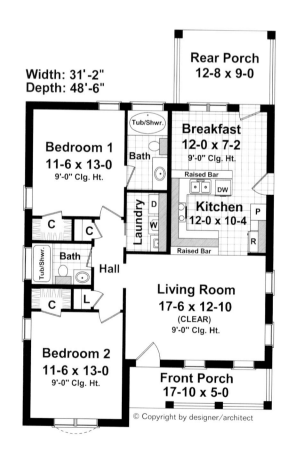

Width: 31'-2"
Depth: 48'-6"

Rear Porch
12-8 x 9-0

Bedroom 1
11-6 x 13-0
9'-0" Clg. Ht.

Tub/Shwr.
Bath

Breakfast
12-0 x 7-2
9'-0" Clg. Ht.

Raised Bar
DW

Laundry
D
W

Kitchen
12-0 x 10-4

P
R

Raised Bar

Bath
Tub/Shwr.
C
C

Hall

Living Room
17-6 x 12-10
(CLEAR)
9'-0" Clg. Ht.

C
L

Bedroom 2
11-6 x 13-0
9'-0" Clg. Ht.

Front Porch
17-10 x 5-0

LOWE'S
LEGACY
SERIES

SPECIAL FEATURES

1,770 total square feet of living area

An open and airy breakfast room features decorative columns allowing it to maintain a feeling of spaciousness

A screened porch is easily accessible from both the master bedroom and the family room

Optional bonus room has an additional 762 square feet of living area

3 bedrooms, 2 baths, 2-car garage

Crawl space foundation

© Copyright by designer/architect

SPECIAL FEATURES

2,024 total square feet of living area

Energy efficient home with
2" x 6" exterior walls

King-size master bedroom
includes a sitting area

Living room features a corner
fireplace, access to the covered rear
porch, 18' ceiling and a balcony

Closet for handling recyclables

Future bonus room has an additional
475 square feet of living area

3 bedrooms, 2 1/2 baths,
2-car side entry garage

Crawl space foundation, drawings also
include slab and basement foundations

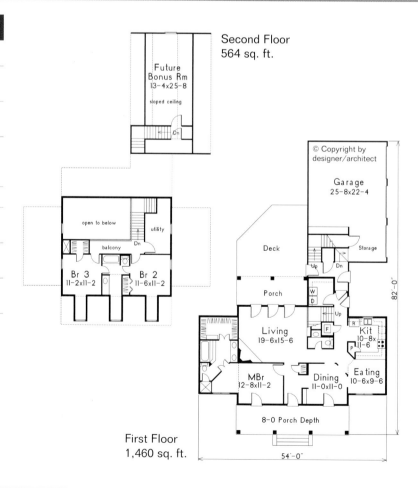

Second Floor
564 sq. ft.

Future
Bonus Rm
13-4x25-8
sloped ceiling

© Copyright by
designer/architect

Garage
25-8x22-4

Deck

Storage

open to below

utility

balcony
Dn

Porch

Br 3
11-2x11-2

Br 2
11-6x11-2

Living
19-6x15-6

Kit
10-8x
11-6

MBr
12-8x11-2

Dining
11-0x11-0

Eating
10-6x9-6

8-0 Porch Depth

First Floor
1,460 sq. ft.

54'-0"

82'-0"

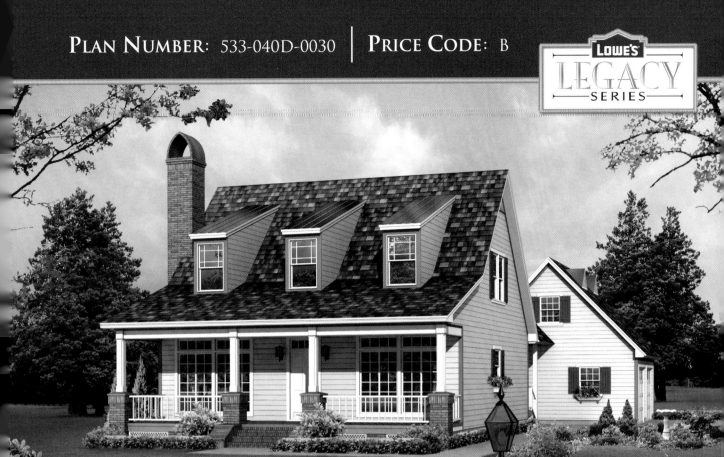

SPECIAL FEATURES

1,543 total square feet of living area

Fireplace serves as the focal point of the large family room

Efficient floor plan keeps hallways at a minimum

Laundry room connects the kitchen to the garage

Private first floor master bedroom has a walk-in closet and bath

3 bedrooms, 2 1/2 baths, 2-car detached side entry garage

Slab foundation, drawings also include crawl space foundation

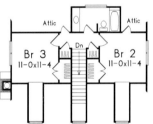

Second Floor
503 sq. ft.

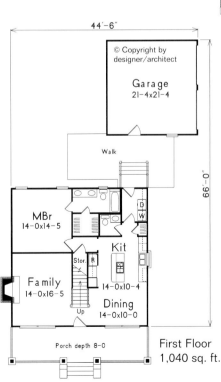

First Floor
1,040 sq. ft.

Lowe's LEGACY SERIES

SPECIAL FEATURES

1,533 total square feet of living area

Multiple gables and stonework deliver a warm and inviting exterior

The vaulted great room has a fireplace and spectacular views accomplished with a two-story atrium window wall

A covered rear porch is easily accessed from the breakfast room or garage

The atrium provides an ideal approach to an optional finished lower level

3 bedrooms, 2 baths, 2-car garage

Walk-out basement foundation

Rear View

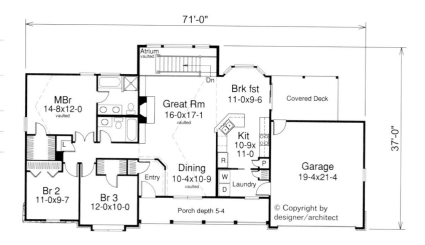

71'-0"

37'-0"

Atrium vaulted

MBr 14-8x12-0 vaulted

Great Rm 16-0x17-1 vaulted

Brk fst 11-0x9-6

Covered Deck

Kit 10-9x 11-0

Dining 10-4x10-9 vaulted

Garage 19-4x21-4

Entry

Laundry

Br 2 11-0x9-7

Br 3 12-0x10-0

Porch depth 5-4

Dn

W D

R

P

L

© Copyright by designer/architect

SPECIAL FEATURES

2,179 total square feet of living area

Energy efficient home with
2" x 6" exterior walls

Open floor plan and minimal halls eliminate
wasted space and create efficiency

First floor master bedroom is conveniently
located near the large kitchen

Three bedrooms on the second floor share
a large bath and nearby linen closet

4 bedrooms, 2 1/2 baths, 2-car garage

Basement foundation

48'-0"

45'-0"

MBr
13-5x14-11

Country Kitchen
26-3x13-7

Lndry

D
W

Dn
R P

Family
16-2x17-3

Entry   Up

Garage
19-4x20-0

© Copyright by
designer/architect

First Floor
1,409 sq. ft.

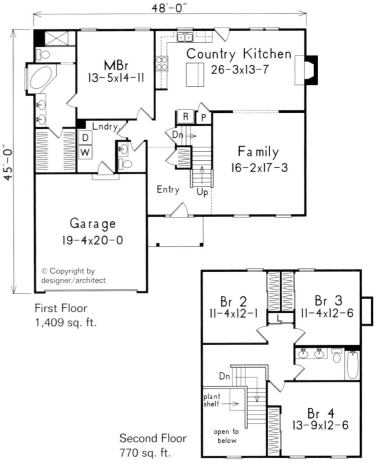

Br 2
11-4x12-1

Br 3
11-4x12-6

L

Dn

plant
shelf

Br 4
13-9x12-6

open to
below

Second Floor
770 sq. ft.

SPECIAL FEATURES

1,880 total square feet of living area

Master bedroom is enhanced
with a coffered ceiling

Generous family and breakfast
areas are modern and functional

The front porch complements
the front facade

3 bedrooms, 2 1/2 baths,
2-car drive under garage

Basement foundation

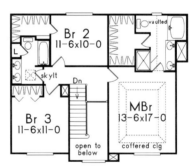

Second Floor
899 sq. ft.

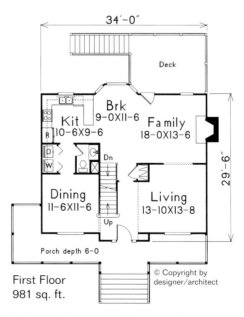

First Floor
981 sq. ft.

SPECIAL FEATURES

1,704 total square feet of living area

Open living and dining areas
combine for added spaciousness

Master bedroom features a private
bath and walk-in closet

Sunny kitchen/nook has space for dining

Cabinet bar in hallway leading to the
living area is designed for entertaining

3 bedrooms, 2 baths, 2-car garage

Basement foundation

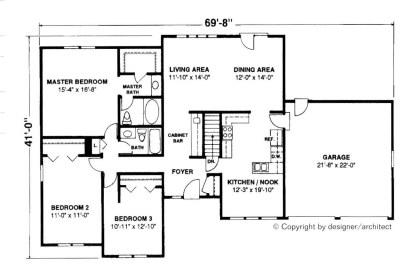

© Copyright by designer/architect

SPECIAL FEATURES

2,013 total square feet of living area

Energy efficient home with 2" x 6" exterior walls

Sliding doors in dinette allow convenient access outdoors

Family room includes a cozy fireplace for informal gathering

All bedrooms are located on the second floor for privacy

Master bath includes a dressing area, walk-in closet and separate tub and shower

4 bedrooms, 2 1/2 baths, 2-car garage

Basement foundation

Second Floor
988 sq. ft.

First Floor
1,025 sq. ft.

LOWE'S
LEGACY
SERIES

SPECIAL FEATURES

1,752 total square feet of living area

The gas fireplace is framed by elegant built-in cabinets

The media/hobby room is a great workspace and overlooks the front yard

The large island in the kitchen provides extra counterspace as well as a snack bar for casual meals

3 bedrooms, 2 baths, 2-car side entry garage

Slab foundation, drawings also include basement and crawl space foundations

© Copyright by designer/architect

Floor plan labels:

Garden Tub
M. Bath 15-0 x 10-0
Master Bedroom 14-6 x 16-0
VAULT
VAULT
Covered Porch 23-0 x 5-0
Kitchen 12-0 x 11-0
Island
BAR
Eating 11-0 x 11-0 9-0 Ceiling
Bedroom 2 12-0 x 12-0 9-0 Ceiling
C 8-0 x 6-0
C 7-0 x 6-0
Brm
C
Hall
Hall Bath
Tub/Shr
Stor. 8-0 x 7-0
F
Utility 9-6 x 8-0
Entry
C
Trayed Ceiling
9-0 Ceiling
10-0 Ceiling
Great Room 23-0 x 16-0
Cabs
Gas Logs
Lin
C
OPTIONAL STAIRS TO BASEMENT
Media/Hobby 9-0 x 8-0
Cabs
Bedroom 3 12-0 x 12-0 9-0 Ceiling
2 Car Garage 21-0 x 22-0
Covered Porch 23-0 x 4-0
Width: 64'-0"
Depth: 46'-0"
OPTIONAL EXTENSION OF GARAGE IF BASEMENT OPTION IS CHOSEN

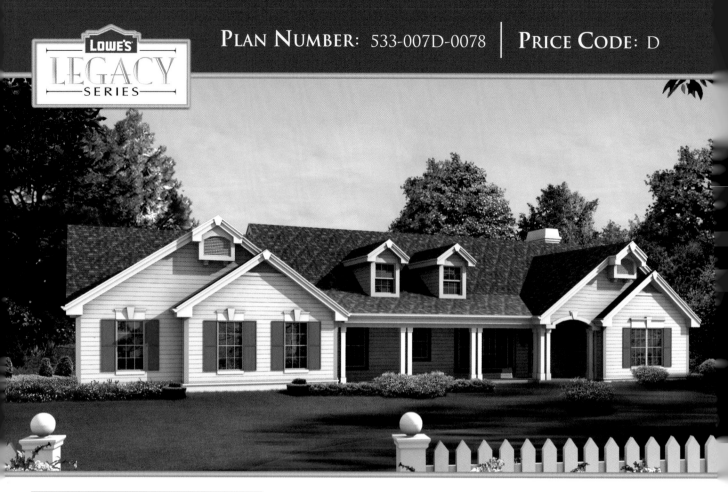

SPECIAL FEATURES

2,514 total square feet of living area

An expansive porch welcomes you into the foyer, spacious dining area with bay and a gallery-sized hall with plant shelf above

A highly functional U-shaped kitchen is open to a bayed breakfast room, study and family room with a 46' vista

The family will enjoy time spent in the vaulted rear sunroom with fireplace

1,509 square feet of optional living area on the lower level with recreation room, bedroom #4 with bath and an office with storage closet

3 bedrooms, 2 baths, 3-car side entry garage with workshop/storage area

Walk-out basement foundation

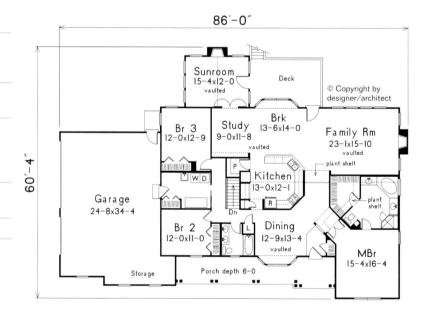

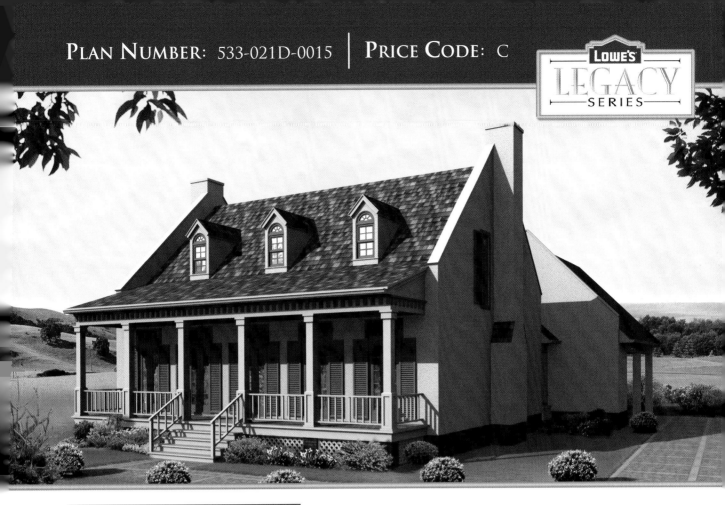

SPECIAL FEATURES

- 1,700 total square feet of living area
- Energy efficient home with 2" x 6" exterior walls
- Fully appointed kitchen with wet bar
- Linen drop from the second floor bath to utility room
- Master bath includes raised marble tub and a sloped ceiling
- 3 bedrooms, 2 1/2 baths, 2-car attached carport
- Crawl space foundation, drawings also include basement and slab foundations

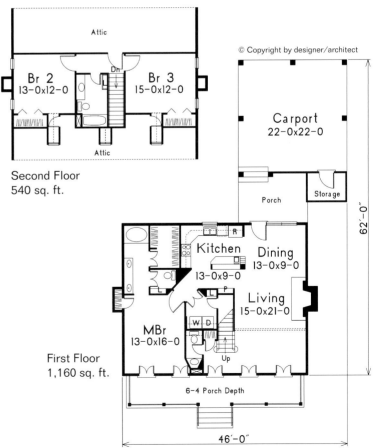

Attic

Br 2
13-0x12-0

Br 3
15-0x12-0

Dn

Attic

Second Floor
540 sq. ft.

© Copyright by designer/architect

Carport
22-0x22-0

Porch

Storage

62'-0"

Kitchen
13-0x9-0

Dining
13-0x9-0

Living
15-0x21-0

MBr
13-0x16-0

W D

P

Up

First Floor
1,160 sq. ft.

6-4 Porch Depth

46'-0"

SPECIAL FEATURES

- 2,351 total square feet of living area

- Coffered ceiling in dining room adds elegant appeal

- Wrap-around porch creates a pleasant escape

- Cozy study features a double-door entry and extra storage

- Double walk-in closets balance and organize the master bedroom

- 3 bedrooms, 2 1/2 baths, 2-car garage

- Basement foundation

Second Floor
1,015 sq. ft.

Br 3
11-2x10-10

MBr
18-4x13-6
vaulted

open to below

Br 2
11-0x13-2

plant shelf

Dn

© Copyright by designer/architect

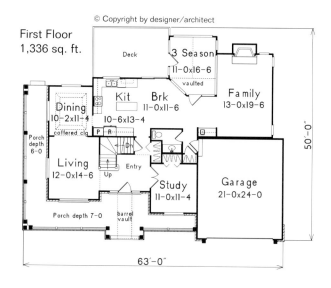

First Floor
1,336 sq. ft.

Deck

3 Season
11-0x16-6
vaulted

Family
13-0x19-6

Kit

Brk
11-0x11-6

Dining
10-2x11-4
coffered clg.

Porch depth 6-0

Living
12-0x14-6

Entry

Study
11-0x11-4

Garage
21-0x24-0

Up

Porch depth 7-0

barrel vault

50'-0"

63'-0"

SPECIAL FEATURES

1,664 total square feet of living area

L-shaped country kitchen includes pantry and cozy breakfast area

Bedrooms are located on the second floor for privacy

Master bedroom includes a walk-in closet, dressing area and bath

2" x 6" exterior walls available, please order plan #533-001D-0122

3 bedrooms, 2 1/2 baths, 2-car garage

Crawl space foundation, drawings also include basement and slab foundations

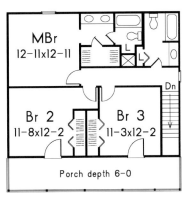

MBr
12-11x12-11

Br 2
11-8x12-2

Br 3
11-3x12-2

Dn

Porch depth 6-0

Second Floor
832 sq. ft.

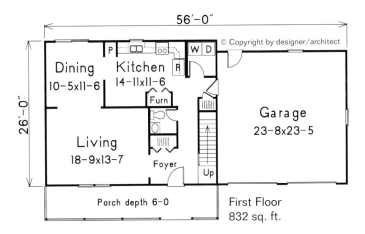

56'-0"

© Copyright by designer/architect

26'-0"

P

W D

Dining
10-5x11-6

Kitchen
14-11x11-6

R

Furn

Garage
23-8x23-5

Living
18-9x13-7

Foyer

Up

Porch depth 6-0

First Floor
832 sq. ft.

LOWE'S LEGACY SERIES

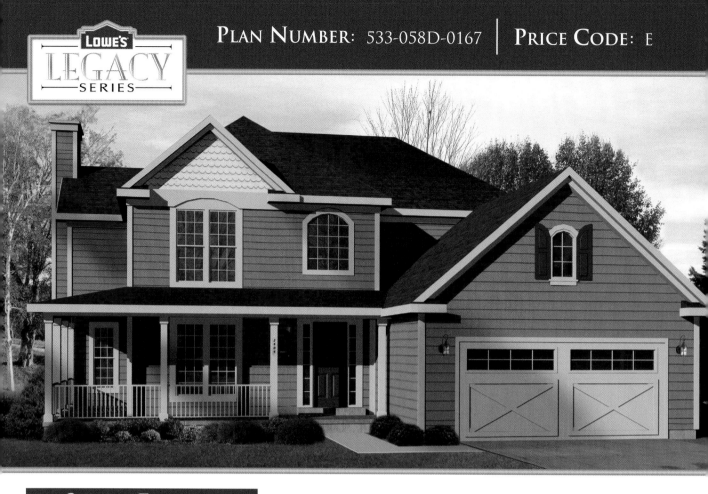

SPECIAL FEATURES

2,224 total square feet of living area

The covered porch welcomes all into this lovely two-story home

A snack bar island and walk-in pantry add efficiency to the open kitchen

The second floor master bedroom enjoys a luxurious bath with twin vanities, a whirlpool tub and massive walk-in closet

3 bedrooms, 2 1/2 baths, 2-car garage

Basement foundation

Second Floor
1,050 sq. ft.

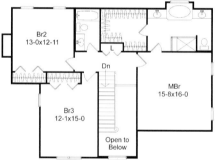

Br2
13-0x12-11

L

Dn

MBr
15-8x16-0

Br3
12-1x15-0

Open to
Below

First Floor
1,174 sq. ft.

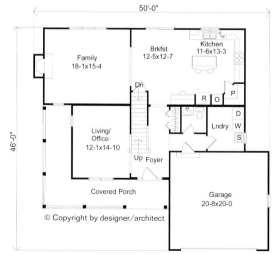

50'-0"

46'-0"

Family
18-1x15-4

Brkfst
12-5x12-7

Kitchen
11-6x13-3

Dn

Living/
Office
12-1x14-10

Lndry

Up Foyer

Covered Porch

Garage
20-8x20-0

© Copyright by designer/architect

SPECIAL FEATURES

1,992 total square feet of living area

Interesting angled walls add drama to many of the living areas including the family room, master bedroom and breakfast area

Covered porch includes a spa and an outdoor kitchen with sink, refrigerator and cooktop

Enter the majestic master bath to find a dramatic corner oversized tub

4 bedrooms, 3 baths, 2-car side entry garage

Basement foundation, drawings also include crawl space and slab foundations

© Copyright by designer/architect

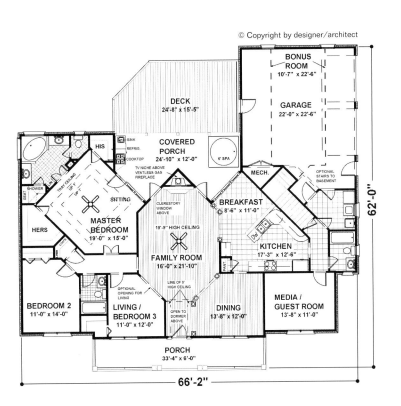

Lowe's LEGACY SERIES

SPECIAL FEATURES

2,054 total square feet of living area

A sweeping porch leads to the large foyer with staircase, powder room and handy coat closet

Spacious living room has a fireplace, triple door to patio and an adjacent computer room

Kitchen features a snack bar, island counter, pantry and breakfast area with bay window

Large master bedroom has two spacious closets and accesses a luxury bath with separate toilet and corner tub

3 bedrooms, 2 1/2 baths, 2-car detached garage

Basement foundation

Second Floor
1,020 sq. ft.

Br 3
12-9x12-8

Dn

MBr
12-6x16-4

Br 2
12-10x13-0

34'-0"

Patio

First Floor
1,034 sq. ft.

30'-0"

Brk fst

W
D

Dn

Living
12-6x20-0

L

Kit
13-0x18-0

Up

Computer
11-0x9-0

Dining
12-8x10-8

Porch depth 6-4

© Copyright by designer/architect

LOWE'S
LEGACY
SERIES

SPECIAL FEATURES

1,685 total square feet of living area

An extra-large, open family area is created with the living and dining rooms combining and featuring a lovely fireplace, window wall and deck access

The kitchen features a sunny breakfast room with corner windows, and has handy access to the attached double garage through the mud/laundry area

On the second floor a spacious, vaulted master bedroom with a private bath and a sitting area is flanked by two additional bedrooms and a second full bath

4 bedrooms, 3 baths, 2-car garage

Basement foundation

Second Floor
708 sq. ft.

BEDRM 3
10'-8"x10'-0"

MASTER BEDRM
12'-4"x14'-6"
14'-0" vaulted clg

BEDRM 2
10'-0"x10'-0"

SITTING LOFT

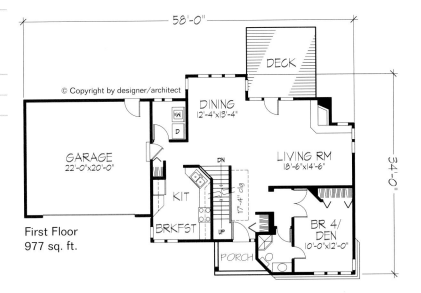

© Copyright by designer/architect

First Floor
977 sq. ft.

58'-0"

34'-0"

DECK

DINING
12'-4"x13'-4"

GARAGE
22'-0"x20'-0"

LIVING RM
18'-6"x14'-6"

KIT

17'-4" clg

BRKFST

BR 4/ DEN
10'-0"x12'-0"

PORCH

SPECIAL FEATURES

1,904 total square feet of living area

The dining/study opens into the family room providing a large area to entertain

The bayed breakfast room offers an enchanting atmosphere with nearby French doors leading onto the covered porch

Three bedrooms, including the luxurious master bedroom, comprise the second floor

3 bedrooms, 2 1/2 baths, 2-car garage

Basement foundation

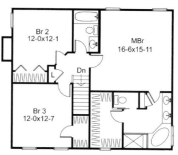

Second Floor
924 sq. ft.

Br 2
12-0x12-1

MBr
16-6x15-11

Br 3
12-0x12-7

Dn

L

© Copyright by designer/architect

44'-0"

52'-4"

First Floor
980 sq. ft.

Family Rm
13-5x15-4

Covered Porch

Dining/Study
12-0x11-8

Dn

Up

Brkfst
11-6x10-6

Kitchen
11-8x11-8

P

Covered Porch

Garage
20-8x19-8

S
D
W

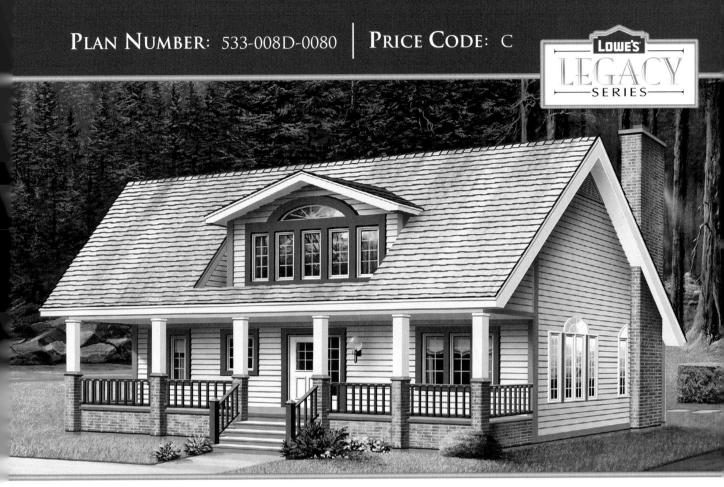

LOWE'S **LEGACY** SERIES

SPECIAL FEATURES

2,009 total square feet of living area

Spacious master bedroom has a dramatic sloped ceiling and private bath with a double-bowl vanity and walk-in closet

Bedroom #3 has an extra storage area behind the closet

Versatile screened porch is ideal for entertaining year-round

Sunny breakfast area is located near the kitchen and screened porch for convenience

3 bedrooms, 2 1/2 baths

Basement foundation

Second Floor
847 sq. ft.

STORAGE

BEDROOM #3
10'-6" x 10'-6"

BEDROOM #2
10'-6" x 11'-6"

OPEN TO REC. RM. BELOW

DN.

BATH

SLOPE CLG.

SLOPE CLG.

OPEN TO LIVING ROOM BELOW

MASTER BATH

MASTER BEDROOM
18'-0" x 13'-0"

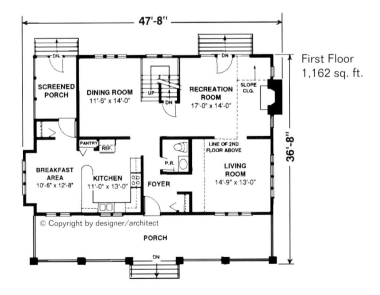

First Floor
1,162 sq. ft.

47'-8"

36'-8"

SCREENED PORCH

DINING ROOM
11'-6" x 14'-0"

UP

DN

DN

RECREATION ROOM
17'-0" x 14'-0"

SLOPE CLG.

PANTRY

REF.

LINE OF 2ND FLOOR ABOVE

P.R.

BREAKFAST AREA
10'-6" x 12'-8"

KITCHEN
11'-0" x 13'-0"

FOYER

LIVING ROOM
14'-9" x 13'-0"

© Copyright by designer/architect

PORCH

DN

SPECIAL FEATURES

1,568 total square feet of living area

A classic hip roof with multiple gables, roof dormers and decorative circular windows are all combined to create this home's stylish facade

The living room includes a vaulted ceiling with plant shelf, fireplace and is open to a bayed breakfast room

A walk-in pantry is featured in the well-designed kitchen and is adjacent to a convenient laundry room

The master bedroom with double entry doors is nicely appointed with an over-sized bath and large walk-in closet

3 bedrooms, 2 baths, 2-car garage

Crawl space foundation, drawings also include slab foundation

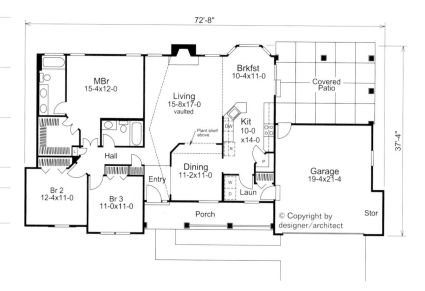

SPECIAL FEATURES

1,364 total square feet of living area

Master bedroom includes a full bath

Pass-through kitchen opens into breakfast room with laundry closet and access to deck

Adjoining dining and living rooms with vaulted ceilings and a fireplace create an open living area

Dining room features a large bay window

3 bedrooms, 2 baths, 2-car drive under garage

Basement foundation

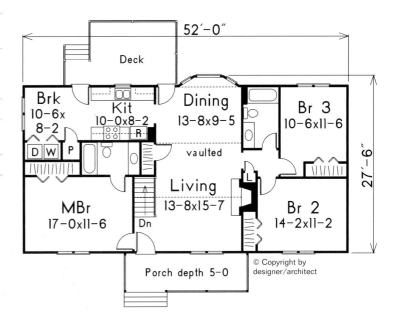

52'-0"

Deck

Brk 10-6x 8-2

Kit 10-0x8-2

Dining 13-8x9-5

Br 3 10-6x11-6

27'-6"

D W P

R

vaulted

MBr 17-0x11-6

Dn

Living 13-8x15-7

Br 2 14-2x11-2

Porch depth 5-0

© Copyright by designer/architect

SPECIAL FEATURES

2,239 total square feet of living area

Two sets of French doors in the family room lead to a covered porch ideal for relaxing

The master bedroom has a spacious bath with an oversized tub placed in a sunny bay window

Both second floor bedrooms have storage closets for terrific organizing

3 bedrooms, 2 1/2 baths, 2-car detached garage

Basement foundation, drawings also include crawl space foundation

Second Floor
607 sq. ft.

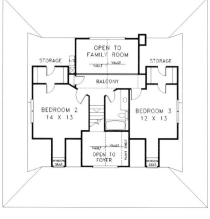

© Copyright by designer/architect

First Floor
1,632 sq. ft.

SPECIAL FEATURES

1,510 total square feet of living area

The decorative porch arches, wood columns and stone walls combine to create an exterior that demands attention

Open living and dining areas feature a vaulted ceiling, fireplace and French doors to rear patio

The well-planned kitchen has a large built-in corner pantry and a snack counter, all open to the living areas

Convenient to the kitchen is a nice sized laundry room with sink

The garage comes complete with a very useful storage room

3 bedrooms, 2 baths, 2-car garage

Slab foundation, drawings also include crawl space foundation

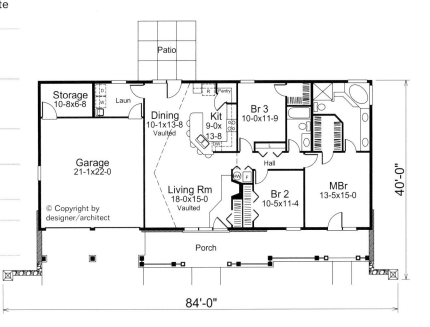

SPECIAL FEATURES

1,714 total square feet of living area

Master bedroom has a luxurious
bath and private rear porch

Angled kitchen counter allows for views
into the family room and breakfast area

Spacious secondary bedrooms
enjoy walk-in closets

3 bedrooms, 2 baths, 2-car
detached side entry garage

Slab foundation, drawings also
include crawl space foundation

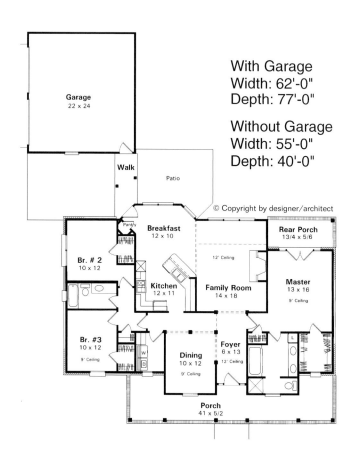

With Garage
Width: 62'-0"
Depth: 77'-0"

Without Garage
Width: 55'-0"
Depth: 40'-0"

© Copyright by designer/architect

SPECIAL FEATURES

1,508 total square feet of living area

This split-bedroom design offers privacy for the homeowners

The central living area includes a vaulted great room with fireplace, the kitchen with pantry and the spacious eating area

The two-car garage includes an essential storage area

3 bedrooms, 2 baths, 2-car side entry garage

Slab foundation, drawings also include basement and crawl space foundations

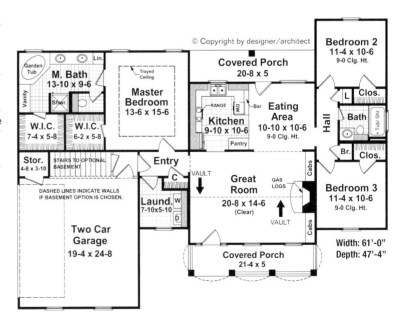

© Copyright by designer/architect

Width: 61'-0"
Depth: 47'-4"

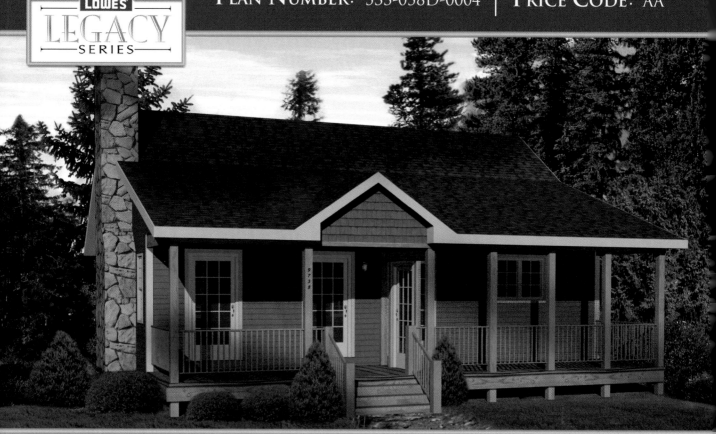

SPECIAL FEATURES

962 total square feet of living area

Both the kitchen and family room share warmth from the fireplace

Charming facade features a covered porch on one side, screened porch on the other and attractive planter boxes

L-shaped kitchen boasts a convenient pantry

2 bedrooms, 1 bath

Crawl space foundation

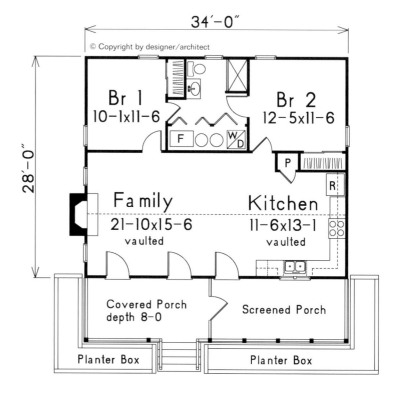

© Copyright by designer/architect

34'-0"

28'-0"

Br 1
10-1x11-6

Br 2
12-5x11-6

F   W/D   P   R

Family
21-10x15-6
vaulted

Kitchen
11-6x13-1
vaulted

Covered Porch
depth 8-0

Screened Porch

Planter Box   Planter Box

SPECIAL FEATURES

1,344 total square feet of living area

Energy efficient home with
2" x 6" exterior walls

Family/dining room has sliding
glass doors to the outdoors

Master bedroom features a
private bath with shower

Hall bath includes double vanity
for added convenience

Kitchen features U-shaped design,
large pantry and laundry area

3 bedrooms, 2 baths, 2-car garage

Crawl space foundation, drawings also
include basement and slab foundations

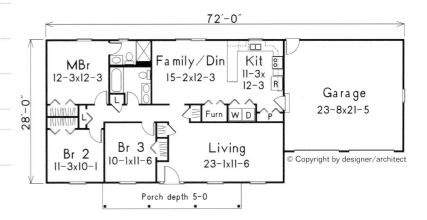

© Copyright by designer/architect

SPECIAL FEATURES

2,727 total square feet of living area

Wrap-around porch and large foyer create an impressive entrance

A state-of-the-art vaulted kitchen has a walk-in pantry and is open to the breakfast room and adjoining screen-in-porch

A walk-in wet bar, fireplace, bay window and deck access are features of the family room

Vaulted master bedroom enjoys a luxurious bath with skylight and an enormous 13' deep walk-in closet

4 bedrooms, 2 1/2 baths, 2-car side entry garage

Walk-out basement foundation

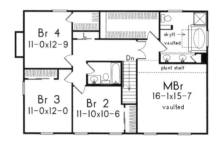

Second Floor
1,204 sq. ft.

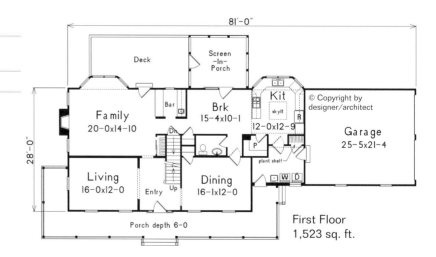

First Floor
1,523 sq. ft.

SPECIAL FEATURES

2,795 total square feet of living area

Second floor has a cozy vaulted family room

Formal dining room is directly off the kitchen

Spacious great room with fireplace has a built-in entertainment center

Bonus room on the second floor has an additional 387 square feet of living area

4 bedrooms, 3 1/2 baths, 2-car side entry garage

Basement foundation, drawings also include crawl space and slab foundations

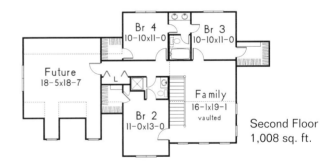

Br 4
10-10x11-0

Br 3
10-10x11-0

Future
18-5x18-7

Family
16-1x19-1
vaulted

Br 2
11-0x13-0

Second Floor
1,008 sq. ft.

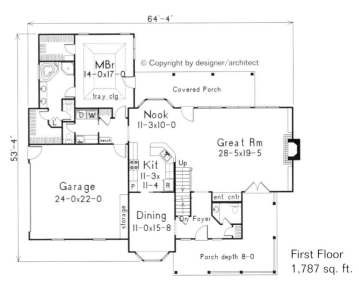

64'-4"

MBr
14-0x17-0
tray clg

© Copyright by designer/architect

Covered Porch

53'-4"

Nook
11-3x10-0

Great Rm
28-5x19-5

Garage
24-0x22-0

Kit
11-3x
11-4

storage

ent. cntr

Dining
11-0x15-8

Dn Foyer

Porch depth 8-0

First Floor
1,787 sq. ft.

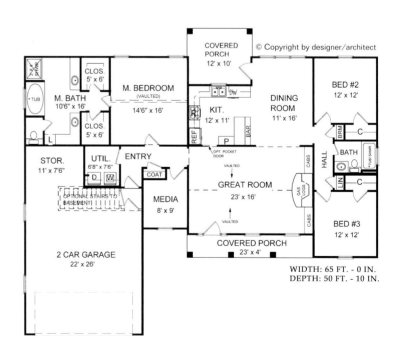

© Copyright by designer/architect

LEGACY SERIES — Lowe's

SPECIAL FEATURES

1,800 total square feet of living area

9' ceilings throughout the home and a vaulted ceiling in the great room create wonderful air flow

The dining room opens onto the covered porch, which is perfect for sheltered outdoor eating

A quiet media room is tucked away from the crowd and can be used as a flex space to use as your family needs

3 bedrooms, 2 baths, 2-car garage

Slab foundation, drawings also include basement and crawl space foundations

COVERED PORCH 12' x 10'

M. BATH 10'6" x 16'

CLOS. 5' x 6'

CLOS. 5' x 6'

M. BEDROOM (VAULTED) 14'6" x 16'

KIT. 12' x 11'

DINING ROOM 11' x 16'

BED #2 12' x 12'

STOR. 11' x 7'6"

UTIL. 6'8" x 7'6"

ENTRY

COAT

OPTIONAL STAIRS TO BASEMENT

MEDIA 8' x 9'

OPT. POCKET DOOR

VAULTED

GREAT ROOM 23' x 16'

GAS LOGS

CABS

CABS

HALL

BATH

BED #3 12' x 12'

2 CAR GARAGE 22' x 26'

COVERED PORCH 23' x 4'

VAULTED

WIDTH: 65 FT. - 0 IN.
DEPTH: 50 FT. - 10 IN.

SPECIAL FEATURES

2,972 total square feet of living area

Extra storage is available off
bedroom #2 on the second floor

Angled staircase in entry adds interest

Charming screened porch is accessible
from the breakfast room

Bonus room above the garage has an
additional 396 square feet of living area

4 bedrooms, 3 1/2 baths,
3-car side entry garage

Walk-out basement foundation,
drawings also include slab and
crawl space foundations

Second Floor
986 sq. ft.

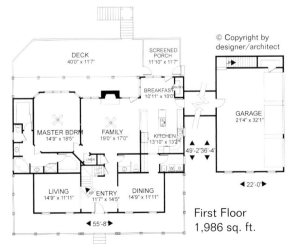

© Copyright by
designer/architect

First Floor
1,986 sq. ft.

SPECIAL FEATURES

1,682 total square feet of living area

A covered porch adds charm to the facade and invites guests into this beautiful home

A vaulted ceiling tops the adjoining kitchen, family and dining rooms adding to the spaciousness of this living area

Retreat to the master bedroom and find amenities including an oversized walk-in closet and a private bath with double-bowl vanity

3 bedrooms, 2 baths, 2-car garage

Basement foundation

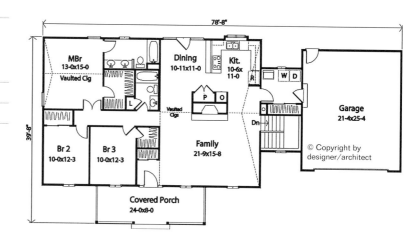

SPECIAL FEATURES

2,560 total square feet of living area

Numerous bay windows create
a design unlike any other

Enormous master bedroom has a private
bath with step-up tub-in-a-bay

Second floor laundry room is
located near all the bedrooms

Cheerful breakfast room extends
onto the covered private porch

4 bedrooms, 2 1/2 baths, 2-car garage

Basement foundation

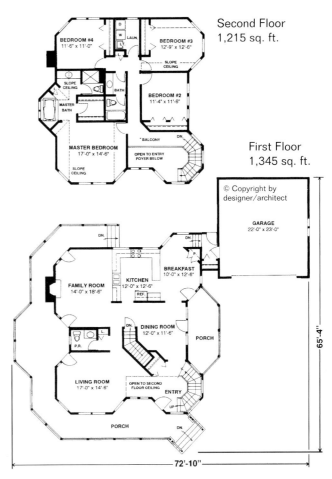

Second Floor
1,215 sq. ft.

First Floor
1,345 sq. ft.

© Copyright by
designer/architect

LOWE'S LEGACY SERIES

SPECIAL FEATURES

2,400 total square feet of living area

All the bedrooms feature walk-in closets for extra organization

The master bedroom with private bath and two walk-in closets is separated from the other bedrooms for privacy

The flex space is a versatile room that can adapt to your needs whether it be an office or formal dining room

The unfinished bonus room has an additional 452 square feet of living area

4 bedrooms, 2 1/2 baths, 2-car side entry garage

Basement foundation

Optional Second Floor

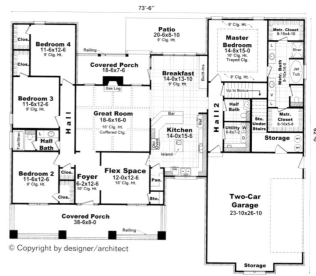

First Floor
2,400 sq. ft.

© Copyright by designer/architect

Special Features

- 2,932 total square feet of living area

- 9' ceilings throughout home

- Rear stairs provide convenient access to the second floor from living area

- Spacious kitchen has a pass-through to the living room, a convenient island and pantry

- Cozy built-in table in breakfast area

- Secluded master bedroom has a luxurious bath and patio access

- 4 bedrooms, 3 1/2 baths, 2-car side entry garage

- Slab foundation

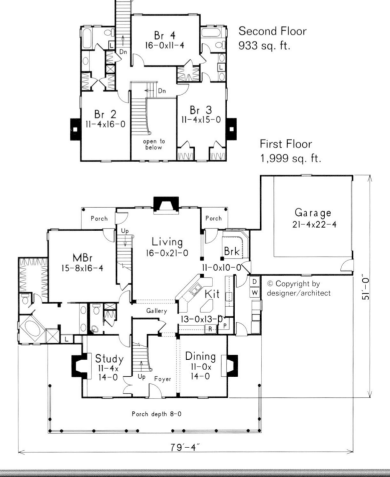

Br 4
16-0x11-4

Second Floor
933 sq. ft.

Br 2
11-4x16-0

Br 3
11-4x15-0

open to below

First Floor
1,999 sq. ft.

Porch

Living
16-0x21-0

Brk
11-0x10-0

Garage
21-4x22-4

MBr
15-8x16-4

Kit
13-0x13-0

© Copyright by designer/architect

Gallery

51'-0"

Study
11-4x
14-0

Dining
11-0x
14-0

Foyer

Porch depth 8-0

79'-4"

LOWE'S
LEGACY
SERIES

SPECIAL FEATURES

2,400 total square feet of living area

Energy efficient home with
2" x 6" exterior walls

Use of T-stair makes efficient room travel

Large kitchen/breakfast area has planning
desk, center island and a walk-in pantry

Generous closets are found
in every bedroom

3 bedrooms, 2 1/2 baths,
3-car side entry garage

Basement foundation

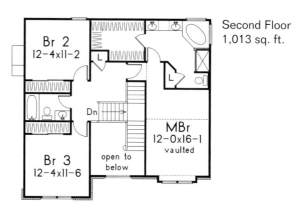

Br 2
12-4x11-2

Br 3
12-4x11-6

Dn

open to
below

MBr
12-0x16-1
vaulted

Second Floor
1,013 sq. ft.

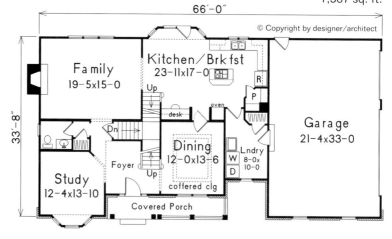

First Floor
1,387 sq. ft.

66'-0"

© Copyright by designer/architect

Family
19-5x15-0

Kitchen/Brkfst
23-11x17-0

Up

oven

R

P

Garage
21-4x33-0

33'-8"

Dn

desk

Dn

Dining
12-0x13-6
coffered clg

Lndry
8-0x
10-0

W
D

Foyer

Up

Study
12-4x13-10

Covered Porch

SPECIAL FEATURES

1,991 total square feet of living area

A large porch with roof dormers and flanking stonework creates a distinctive country appeal

The highly functional U-shaped kitchen is open to the dining and living rooms defined by a colonnade

Large bay windows are enjoyed by both the living room and master bedroom

Every bedroom features spacious walk-in closets and their own private bath

3 bedrooms, 3 1/2 baths, 2-car side entry garage

Basement foundation

© Copyright by designer/architect

Patio

MBr
17-0x12-8

Living
21-0x16-6

Br 2
11-8x14-6

Dn

Garage
21-4x23-3

Kit
10-0 x
10-9

Brk fst
10-0x11-10

Br 3
15-8x12-6

Entry

Porch depth 6-0

38'-4"

85'-6"

SPECIAL FEATURES

1,430 total square feet of living area

All bedrooms enjoy spacious walk-in closets

A large dining room enjoys close proximity to the kitchen

Varied ceiling heights throughout help add character to the interior

3 bedrooms, 2 baths, 2-car detached garage

Crawl space foundation, drawings also include slab foundation

© Copyright by designer/architect

Garage
22 x 24

Patio

Walk
8/8 x 10

Dining
13/8 x 10
9' Clg.

Master
12/10 x 15
Recessed Clg. 10'

Kitchen
15/10 x 10

Pantry

Utility

W
D

Family Room
17/2 x 14/8
12' Clg.

Sloped Ceiling

Sloped

Porch
13 x 6

Bedroom #2
10 x 11/8
9' Clg.

Bedroom #3
10 x 12/8
9' Clg

Width: 34'-0"
Depth: 60'-0"

SPECIAL FEATURES

1,687 total square feet of living area

Family room with built-in cabinet and fireplace is the focal point of this home

U-shaped kitchen has a bar that opens to the family room

Back porch opens to the dining room and leads to the garage via a walkway

Convenient laundry room is located near the center of activity

4 bedrooms, 2 1/2 baths, 2-car detached garage

Basement foundation

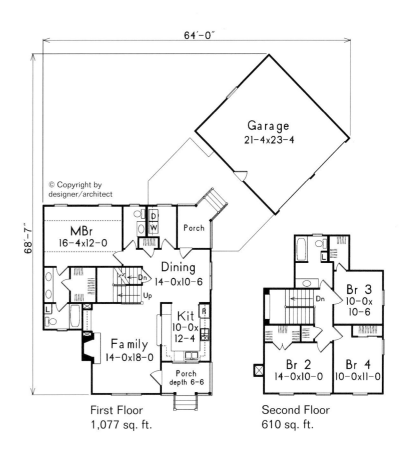

64'-0"

68'-7"

© Copyright by designer/architect

Garage 21-4x23-4

Porch

MBr 16-4x12-0

Dining 14-0x10-6

Dn

Up

Kit 10-0x 12-4

Family 14-0x18-0

Porch depth 6-6

Br 3 10-0x 10-6

Dn

Br 2 14-0x10-0

Br 4 10-0x11-0

First Floor 1,077 sq. ft.

Second Floor 610 sq. ft.

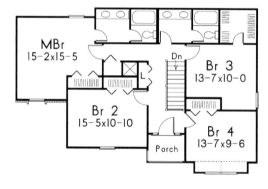

SPECIAL FEATURES

2,352 total square feet of living area

Separate family and living rooms for casual and formal entertaining

Master bedroom features a private dressing area and bath

Bedrooms are located on the second floor for privacy

2" x 6" exterior walls available, please order plan #533-001D-0125

4 bedrooms, 2 1/2 baths, 2-car rear entry garage

Crawl space foundation, drawings also include basement and slab foundations

MBr
15-2x15-5

Br 3
13-7x10-0

Br 2
15-5x10-10

Br 4
13-7x9-6

Dn

Porch

Second Floor
1,182 sq. ft.

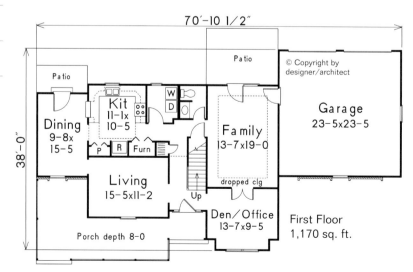

70'-10 1/2"

38'-0"

Patio

Patio

© Copyright by designer/architect

Kit
11-1x
10-5

W
D

Family
13-7x19-0

Garage
23-5x23-5

Dining
9-8x
15-5

P R Furn

Living
15-5x11-2

Up

dropped clg

Den/Office
13-7x9-5

Porch depth 8-0

First Floor
1,170 sq. ft.

SPECIAL FEATURES

1,635 total square feet of living area

This country-style ranch is sure to please with an open living area and private bedrooms

The great room enjoys the openness to the kitchen, a grand fireplace and access to the backyard

A walk-in closet, deluxe bath with whirlpool tub and a vaulted ceiling creates a luxurious master bedroom suite

3 bedrooms, 2 1/2 baths, 2-car garage

Basement foundation

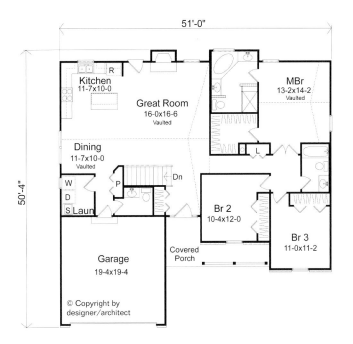

LOWE'S
LEGACY
SERIES

SPECIAL FEATURES

1,800 total square feet of living area

9' ceilings create a spacious home

The great room with its gas fireplace
is a cozy place to gather

The screen porch offers an enchanting
space to relax outdoors in any weather

3 bedrooms, 3 baths, 2-car side entry garage

Slab foundation, drawings also
include crawl space foundation

© Copyright by designer/architect

Width: 64'-0"
Depth: 53'-0"

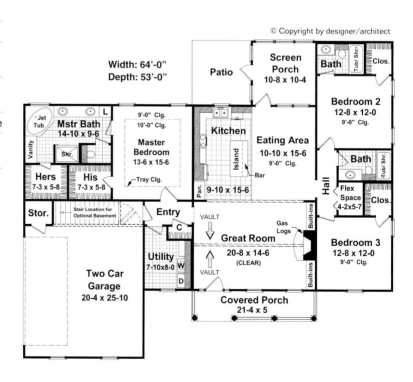

Lowe's LEGACY SERIES

SPECIAL FEATURES

2,445 total square feet of living area

Sunken living room has a corner fireplace, vaulted ceiling and is adjacent to the dining room for entertaining large groups

Large vaulted open foyer with triple skylights provides an especially bright entry

Loft area overlooks foyer and features a decorative display area

Bedrooms are located on the second floor for privacy and convenience, with a vaulted ceiling in the master bedroom

4 bedrooms, 2 1/2 baths, 3-car garage

Basement foundation

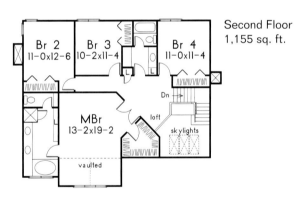

Second Floor
1,155 sq. ft.

Br 2
11-0x12-6

Br 3
10-2x11-4

Br 4
11-0x11-4

Dn

loft

MBr
13-2x19-2

skylights

vaulted

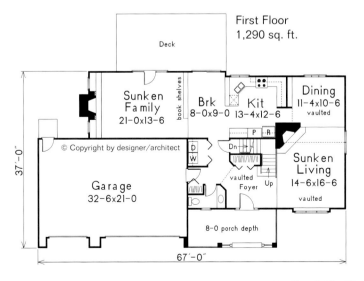

First Floor
1,290 sq. ft.

Deck

Sunken Family
21-0x13-6

book shelves

Brk
8-0x9-0

Kit
13-4x12-6

Dining
11-4x10-6
vaulted

© Copyright by designer/architect

D W

Dn

P R

Sunken Living
14-6x16-6
vaulted

Garage
32-6x21-0

vaulted Foyer

Up

37'-0"

8-0 porch depth

67'-0"

SPECIAL FEATURES

2,409 total square feet of living area

Double two-story bay windows
adorn the wrap-around porch

A grand-scale foyer features a 40'
view through morning room

An eating area, fireplace, palladian
windows, vaulted ceiling and balcony
overlook are among the many amenities
of the spacious morning room

Two large second floor bedrooms
and an enormous third bedroom
enjoy two walk-in closets, a bay
window and access to hall bath

4 bedrooms, 2 1/2 baths, 2-car
side entry garage with storage

Basement foundation

Second Floor
799 sq. ft.

First Floor
1,610 sq. ft.

© Copyright by designer/architect

SPECIAL FEATURES

3,556 total square feet of living area

Jack and Jill bath is located between two of the bedrooms on the second floor

Second floor features three bedrooms and overlooks the great room

Formal entrance and additional family entrance from covered porch to laundry/mud room

First floor master bedroom features a coffered ceiling, double walk-in closets, luxury bath and direct access to the study

4 bedrooms, 3 1/2 baths, 3-car side entry garage

Basement foundation

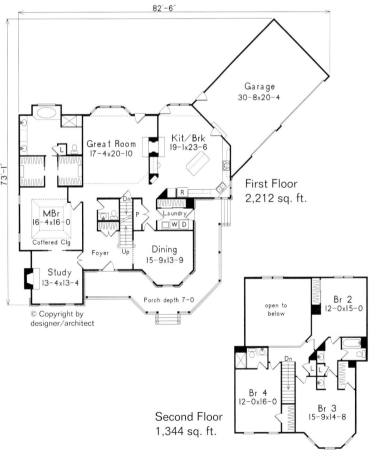

82'-6"

73'-1"

Garage 30-8x20-4

Great Room 17-4x20-10

Kit/Brk 19-1x23-6

First Floor 2,212 sq. ft.

MBr 16-4x16-0
Coffered Clg

Laundry
W D

Foyer

Up

Dining 15-9x13-9

Study 13-4x13-4

Porch depth 7-0

© Copyright by designer/architect

open to below

Br 2 12-0x15-0

Dn

Br 4 12-0x16-0

Br 3 15-9x14-8

Second Floor 1,344 sq. ft.

LOWE'S
LEGACY
SERIES

SPECIAL FEATURES

2,420 total square feet of living area

Master bedroom is filled with extras such as a unique master bath and lots of storage

Extending off the great room is a bright sunroom with access to an optional deck

Compact kitchen with nook creates a useful breakfast area

4 bedrooms, 2 1/2 baths, 2-car garage

Basement foundation

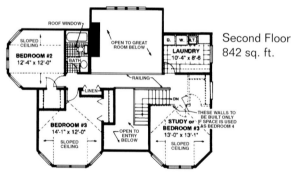

Second Floor
842 sq. ft.

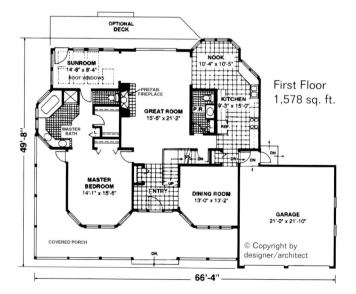

First Floor
1,578 sq. ft.

© Copyright by
designer/architect

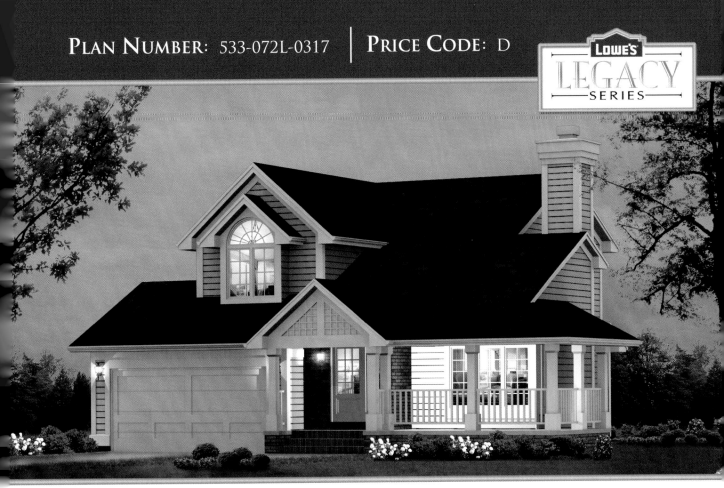

SPECIAL FEATURES

1,550 total square feet of living area

Greenhouse windows in the kitchen create the perfect place to grow herbs or vegetables

The sunken great room has a cozy corner fireplace and a vaulted ceiling

The second floor includes a large loft area that could make an excellent place for a home office

2 bedrooms, 2 1/2 baths, 2-car garage

Basement foundation

Mas. Suite
12-4x14
vaulted

Loft
12-8x11-2

Br 2
12-4x10-2

open to below

Second Floor
732 sq. ft.

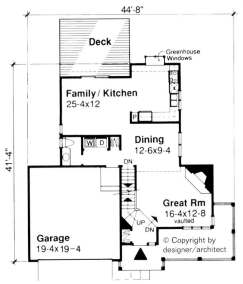

44'-8"

41'-4"

Deck

Greenhouse
Windows

Family / Kitchen
25-4x12

Dining
12-6x9-4

Great Rm
16-4x12-8
vaulted

Garage
19-4x19-4

© Copyright by
designer/architect

First Floor
818 sq. ft.

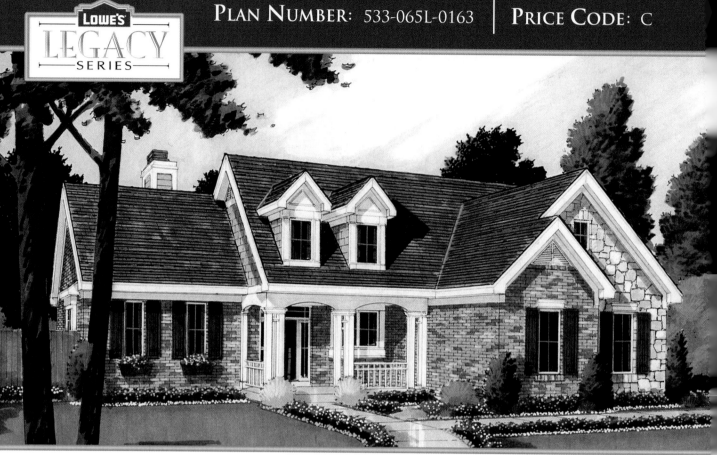

PLAN NUMBER: 533-065L-0163 | **PRICE CODE:** C

SPECIAL FEATURES

1,876 total square feet of living area

Excitement is easily achieved in the central great room with a high sloping ceiling, corner fireplace and multiple rear windows

The deluxe master bedroom offers a walk-in closet and plush bath, creating a private retreat

Two bedrooms and a bonus room comprise the second floor making this design perfect for a growing family

The second floor bonus room has an additional 182 square feet of living area

3 bedrooms, 2 1/2 baths, 2-car side entry garage

Basement foundation

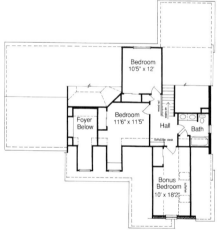

Second Floor
528 sq. ft.

© Copyright by designer/architect

First Floor
1,348 sq. ft.

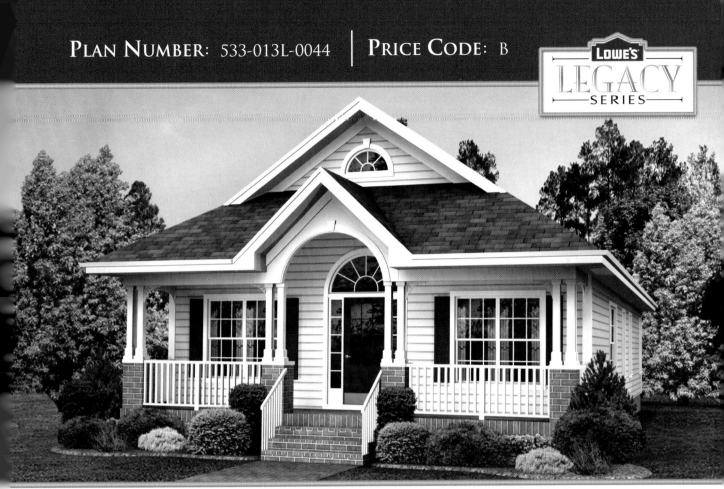

LEGACY SERIES — Lowe's

SPECIAL FEATURES

1,420 total square feet of living area

Energy efficient home with
2" x 6" exterior walls

Windowed wall in the master
suite lets in plenty of light and
creates an open atmosphere

High ceiling connects the family room
and dining area into a large, airy room

Large corner counter in kitchen provides
an easy place for quick meals

3 bedrooms, 2 baths, optional 2-car garage

Crawl space foundation, drawings
also include slab foundation

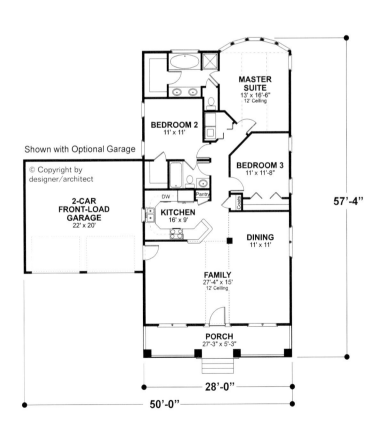

Shown with Optional Garage

© Copyright by
designer/architect

MASTER SUITE
13' x 16'-6"
12' Ceiling

BEDROOM 2
11' x 11'

BEDROOM 3
11' x 11'-8"

2-CAR
FRONT-LOAD
GARAGE
22' x 20'

DW

Pantry

Coats

KITCHEN
16' x 9'

DINING
11' x 11'

FAMILY
27'-4" x 15'
12' Ceiling

PORCH
27'-3" x 5'-3"

57'-4"

28'-0"

50'-0"

SPECIAL FEATURES

1,681 total square feet of living area

A formal dining room has a built-in alcove perfect for a china cabinet or buffet table

Varied ceiling heights throughout add overall appeal to the interior

A useful snack bar attached to the kitchen counter makes mealtime a breeze

3 bedrooms, 2 baths, 2-car garage

Basement foundation

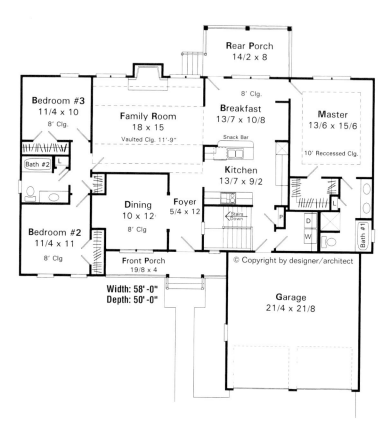

Rear Porch
14/2 x 8

8' Clg.

Bedroom #3
11/4 x 10
8' Clg.

Family Room
18 x 15
Vaulted Clg. 11'-9"

Breakfast
13/7 x 10/8

Master
13/6 x 15/6

Snack Bar

10' Reccessed Clg.

Kitchen
13/7 x 9/2

Bath #2   L

Dining
10 x 12
8' Clg

Foyer
5/4 x 12

Stairs
Down

P   D
W

Bath #1

Bedroom #2
11/4 x 11
8' Clg

© Copyright by designer/architect

Front Porch
19/8 x 4

Width: 58'-0"
Depth: 50'-0"

Garage
21/4 x 21/8

SPECIAL FEATURES

1,659 total square feet of living area

The large family room enjoys the warmth of the fireplace flanked by built-in bookcases

The porte-cochere has extra storage and access into the home near the utility room

The cheerful dining area provides accessibility to the covered rear porch

3 bedrooms, 2 1/2 baths, 2-car carport

Slab foundation

Second Floor
422 sq. ft.

First Floor
1,237 sq. ft.

© Copyright by designer/architect

SPECIAL FEATURES

2,547 total square feet of living area

Grand-sized great room features a 12' volume ceiling, fireplace with built-in wrap-around shelving and patio doors with sidelights and transom windows

The walk-in pantry, computer desk, large breakfast island for seven and bayed breakfast area are the many features of this outstanding kitchen

The master bedroom suite enjoys a luxurious bath, large walk-in closets and patio access

4 bedrooms, 2 1/2 baths, 3-car side entry garage

Basement foundation

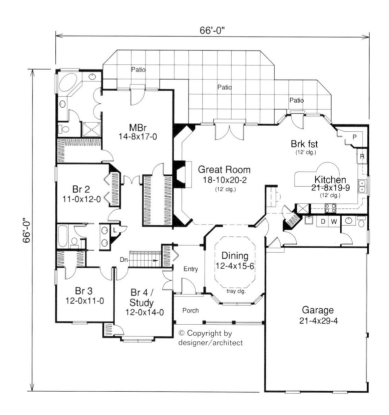

66'-0"

66'-0"

Patio

Patio

Patio

MBr
14-8x17-0

Br 2
11-0x12-0

Br 3
12-0x11-0

Br 4 / Study
12-0x14-0

Dn

Great Room
18-10x20-2
(12' clg.)

Brk fst
(12' clg.)

Kitchen
21-8x19-9
(12' clg.)

D W

Dining
12-4x15-6
tray clg.

Entry

Porch

Garage
21-4x29-4

P

R

L

© Copyright by designer/architect

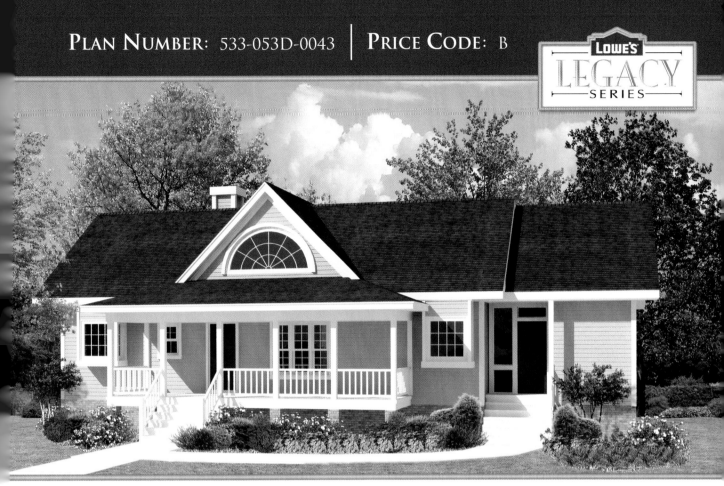

SPECIAL FEATURES

1,732 total square feet of living area

Spacious great room has a vaulted ceiling and fireplace that overlooks the large sundeck

Dramatic dining room boasts extensive windows and angled walls

Vaulted master bedroom includes a private bath with laundry area and accesses the sundeck

Convenient second entrance leads to the screen porch and dining area

3 bedrooms, 2 1/2 baths, 2-car drive under garage

Basement foundation

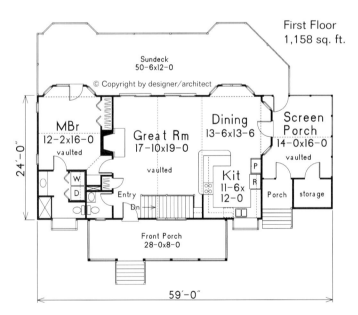

First Floor
1,158 sq. ft.

© Copyright by designer/architect

Sundeck 50-6x12-0

MBr 12-2x16-0 vaulted

Great Rm 17-10x19-0 vaulted

Dining 13-6x13-6

Screen Porch 14-0x16-0 vaulted

Kit 11-6x 12-0

Entry Dn

Porch

storage

Front Porch 28-0x8-0

24'-0"

59'-0"

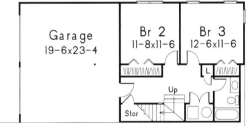

Lower Level
574 sq. ft.

Garage 19-6x23-4

Br 2 11-8x11-6

Br 3 12-6x11-6

Stor

Up

SPECIAL FEATURES

2,501 total square feet of living area

The front covered porch offers a central entry and two additional entries through French doors into either bedroom #2 or the dining room/study

The kitchen enjoys a walk-in pantry and angled snack bar open to the great room and bayed breakfast nook

The unfinished bonus room on the second floor has an additional 426 square feet of living space

4 bedrooms, 3 baths, 2-car side entry garage

Slab foundation, drawings also include basement and crawl space foundations

Optional Second Floor

UNFINISHED BONUS ROOM
23' X 18'-8"
(CLEAR)

8'-0" C.H.

Width: 84'-0"
Depth: 54'-0"

© Copyright by designer/architect

First Floor
2,501 sq. ft.

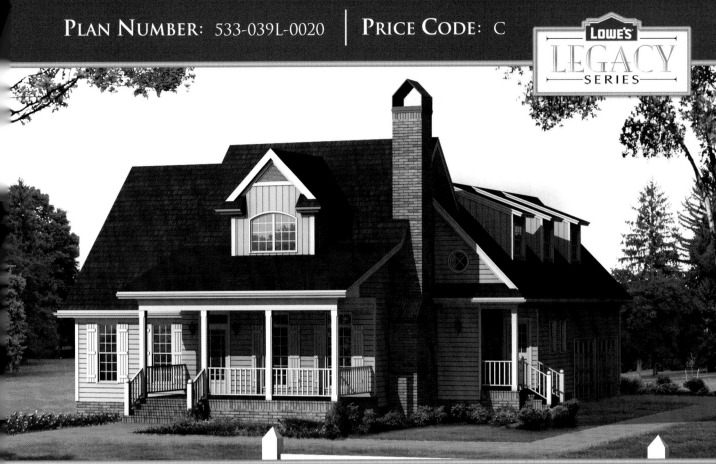

SPECIAL FEATURES

2,010 total square feet of living area

Oversized kitchen is a great gathering place with eat-in island bar, dining area nearby and built-in desk

First floor master bedroom has privacy

Unique second floor kid's living area for playroom

Optional bonus room has an additional 313 square feet of living area

3 bedrooms, 2 1/2 baths, 2-car side entry garage

Basement foundation

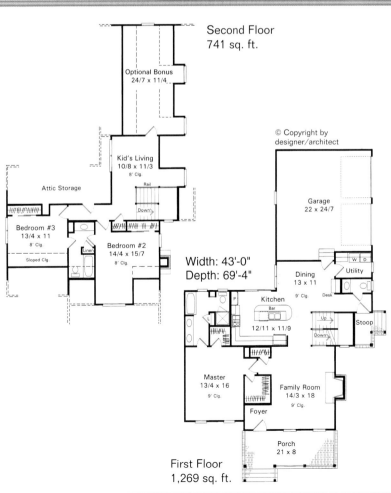

Second Floor
741 sq. ft.

Optional Bonus
24/7 x 11/4

© Copyright by
designer/architect

Kid's Living
10/8 x 11/3
8' Clg.

Attic Storage

Rail

Down

Garage
22 x 24/7

Bedroom #3
13/4 x 11
8' Clg.

Bedroom #2
14/4 x 15/7
8' Clg.

Linen

Sloped Clg.

Width: 43'-0"
Depth: 69'-4"

Dining
13 x 11
9' Clg.

Utility
W D

Kitchen
Bar
12/11 x 11/9

Desk

Up
Down

Stoop

Master
13/4 x 16
9' Clg.

Family Room
14/3 x 18
9' Clg.

Foyer

Porch
21 x 8

First Floor
1,269 sq. ft.

Lowe's LEGACY SERIES

SPECIAL FEATURES

2,059 total square feet of living area

Large desk and pantry add
to the breakfast room

The laundry room is located on the
second floor near the bedrooms

Vaulted ceiling in the master bedroom

Mud room is conveniently
located near the garage

3 bedrooms, 2 1/2 baths, 2-car garage

Basement foundation

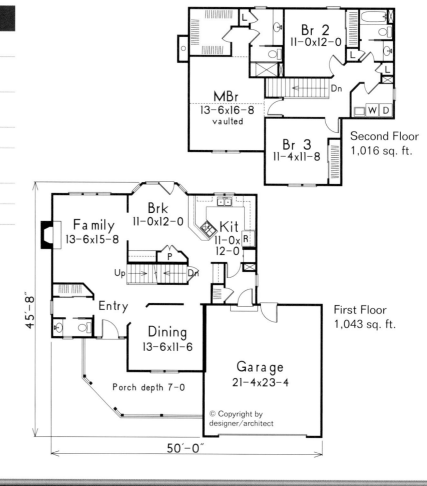

Br 2
11-0x12-0

MBr
13-6x16-8
vaulted

Br 3
11-4x11-8

Second Floor
1,016 sq. ft.

Brk
11-0x12-0

Family
13-6x15-8

Kit
11-0x
12-0

Up
Dn
P

Entry

Dining
13-6x11-6

First Floor
1,043 sq. ft.

Garage
21-4x23-4

45'-8"

Porch depth 7-0

© Copyright by
designer/architect

50'-0"

SPECIAL FEATURES

2,360 total square feet of living area

Energy efficient home with
2" x 6" exterior walls

Master bedroom includes a
sitting area and large bath

Sloped family room ceiling provides a
view from the second floor balcony

Kitchen features an island bar
and walk-in butler's pantry

3 bedrooms, 2 1/2 baths,
2-car side entry garage

Crawl space foundation, drawings also
include slab and basement foundations

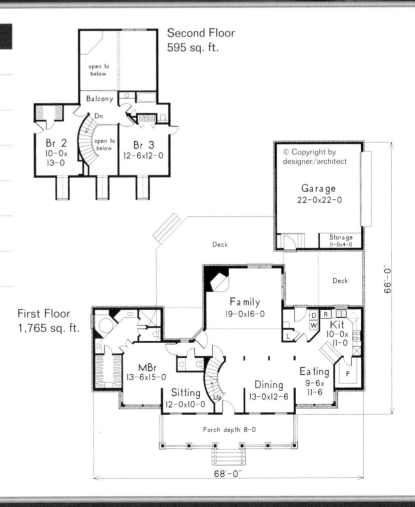

Second Floor
595 sq. ft.

open to below

Balcony

Dn

open to below

Br 2
10-0x
13-0

Br 3
12-6x12-0

© Copyright by
designer/architect

Garage
22-0x22-0

Storage
11-0x4-0

Deck

Deck

First Floor
1,765 sq. ft.

Family
19-0x16-0

Kit
10-0x
11-0

MBr
13-6x15-0

Sitting
12-0x10-0

Dining
13-0x12-6

Eating
9-6x
11-6

Porch depth 8-0

66-0"

68-0"

SPECIAL FEATURES

1,344 total square feet of living area

Energy efficient home with
2" x 6" exterior walls

Family/dining room has sliding
glass doors to the outdoors

Master bedroom features a
private bath with shower

Hall bath includes double-bowl
vanity for added convenience

Kitchen features U-shaped design,
large pantry and laundry area

3 bedrooms, 2 baths, 2-car garage

Crawl space foundation, drawings also
include basement and slab foundations

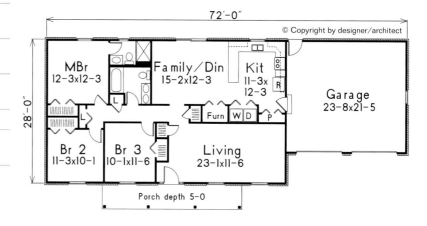

LOWE'S
LEGACY
SERIES

SPECIAL FEATURES

1,542 total square feet of living area

The large bayed dining room enjoys direct access to the outdoors and close proximity to the kitchen

Two vaulted bedrooms and a full bath complete the second floor

Both a separate shower and tub add great function to the master bath

The future expansion on the second floor has an additional 226 square feet of living area

3 bedrooms, 2 1/2 baths, 2-car garage

Slab foundation

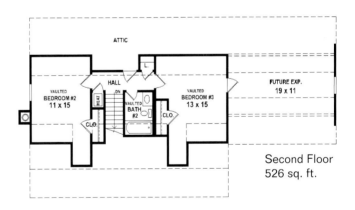

Second Floor
526 sq. ft.

First Floor
1,016 sq. ft.

© Copyright by designer/architect

SPECIAL FEATURES

1,777 total square feet of living area

Large master bedroom has a bath
with whirlpool tub, separate shower
and spacious walk-in closet

Large island kitchen features a breakfast
bay and access to the three-season porch

Convenient laundry room
includes a half bath

3 bedrooms, 2 1/2 baths, 2-car garage

Basement foundation

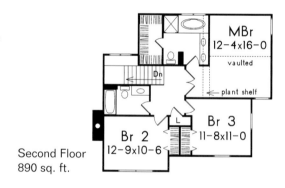

MBr
12-4x16-0
vaulted

plant shelf

Dn

Br 3
11-8x11-0

Br 2
12-9x10-6

Second Floor
890 sq. ft.

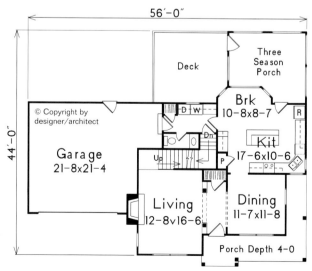

56'-0"

Three
Season
Porch

Deck

Brk
10-8x8-7

© Copyright by
designer/architect

44'-0"

Kit
17-6x10-6

Garage
21-8x21-4

Dn

Up

P

Living
12-8v16-6

Dining
11-7x11-8

First Floor
887 sq. ft.

Porch Depth 4-0

SPECIAL FEATURES

- 2,280 total square feet of living area
- Laundry area is conveniently located on the second floor
- Compact, yet efficient kitchen
- Unique shaped dining room overlooks the front porch
- Cozy living room is enhanced with a sloped ceiling and fireplace
- 4 bedrooms, 2 1/2 baths, 2-car side entry garage
- Basement foundation

Second Floor
1,049 sq. ft.

Br 3 10-0x 10-8

Br 4 10-0x 10-0

MBr 16-9x15-4

Br 2 12-4x13-4

open to below

plant shelf

Dn

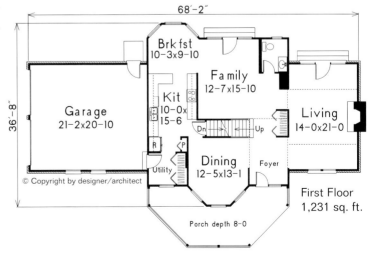

68'-2"

36'-8"

Garage 21-2x20-10

Brk fst 10-3x9-10

Family 12-7x15-10

Kit 10-0x 15-6

Living 14-0x21-0

Dining 12-5x13-1

Utility

Foyer

Dn   Up

© Copyright by designer/architect

First Floor
1,231 sq. ft.

Porch depth 8-0

LOWE'S LEGACY SERIES

SPECIAL FEATURES

2,100 total square feet of living area

A large courtyard with stone walls, lantern columns and covered porch welcomes you into open spaces

The great room features a stone fireplace, built-in shelves, vaulted ceiling and atrium with dramatic staircase and a two and a half story window wall

Two walk-in closets, vaulted ceiling with plant shelf and a luxury bath adorn the master bedroom suite

1,391 square feet of optional living area on the lower level with family room, walk-in bar, sitting area, bedroom #3 and a bath

2 bedrooms, 2 baths, 3-car side entry garage

Walk-out basement foundation

© Copyright by designer/architect

First Floor
2,100 sq. ft.

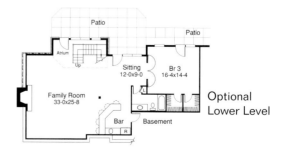

Optional Lower Level

SPECIAL FEATURES

2,750 total square feet of living area

Oversized rooms throughout

9' ceilings on the first floor

Unique utility bay workshop off garage

Spacious master bedroom is adorned with a luxurious bath

Optional six bedroom plan is also included

5 bedrooms, 3 baths, 2-car side entry garage

Basement foundation, drawings also include crawl space and slab foundations

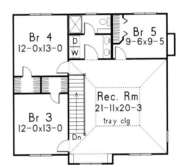

Second Floor
1,050 sq. ft.

Br 4
12-0x13-0

Br 5
9-6x9-5

Br 3
12-0x13-0

Rec. Rm
21-11x20-3
tray clg

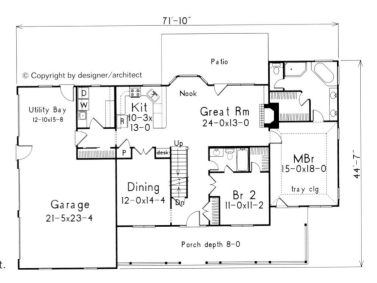

First Floor
1,700 sq. ft.

71'-10"

44'-7"

© Copyright by designer/architect

Patio

Utility Bay
12-10x15-8

Kit
10-3x13-0

Nook

Great Rm
24-0x13-0

MBr
15-0x18-0
tray clg

Dining
12-0x14-4

Br 2
11-0x11-2

Garage
21-5x23-4

Porch depth 8-0

SPECIAL FEATURES

3,493 total square feet of living area

Formal living and dining rooms comprise the front of the home

Casual screened porch located off the breakfast area

A large corner fireplace warms the family room

Lots of extra storage located on the second floor

4 bedrooms, 3 1/2 baths, 3-car side entry garage

Basement foundation, drawings also include slab foundation

Second Floor
1,013 sq. ft.

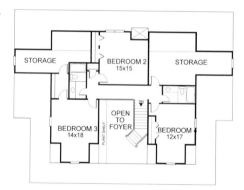

First Floor
2,480 sq. ft.

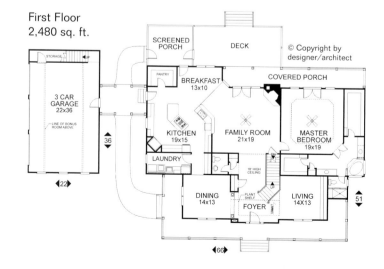

© Copyright by designer/architect

FREE LOWE'S GIFT CARD OFFER

Lowe's Special Rebate Offer

Purchase any plan package featured in this book PLUS at least $15,000 of your materials from Lowe's and receive a gift card for the purchase price of your plans.

To receive the rebate:

1. Purchase any of the plan packages in this publication PLUS at least $15,000 of the materials to build your home at Lowe's before 12/31/10. Requests must be postmarked by 1/31/11. Claims postmarked after this date will not be honored.

2. Limit one gift card per set of plans.

3. Please allow 3-4 weeks for processing. If you do not receive a gift card after 4 weeks, visit www.lowes.com/rebates, or you may call 1-877-204-1223.

4. Please keep a copy of all materials submitted for your records.

5. Copy the entire sale receipt(s), including store name, location, purchase date, and invoice number, showing blueprint purchase and total amount spent.

6. Mail this complete page with your name, address and other information below, along with a copy of the receipt(s).

Name _____

Street Address _____

City _____

State/Zip _____

Daytime phone number (_____) - _____

E-mail address _____

Plan number purchased 533- _____

I purchased a
- ☐ One-Set Plan Package
- ☐ Five-Set Plan Package
- ☐ Eight-Set Plan Package
- ☐ Reproducible Masters
- ☐ Builder's CAD Package

MAIL TO:
Lowe's Free Gift Card Offer
P.O. Box 3029
Young America, MN 55558-3029

Check the status of your rebate at www.lowes.com/rebates

OUR BLUEPRINT PACKAGES INCLUDE...

Quality plans for building your future, with extras that provide unsurpassed value, ensure good construction and long-term enjoyment.

COVER SHEET

Included with many of the plans, the cover sheet is the artist's rendering of the exterior of the home. It will give you an idea of how your home will look when completed and landscaped.

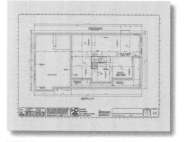

FOUNDATION

The foundation plan shows the layout of the basement, walk-out basement, crawl space, slab or pier foundation. All necessary notations and dimensions are included. See plan page for the foundation types included. If the home plan you choose does not have your desired foundation type, our Customer Service Representatives can advise you on how to customize your foundation to suit your specific needs or site conditions.

FLOOR PLANS

The floor plans show the placement of walls, doors, closets, plumbing fixtures, electrical outlets, columns, and beams for each level of the home.

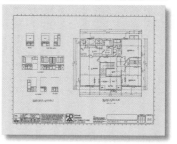

INTERIOR ELEVATIONS

Interior elevations provide views of special interior elements such as fireplaces, kitchen cabinets, built-in units and other features of the home.

EXTERIOR ELEVATIONS

Exterior elevations illustrate the front, rear and both sides of the house, with all details of exterior materials and the required dimensions.

SECTIONS

Show detail views of the home or portions of the home as if it were sliced from the roof to the foundation. This sheet shows important areas such as load-bearing walls, stairs, joists, trusses and other structural elements, which are critical for proper construction.

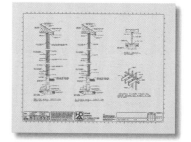

DETAILS

Show how to construct certain components of your home, such as the roof system, stairs, deck, etc.

WHAT KIND OF PLAN PACKAGE DO YOU NEED?

Now that you've found the home you've been looking for, here are some suggestions on how to make your Dream Home a reality. To get started, order the type of plans that fit your particular situation.

YOUR CHOICES

THE ONE-SET STUDY PACKAGE -

We offer a One-set plan package so you can study your home in detail. This one set is considered a study set and is marked "not for construction." It is a copyright violation to reproduce blueprints.

THE MINIMUM 5-SET PACKAGE -

If you're ready to start the construction process, this 5-set package is the minimum number of blueprint sets you will need. It will require keeping close track of each set so they can be used by multiple subcontractors and tradespeople.

THE STANDARD 8-SET PACKAGE -

For best results in terms of cost, schedule and quality of construction, we recommend you order eight (or more) sets of blueprints. Besides one set for yourself, additional sets of blueprints will be required by your mortgage lender, local building department, general contractor and all subcontractors working on foundation, electrical, plumbing, heating/air conditioning, carpentry work, etc.

REPRODUCIBLE MASTERS -

If you wish to make some minor design changes, you'll want to order reproducible masters. These drawings contain the same information as the blueprints but are printed on reproducible paper and clearly indicates your right to alter, copy or reproduce. This will allow your builder or a local design professional to make the necessary drawing changes without the major expense of redrawing the plans. This package also allows you to print copies of the modified plans as needed. The right of building only one structure from these plans is licensed exclusively to the buyer. You may not use this design to build a second or multiple dwelling(s) without purchasing another blueprint. Each violation of the Copyright Law is punishable in a fine.

MIRROR REVERSE SETS -

Plans can be printed in mirror reverse. These plans are useful when the house would fit your site better if all the rooms were on the opposite side than shown. They are simply a mirror image of the original drawings causing the lettering and dimensions to read backwards. Therefore, when ordering mirror reverse drawings, you must purchase at least one set of right-reading plans. Some of our plans are offered mirror reverse right-reading. This means the plan, lettering and dimensions are flipped but read correctly. See the Home Plans Index on pages 285-286 for availability

CAD PACKAGES -

A CAD package is a complete set of construction drawings in an electronic file format. They are beneficial if you have a significant amount of changes to make to the home plan or if you need to make the home plan fit your local codes. If you purchase a CAD Package, you can take the plan to a local design professional who uses AutoCAD or DataCAD and they can modify the design much quicker than with a paper-based drawing, which will help save you time and money. Just like our reproducible masters, with a CAD package you will receive a one-time build copyright release that allows you to make changes and the necessary copies needed to build your home. For more information and availability, please call our Customer Service Department at 1-877-379-3420.

PDF FILE FORMAT -

A complete set of construction drawings in an electronic format that allows you to modify and reproduce the plans to fit your needs. Since these are electronic files, we can send them to you within 24 hours (Mon-Fri, 8-5 CST) via email and save you shipping costs. They also offer printing flexibility by allowing you to print the size and number of sets you need. Note: These are not CAD files and cannot be altered electronically.

Your Blueprint Package will contain the necessary construction information to build your home. We also offer the following products and services to save you time and money in the building process.

EXPRESS DELIVERY

Most orders are processed within 24 hours of receipt. Please allow 7-10 business days for delivery. If you need to place a rush order, please call us by 11:00 a.m. Monday-Friday CST and ask for express service (allow 1-2 business days).

TECHNICAL ASSISTANCE

If you have questions, call our technical support line at 1-314-770-2228 between 8:00 a.m. and 5:00 p.m. Monday-Friday CST. Whether it involves design modifications or field assistance, our designers are extremely familiar with all of our designs and will be happy to help you. We want your home to be everything you expect it to be.

MATERIAL LIST

Material lists are available for all of the plans in this book. Each list gives you the quantity, dimensions and description of the building materials necessary to construct your home. You'll get faster and more accurate bids from your contractor while saving money by paying for only the materials you need. See your Commercial Sales Specialist at your local Lowe's Store to receive a free take-off.

OTHER GREAT PRODUCTS

THE LEGAL KIT -

Avoid many legal pitfalls and build your home with confidence using the forms and contract featured in this kit. Included are request for proposal documents, various fixed price and cost plus contracts, instructions on how and when to use each form, warranty statements and more. Save time and money before you break ground on your new home or start a remodeling project. All forms are reproducible. The kit is ideal for homebuilders and contractors. **Cost: $35.00**

DETAIL PLAN PACKAGES -

Electrical, Plumbing and Framing Packages

Three separate packages offer homebuilders details for constructing various foundations; numerous floor, wall and roof framing techniques; simple to complex residential wiring; sump and water softener hookups; plumbing connection methods; installation of septic systems, and more. Each package includes three dimensional illustrations and a glossary of terms. Purchase one or all three. Note: These drawings do not pertain to a specific home plan.
Cost: $20.00 each or all three for $40.00

(Continued, page 286)

EXCHANGE POLICIES

Since blueprints are printed in response to your order, we cannot honor requests for refunds. However, if for some reason you find that the plan you have purchased does not meet your requirements, you may exchange that plan for another plan in our collection within 90 days of purchase. At the time of the exchange, you will be charged a processing fee of 25% of your original plan package price, plus the difference in price between the plan packages (if applicable) and the cost to ship the new plans to you. Please note: Reproducible drawings can only be exchanged if the package is unopened.

BUILDING CODES & REQUIREMENTS

At the time the construction drawings were prepared, every effort was made to ensure that these plans and specifications meet nationally recognized codes. Our plans conform to most national building codes. Because building codes vary from area to area, some drawing modifications and/or the assistance of a professional designer or architect may be necessary to comply with your local codes or to accommodate specific building site conditions. We advise you to consult with your local building official for information regarding codes governing your area.

ADDITIONAL SETS*

Additional sets of the plan ordered are available for $45.00 each. Five-set, eight-set, and reproducible packages offer considerable savings.

MIRROR REVERSE PLANS*

Available for an additional $15.00 per set, these plans are simply a mirror image of the original drawings causing the dimensions and lettering to read backwards. Therefore, when ordering mirror reverse plans, you must purchase at least one set of right-reading plans. Some of our plans are offered mirror reverse right-reading. This means the plan, lettering and dimensions are flipped but read correctly. To purchase a mirror reverse right-reading set, the cost is an additional $150.00. See the Home Plans Index on pages 285-286 for availability.

ONE-SET STUDY PACKAGE

We offer a one-set plan package so you can study your home in detail. This one set is considered a study set and is marked "not for construction." It is a copyright violation to reproduce blueprints.

*Available only within 90 days after purchase of plan package or reproducible masters of same plan.

BLUEPRINT PRICE SCHEDULE *BEST VALUE*

Price Code	1-Set	Save $80 5-Sets	Save $115 8-Sets	Reproducible/ PDF File
AAA	$310	$410	$510	$610
AA	$410	$510	$610	$710
A	$470	$570	$670	$770
B	$530	$630	$730	$830
C	$585	$685	$785	$885
D	$635	$735	$835	$935
E	$695	$795	$895	$995
F	$750	$850	$950	$1050
G	$1000	$1100	$1200	$1300
H	$1100	$1200	$1300	$1400
I	$1150	$1250	$1350	$1450
J	$1200	$1300	$1400	$1500
K	$1250	$1350	$1450	$1550

**Plan prices are subject to change without notice.
Please note that plans and material lists are not refundable.**

SHIPPING & HANDLING CHARGES

US SHIPPING (AK and HI express only)

	1-4 Sets	5-7 Sets	8 Sets or Reproducibles
Regular (allow 7-10 business days)	$15.00	$17.50	$25.00
Priority (allow 3-5 business days)	$35.00	$40.00	$45.00
Express* (allow 1-2 business days)	$50.00	$55.00	$60.00

CANADA SHIPPING (to/from)**

	1-4 Sets	5-7 Sets	8 Sets or Reproducibles
Standard (allow 8-12 business days)	$35.00	$40.00	$45.00
Express* (allow 3-5 business days)	$75.00	$85.00	$95.00

*For express delivery please call us by 11:00 a.m. Monday-Friday CST
Overseas Shipping/International - Call, fax, or e-mail (plans@hdainc.com) for shipping costs.

**Orders may be subject to custom's fees and or duties/taxes

Note: Shipping and handling does not apply for PDF files. Orders will be emailed within 24 hours (Mon.-Fri., 8am-5pm CST) of purchase.

CAD FORMAT PLANS Many of our plans are available in CAD. For availability, please call our Customer Service Number below.

1-877-379-3420

HOW TO ORDER

1.) **CALL** toll-free 1-877-379-3420 for credit card orders

2.) **FAX** your order to 1-314-770-2226

3.) **MAIL** the Order Form to: *HDA , Inc.*
   944 Anglum Road
   St. Louis, MO 63042
   ATTN: Customer Service Dept.

For fastest service, Call Toll-Free
1-877-379-3420 day or night

ORDER FORM

Please send me -

PLAN NUMBER 533- _____

PRICE CODE _____ (see pages 285-286)

Specify Foundation Type (see plan page for availability)

☐ Slab   ☐ Crawl space   ☐ Pier

☐ Basement   ☐ Walk-out basement

☐ Reproducible Masters $ _____

☐ PDF File Format $ _____

☐ CAD Package (call for availability and pricing) $ _____

☐ Eight-Set Plan Package $ _____

☐ Five-Set Plan Package $ _____

☐ One-Set Study Package (no mirror reverse) $ _____

Additional Plan Sets*

☐ ____ (Qty.) at $45.00 each $ _____

Mirror Reverse*

☐ Right-reading $150 one-time charge $ _____
(see index on pages 285-286 for availability)

                                          $ _____
☐ Print in Mirror Reverse
(where right-reading is not available)

____ (Qty.) at $15.00 each

☐ Legal Kit (see page 284) (002D-9991) $ _____

Detail Plan Packages: (see page 284)

☐ Framing   ☐ Electrical   ☐ Plumbing
(002D-9992)   (002D-9993)   (002D-9994)

SUBTOTAL $ _____

Sales Tax (MO residents add 7%) $ _____

☐ Shipping / Handling (see chart on page 287) $ _____

TOTAL (US funds only - sorry no CODs) $ _____

I hereby authorize HDA, Inc. to charge this purchase to my credit card account (check one):

☐ MasterCard   ☐ VISA   ☐ DISCOVER   ☐ AMERICAN EXPRESS Cards

Prices are subject to change without notice.
Please note plans and material lists are not refundable.

Credit Card number _____

Expiration date _____

Signature _____

Name _____
       (Please print or type)

Street Address _____
          (Please do not use a PO Box)

_____

City _____

State _____

Zip _____

Daytime phone number   (_____) - _____

E-mail address _____

I am a   ☐ Builder/Contractor
          ☐ Homeowner
          ☐ Renter

I ☐ have ☐ have not selected my general contractor.

Thank you for your order!

* Available only within 90 days after purchase of plan package or reproducible masters of the same plan.

Note: Shipping and handling does not apply for PDF files. Orders will be emailed within 24 hours (Mon.-Fri., 8am-5pm CST) of purchase.